THE MAKING OF
THE ENGLISH LANDSCAPE

THE SOMERSET LANDSCAPE

7

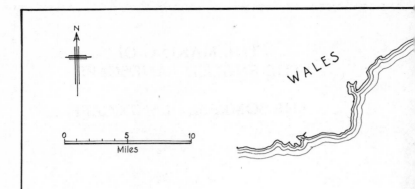

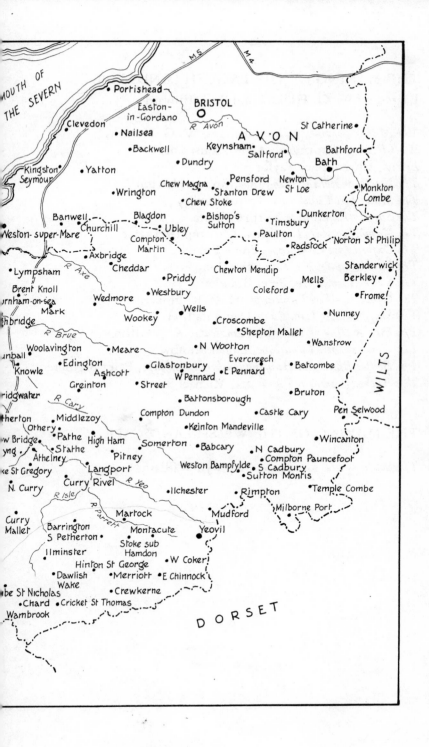

THE MAKING OF THE ENGLISH LANDSCAPE
Edited by W. G. Hoskins and Roy Millward

THE MAKING OF THE WELSH LANDSCAPE

THE MAKING OF THE ENGLISH LANDSCAPE

The Somerset Landscape

by

MICHAEL HAVINDEN

HODDER AND STOUGHTON
LONDON   SYDNEY   AUCKLAND   TORONTO

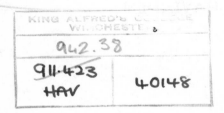

British Library Cataloguing in Publication Data
Havinden, Michael
    The Somerset landscape. — (The Making of the
English landscape)
    1. Somerset — Historical geography
    I. Title.   II. Series
    911'.423'8   DA670.S5

ISBN 0 340 20116 9

For Kate and Jennifer

Editor's Introduction

THIS SERIES OF BOOKS on The Making of the English Landscape originated in 1955 with my own pioneer book under that title. A few county volumes were published under the same format (Cornwall, Leicestershire, Gloucestershire, and Lancashire), but a new and better format was worked out from 1970 onwards, beginning with Arthur Raistrick's *West Riding of Yorkshire* and Christopher Taylor's *Dorset*. Since then there has been a steady flow of such county studies, aiming at covering the whole country eventually. Already there have been volumes as far apart as Northumberland and Sussex; and books are in preparation ranging from Kent in the east to a revised edition of Cornwall in the far west.

Purists might object that the geographical county has no particular unity except for administrative purposes, that the "region" would be more appropriate. Apart from the fact that few would agree about what constituted a "region", the primary fact is that the geographical county is a unity so far as the documentary material is concerned; but, more than that, it evokes local patriotism, and again each English county (one ought to say "British" in view of the fact that Wales has been brought within the orbit of the series) contains a wide variety of landscapes each interesting and appealing in its own right. Every county presents a multitude of problems of Landscape History and their very contrast is illuminating. Even little Rutland has such contrasts, though naturally on a more limited scale; and a large county like Devon has almost every kind of landscape. One other point: when the reorganisation of local government took place a few years ago, and some entirely new names appeared on the administration map of England, such as Avon and Cleveland, I had to consider whether we should stick to the old counties as we have always known them or adopt the new set-up. As the series was by then so far advanced under the old and well-loved names, we decided to retain them and go on as before. There were other good reasons, besides the sentimental one, for sticking to the original plan.

It is a well-worn truism that England is a very small country with an almost infinite variety of rocks, soils, topography, and watercourses by the tens of thousands: all these things create what one might call micro-landscapes at the risk of importing a little professional jargon into something which is meant to be enjoyed and explained in plain English. One look at the coloured map of the geology of England and Wales, and above all the way in which the colours change every few miles, is enough to excite the visual imagination. This is especially true when one crosses the grain of a piece of country, instead of travelling along it. There is for example the major grain, so to speak, which runs from the south-west coast in Dorset north-eastwards to the Yorkshire coast round Whitby. If you cut *across* this geological grain, going from south-east to north-west, the landscapes change every few miles. On a smaller scale but nearly as complicated, the south-eastern corner of England, running from say Newhaven northwards to the Thames estuary, presents rapid and very contrasted changes of landscape—in soils, building stones (and hence buildings themselves), in vernacular building—the architectural equivalent of the once-rich variety of local dialects in this country—in land-forms, in farming, in almost everything that is visible.

Most of us enjoy some widespread view from a hilltop or on some grand coast: we enjoy it as "scenery" but this is really a superficial enjoyment. What I prefer to call "landscape" as distinct from "scenery" is that a landscape to me asks questions: why is something like this at all, why does it differ from another view a few miles away? It is the difference perhaps between what an amateur portrait painter sees and puts on paper and what a skilled surgeon sees when he contemplates and reflects over a human body. He sees things, even on a superficial examination, because of his training and his long experience, that the layman never sees. So it is with *landscape*. To see it thus, seeing beneath the surface and the obvious, is to increase one's enjoyment of the English countryside enormously. The great English painter John Constable makes this point in one simple sentence in one of his *Discourses on Landscape*, a sentence I shall never tire of quoting. *"We see nothing till we truly understand it."* Constable's *Discourses* were an attempt to justify landscape-painting as an end in itself. If we take his great dictum as our text, Landscape History becomes an end in itself, transmuting the textbook facts of rocks and soils, landforms, economic history, industrial archaeology—words calculated to deter all but the most determined reader—into a different way of looking at perhaps commonplace things, into a different language. The art is to use these academic disciplines in a concealed way, never to let them obtrude or, if so, to some essential purpose so that the visual is always paramount.

When I wrote my own book, now more than twenty years ago, I did not answer all the possible questions by a long way, though it still stands as a good introduction to a new field of history. Landscape History is now, I think, a well-accepted and respectable discipline, taught in some universities and in schools, and the subject of theses. I did not answer all the questions for the simple reason that I did not then know what they all were. And even now, after so many books and articles and theses have been written, there is so much that remains unknown, and no doubt questions that I, and others, have still not perceived. This, to me, is one of the great values of these landscape books, treated county by county. Local studies in depth, to use a fashionable phrase, but for once a useful one, will not only enlarge our generalisations about the major changes in the landscape, but also because of their detail bring new lights into the picture. Ideally, as editor of this series, I would like each writer on a particular county to pick out an even smaller area for special examination under the microscope, having in mind such revealing studies as Professor Harry Thorpe's masterly essay on Wormleighton in Warwickshire (*The Lord and the Landscape*, published in 1965) and Dr Jack Ravensdale's *Liable to Floods* (1974) which deals with three Fen-Edge villages in Cambridgeshire. Not only are the topographical settings of these two studies so completely different, but one is concerned with "peasant villages" and the landscapes they created. So social structure also enters into the many hidden creators of a particular bit of England and the vision it presents.

Some major problems remain virtually unsolved. I myself in my first book fell into the trap, or rather accepted the current doctrine, that until the Old English Conquest most of this country was uncleared woodland or undrained marsh or in many parts primaeval moorland. To a large extent I was deceived by the overwhelming evidence of the number of Old English place-names on the map, or, if not these, then the powerful Scandinavian element in the eastern parts of England. I am no longer deceived, or perhaps I should say that I have become much more sceptical about the ultimate value of this treacherous evidence. Thanks to archaeological advances in the past twenty years (and partly thanks to the opportunities offered by the odious onward march of the motorways—their only value in my eyes) we know very much more about the density of settlement and of population in prehistoric times right back to the Mesolithic of seven or eight thousand years ago. There is evidence for forest clearance and to some extent for settled farming as early as this, and to an even greater extent by Neolithic times when one thinks of the axe-factories two thousand or more feet up on the wildest mountains of Lakeland. Forest clearance was going on at this height, and axes were being exported as far south as the coast of Hampshire. We now need a completely fresh study of the distribution of woodland by, say, Romano-British times. Not only woodland clearance, but the river gravels which have been exploited by modern man for his new roads have changed our whole concept of prehistoric settlement. The gravels of the Welland valley, almost in the heart of the Midlands, have been particularly intensively studied and have changed our entire thinking in these parts.

That is one aspect of the English landscape which I greatly under-estimated when I first wrote and I welcome every fresh piece of evidence that proves me misguided. Yet all the same the outlines of the main picture remain unchanged, and I stand by that first book subject to such changes of emphasis as I have mentioned.

There are other problems waiting to be worked out, some special to particular bits of England, others of a more general nature. Of the special problems I think of the number of isolated parish churches in the beautiful county of Norfolk: why are they there, stuck out all alone in the fields? Somebody could write a wonderful book on Churches in the Landscape. And there are other special aspects of the landscape wherever one walks in this most beloved of all countries: so much to do, so little done. These closer studies of England county by county will add enormously to our knowledge. Already the study of Landscape History has attracted a growing literature of its own, a great deal of it scattered in local journals and periodicals. Soon, perhaps in ten years' time, we shall need a Bibliography of the subject. This makes it sound dull and academic, but in the end I look upon it as an enlargement of consciousness, a new way of looking at familiar scenes which adds to the enjoyment of life. For those who have eyes to see, the face of Britain will never look the same again.

Exeter, 1976   W. G. HOSKINS

Preface

ANYONE ATTEMPTING TO write a history of the landscape of Somerset, with its magnificent and varied scenery, is immediately struck by the impossibility of doing justice to it in any conceivable span of time or space. The painful process of compression and omission is inevitable, and if readers find their favourite corner has been omitted or given insufficient attention, I hope they will forgive the author for selecting his own personal choices and enthusiasms. He has no escape from that dilemma.

A few years before I began the study, the historic county of Somerset was truncated and its northern portion was incorporated with Bristol and south Gloucestershire into the new county of Avon. Perhaps one day it will be possible to write a history of the landscape of Avon, but in this book its existence has been ignored, and I have included the ancient county of Somerset in its entirety. No other course would have made sense.

A study such as this is also heavily dependent on all those scholars and enthusiasts, both professional and amateur, who have written about the county in the past, as well as the many dedicated local historians who are happily still at work within it. It is a real pleasure to express my thanks and gratitude to all those who have helped with friendly advice and assistance. They are far too numerous to name individually, but there are some whose kindness deserves a special mention. David Bromwich, the local history librarian of the Somerset County Council and the Somerset Archaeological and Natural History Society was a constant help, as were Derek Shorrocks and Robin Bush and the rest of the friendly staff of the Somerset Record Office in Taunton. Students of Somerset are indeed fortunate to have such an excellent local history library and record office at their service. I am also grateful to Robert Dunning and his colleagues on the Victoria County History of Somerset, whose recent volumes on the Southern hundreds of the county are indispensable for a proper understanding of its landscape history. Joe Bettey of the University of Bristol Extra-Mural Department gave me much helpful advice on the north of the county and his colleague, Michael Aston, was exceptionally generous with his time and expertise on matters archaeological, especially in relation to field systems and medieval deserted villages. The earliest history of the landscape is one of the most difficult and rapidly changing subjects, and I am also grateful to my colleague Bryony Orme at Exeter for help with the Neolithic period, and to Roger Leech of the University of Lancaster for kindly allowing me to consult his unpublished thesis on Roman Somerset. I also benefited from the kindness of Ian Burrow, Somerset County Archaeologist, in reading and commenting on the chapter on the early English settlement. Needless to say, I alone am responsible for all conclusions and interpretations.

Michael Williams' researches on the Levels and the Mendips are of fundamental importance and I am indebted to him for allowing me to draw so freely on them; as I am also to Prof. Ron Neale, the historian of Bath, for a most enjoyable day exploring that incomparable city. His help and advice were invaluable. Clare Austin helped elucidate some of the problems of the vernacular architecture of South Somerset. Lloyd and Ann Jones of West Lyng provided agricultural expertise and their knowledge of farmhouses and manors in the Quantock region revealed much that would otherwise have been missed. My niece and nephew, Julia and Nigel Hunter, lent a cottage in East Lyng, without whose peaceful ambience the book would never have been written. Simon Lamb's superb photographs I think speak for themselves. Margaret Body's tactful and constructive editing at Hodder and Stoughton has also helped to improve the text, the maps and the illustrations. I am also most grateful to the University of Exeter for granting me a year's study leave to complete the writing. Needless to say my debt to Professor W. G. Hoskins for inviting me to write the book, and for his constant inspiration and encouragement, is not only profound, but of long standing. It was he who first introduced me to historical research. Professor Eric Jones kindly read the whole text and I am grateful to him, not only for the many improvements he suggested, but also for his companionship and help during one of those extraordinarily fortunate coincidences that found us both enjoying a sabbatical year in Somerset simultaneously. Finally my greatest debt is to my wife Kate and this is no conventional author's acknowledgement. Without her assistance with archives, field work, and, not least, with typing the manuscript, the book could never have been written. Her constant encouragement drove it forward and only she can know how much it owes to her inspiration.

MICHAEL HAVINDEN

Contents

List of Plates

List of maps and plans

ABBREVIATIONS USED IN FOOTNOTES

SANHS   Proceedings of the Somerset Archaeological and Natural History Society
VCH   The Victoria History of the County of Somerset
SRO   Somerset Record Office

ACKNOWLEDGEMENTS

The author wishes to thank the following for permission to use their photographs:

Michael Aston:	Plate 5
Clare Austin:	Plates 32, 40
Country Life:	Plate 28
Kate Havinden:	Plates 3, 7, 14, 17, 18, 33, 43, 47
A. F. Kersting:	Plates 35, 46
Simon Lamb:	Plates, 2, 6, 8, 9, 10, 11, 12, 13, 15, 16, 19, 20, 21, 22, 23, 24, 25, 26, 27, 29, 30, 31, 34, 35, 37, 38, 39, 42, 44, 45, 48, 49, 50, 51, 52, 53
West Air Photography:	Plates 1, 4, 41

The author wishes to acknowledge the following map sources on which his figures were based:
Figs. 2, 3, 4, 5: After R. H. Leech, "Romano-British rural settlement in S. Somerset and N. Dorset", Bristol University Ph.D thesis, 1977; Fig. 6: Based on W. G. Hoskins' *The Westward Expansion of Wessex*, 1966; Fig. 11: "Population" and "Values" maps from Roy Millward, Dept. of Geography, Leicester University; "Well Wooded" map based on H. C. Darby and R. Welldon Finn, *The Domesday Geography of South-West England*, 1967; Figs. 12, 17, 19, 24 (right): Adapted from Michael Williams' *The Draining of the Somerset Levels*; Fig. 15: Adapted from T. J. Hunt and R. R. Sellman's *Aspects of Somerset History*; Figs. 16, 20: Adapted from "The Brue Drainage", a plan by William White, 1803 (SRO); Fig. 18: Adapted from "A map of Grenton Manor and its share of Sedgemoore", (SRO); Fig. 23: Adapted from Roger Miles' *The Trees and Woods of Exmoor* (Exmoor Press, Dulverton, 1972); Fig. 24 (left): After

Day and Masters' map of 1782; Fig. 25: After Michael Aston and Roger Leech's *Historic Towns in Somerset* and Strachey's map of 1736; Fig. 26: After Aston and Leech; Fig. 27: After Aston and Leech and maps in the Victoria History of the County of Somerset, Vol. III.

ONE

Somerset's changing landscape, an overview

1. The landscape yesterday and today

The landscape today—a journey through the county. The main phases in the evolution of the landscape

THE SOMERSET LANDSCAPE is one of the most varied and beautiful in England, and it is this variety which presents the most intriguing problems for anyone trying to explain its history. Historic Somerset was a large county, containing over one million acres and stretching seventy miles from east to west, and fifty from north to south at its broadest point. The contrast between the bleak, windswept uplands of Mendip, the lush flat emerald meadows of the central plain, and the wild, romantic grandeur of Exmoor and the western hills, is so great that the history of their creation cannot be understood as a unified whole. Hence the major part of this book is devoted to regional studies. Yet they were all part of one historic county, and so in the first part of the book an attempt will be made to give an overview of the creation of the landscape as it happened through time, so that the common historical forces which acted on all the regions will not be lost sight of. It is hoped that this initial unified study will enable the regional chapters to be fitted into a general framework.

We of course begin at the end of the story. The landscape which surrounds us is the product of thousands of years of slow and laborious work by our ancestors. We need to examine it in all its charm and variety before we can fully appreciate how it came to have its present shape and form. We may start by making an imaginary journey through the county, beginning in the north. If a traveller enters the county at its northernmost point, he journeys along the crest of the Cotswold Hills at a height of some 800 feet, and from that rolling plateau looks down steep-sided, wooded combes to the Avon valley twisting beneath him. From the vantage point of Lansdown racecourse, above Bath, he can see the great curve of the Avon as it circles the hills behind Bath (Plate 41), and he can look down on that dignified ancient city astride the river. A metropolis since Roman times, Bath was the largest city in Somerset (before its inclusion in the new county of Avon in 1974), but even so it was only a medium-sized town with a population of nearly 85,000 in 1971 (compared with somewhat less than 40,000 in Taunton, the county capital).

No other town in England has such a wealth of Georgian architecture as Bath. Its ordered streets, charming ambience, and its beautiful setting amidst the wooded hills of the Avon valley make it a gateway of which any county could be proud. Bath is a truly exceptional town, with its Roman plan (and surviving baths) and its medieval abbey church as well as its Georgian elegance.[1] West of Bath the Avon flows through undulating pasture-lands favoured for country seats. The handsome Georgian houses and parks of Newton St Loe (now a teachers' training college) and Kelston, on a bluff overlooking the northern bank of the Avon, are good examples of the Palladian style in England. Next comes Keynsham, another small industrial town, rather knocked about by modern development, and then the vast, sprawling suburbs of southern Bristol, under which the ancient parishes of Bedminster and Brislington have disappeared as separate entities. The suburbs now reach to the foot of the Dundry Hills, which fortunately are too steep for them to climb.

South-west of Keynsham is the pretty valley of the river Chew with its handsome stone villages with their elegant churches, like Chew Magna and Chew Stoke. This rural calm, however, conceals a busy industrial past, for this valley once boasted many water-powered mills engaged in copper, brass, leather and other trades, and it embodies an exceptionally important and yet little recognised feature of the Somerset landscape—the fact that much of it is post-industrial. This is most noticeable a little farther east in the area between Bath and the Mendips, which is one of Britain's largest totally-disused coalfields. Although the remains of industrial activity (and its current continuance in new forms) are much more noticeable here than in the Chew

[1] C. Robertson, *Bath, an Architectural Guide* (1975).

valley, it is still difficult to believe that this deeply-indented hill country with its fine views and wooded valleys once contained hundreds of coal-mines, and was criss-crossed with canals and railways, now all gone. One of the most astonishing aspects of the Somerset landscape is the way in which nature has reasserted itself, and converted areas once gashed and torn by mining activity back into quiet agricultural landscapes. Towns and villages like Radstock, Paulton, Timsbury and Dunkerton now house workers in prosperous light industries such as printing, plastics, electronics and textiles in a region where most of the mining spoil-heaps have been rapidly overgrown, and only the neat rows of stone cottages evoke the coal-laden past. Yet the last mines closed as recently as 1973.

South of the variegated hill and valley landscape between the Avon and the Mendips, the bleak upland solidity of the lime-stone range presents a stark contrast. Almost uninhabited on its broad plateau, except for the ancient lead-mining settlement of Priddy and the scattered farms created during the enclosures (1700–1840), the windswept hilltop yields the most breath-taking views southwards. On a clear day the whole of Somerset right to the limits of Exmoor on the far western horizon is laid out before the traveller. This stupendous view has struck countless writers, and none more forcibly than Edward Hutton, author of *Highways and Byways in Somerset*, who saw it in 1912, after many years' residence in Italy. On Beacon Hill above Wells the traveller comes upon

. . . one of the most astonishing views in all Southern England. For suddenly and without warning from that great height he will see spread out beneath him a vast and mysteri-ous plain, blue and grey and gold in the setting sun, and beyond, far and far away, the great broken hills of the West Country. To one returning after long absence that view must be the most consoling in the world . . . much else doubtless he may see as he lingers there: the boundaries of his beloved kingdom, the chalk hills of Wiltshire in the east, the shining Channel to the west, to the south the dark highlands of Dorset and Devon, and to the north the spurs of the Cots-wolds; but this chiefly—his home, the county of Somerset

31

from Bath and Bristol to Dunkery Beacon, from Penselwood and the Blackdown Hills to the Severn Sea.[2]

Along the southern base of Mendip, in the immediate foreground is a line of ancient towns and villages taking advantage of the streams which issue from underground at the foot of the pervious limestone hills. Farthest to the west is Axbridge, a medieval borough which still retains its ancient character. Nearby is Cheddar, at the foot of its magnificent gorge and guarding its famous caves where the strange behaviour of water on limestone has created beautiful stalactites and stalagmites. In the centre is Wells, the ancient cathedral city, and one of the most attractive small towns in England, set next to its moated bishop's palace. A few miles farther east is Shepton Mallet, now somewhat marred by redevelopment, but still possessing the character of an old Somerset woollen town, much of it built from the mellow oolitic limestone from the quarries of the neighbouring village of Doulting.

Out beyond this line of towns lies the strange landscape of the Somerset Levels, a vast reclaimed swamp, where the brilliant emerald green pastures are separated not by hedges or walls, but by a huge network of irrigation ditches (known locally as rhynes, pronounced reens). Each is about six feet wide and filled with water, which, when caught by the setting sun, glistens a brilliant silver or gold, so that the whole basin of some 250 square miles looks like a huge green fishing-net with its translucent ribs shimmering and glistening. Rivers wind and twist their way through the plain, which is always liable to flooding in winter (see Plate 1), both because the rainfall which falls on the surrounding hills can be very heavy, and because there is a barely perceptible ridge of clays which stretches along the coast and is a few feet higher than the surrounding plain. This clay ridge impedes the drainage of the Levels and makes it difficult for the rivers and artificial drainage cuts to carry off excess water. When the tides are high in the Bristol Channel, the sea can be higher than the water level in the rivers, and only the existence of one-way trap-gates (known as clyses) prevents

[2] E. Hutton, *Highways and Byways in Somerset* (Macmillan, 1924 ed.), p. vii.

the sea from flowing up the rivers and causing more serious flooding. All the river mouths are fitted with clyses except the Parrett, whose estuary is too wide. Coastal trade up to Bridg-water was also a factor until recently.

Narrow hills divide the Levels into three sections. The northernmost, and smallest, lies between the Failand Hills, just south of Bristol, and the Mendips, and is dominated by Weston-super-Mare, the popular tourist and commuter town which has spread all along the reclaimed land fronting Weston Bay between the great wooded mound of Worlebury Hill to its north and the cliffs of Uphill to its south, and now houses over 50,000 people. Between the Mendips and the Poldens lie the central Levels, drained by the rivers Axe and Brue. It is here in the Brue valley between Glastonbury and Meare that the peat is thickest and crops out on the surface. Scattered amongst the Levels are a series of hills and ridges which were once islands in the swamp. The most celebrated of these is Glastonbury Tor (Plate 19), the majestic cone which draws the eye from all parts of central Somerset. At its foot lies the little town of Glaston-bury clustered round the ruins of its famous abbey. This is reputed to be the oldest Christian shrine in England, with legends going back to Roman times. Whatever their truth, the countryside around Glastonbury evokes the remote past in a mysterious way of its own. Nearby, to the south-east, a larger range of attractively wooded hills has a special significance for Somerset history. For here lies Somerton, the ancient heartland settlement from which the county derives its name. It is thought that the earliest Saxon settlers around here may have migrated during the summer into the rich marshland pastures surrounding their villages, and hence have earned the name of *sumorsaetas*—the summer dwellers in the marshes. But the hills themselves have been permanently settled for much longer. As we shall see, this was the centre of one of the densest con-centrations of Roman villas anywhere in England.

The narrow ridge of the Polden Hills, running from near the coast at Dunball eastwards to join the Somerton Hills south of Street, separates the central Levels from the southern Levels, sometimes known as Sedgemoor from their most extensive floodable area lying athwart the rivers Cary, Parrett, and Tone, between the Poldens and the Quantocks. It was on a small "island" here at Athelney (Plate 16) that King Alfred took refuge from the Danes before defeating them in the historic campaign of 878. The subsequent peace was signed at another "island", Wedmore, a few miles south of Cheddar. This flat landscape of drained marshland with its roads fringed with pollarded willows is a world of its own—remote and slightly secretive and yet possessing a curious charm, felt best perhaps amongst the ruins of the ancient abbeys of Muchelney and Athelney, once islands surrounded by swamps (though no visible remains survive at Athelney). So flat is this country that even a low hill like Athelney, only twelve metres high, can seem formidable by contrast with the miles of surrounding flatness.

The rivers of the southern Levels, the Yeo, the Parrett and the Isle, carry tongues of the wetlands deep into southern Somerset, where a long, narrow arc of rolling vales and scarps stretches from beneath the Wiltshire Downs below PenSelwood westwards through the vicinities of Yeovil and Ilminster, and into the Vale of Taunton Deane. Here it divides into two parts, one reaching westwards between the Blackdown Hills (on the south) and the Brendons and Quantocks (on the north) to Wellington and Wiveliscombe. The other part skirts the north side of the Quantocks and reaches the sea between the Parrett and Quantoxhead. On this flat plain may be found some of the most fertile land and most prosperous farms in this whole rich arable arc. Although the Vale of Taunton Deane was famous for its early enclosures and its lush orchards as early as the sixteenth century, the central and easterly part of the arc presents a quite different landscape. Here the enclosure process was very slow and long-drawn-out. Even today, in the villages between Ilminster and Ilchester vast open fields of corn stretch to the horizon. Technically they are enclosed, and most traces of the semi-communal farming of the open-field system have long since vanished, but although the individually-owned fields are large, they are often still only separated from one another by the grassy balks of medieval times. Most of the farms still cluster in the villages, and it does not require much imagination in a place like Shepton Beauchamp to transport oneself back to Tudor times; yet this is the centre of highly mechanised and prosperous modern farming.

This is also a region of fine country houses and beautifully built stone villages, using the magnificent honey-coloured limestone from the ancient Ham Hill quarries near Montacute. An Iron Age hill-fort stands above the quarries whose stone has been used since Roman times, if not earlier. Nearby stands Montacute House, home of Sir Edward Phelips, an Elizabethan judge, who celebrated his success by building Somerset's most ostentatious Tudor manor house. A few miles to the south-west a rival family, the Earls Poulett, built an imposing seat of many architectural periods at Hinton St George, and owned one of the most beautiful villages in Somerset. At Hinton the stone vernacular architecture of the Tudor and Stuart period may be seen at its finest.

Although this southern arc shares common characteristics in being devoted to arable farming and in its absence of either marshland or high hills, it is by far the least homogeneous of Somerset's regions, and the geological complexity of clays, limestones, sandstones and marls, especially in the eastern part, gives it a variety of localised topography which cannot be fully appreciated in a generalised description.

One of its strangest scenes occurs in the zone of porous yellow sandstones, known as the Yeovil sands, where the rocks are so soft that the roads and lanes have cut gorges in them which are sometimes as much as twenty feet high. The A30 main road passes through such gorges between West Coker and Yeovil, and there are many more in the neighbourhood.

Finally we come to the western hills, and here again there is much variety in local topography. The Blackdown Hills, whose north-facing scarp stretches from Chard to west of Wellington, are shared with Devon, and the border runs along an ancient trackway on their crest. Seen from the Levels, their steep, forbidding scarp looms like a true frontier, and may well have been the ancient eastern border of *Dumnonia*, the Celtic kingdom based on Devon and Cornwall. The scarp is steep and heavily wooded, and the underlying rocks of chalk, greensand and clay help to produce a very different landscape from the open rolling moorland of the Brendons, Exmoor and the higher parts of the Quantocks. The remains of the great medieval forest of Neroche survive around Staple Fitzpaine, and amongst the winding lanes and the magnificent beech trees of the Blackdowns one is in deep and remote country which seems worlds away from the bustle of Taunton, only a few miles to the north.

As we look across the Vale of Taunton Deane from the Duke of Wellington's monument, 800 feet above sea level, the graceful line of the Quantocks can be seen receding north-westwards towards the sea. Here again is another unique landscape, with a line of parishes like Cothelstone, West Bagborough and Crowcombe situated beneath the western scarp of the Quantocks in the undulating vale separating the latter hills from the Brendons, and all having a scatter of small fields enclosed behind large hedgerows and banks of the Devon type, and extensive grazing-commons on the Quantock heights. The hills are less bare now than formerly, when they were great unfenced sheepwalks. In recent years much afforestation with conifers has taken place (Plate 17), especially on the eastern dip slope where the hills recede gently towards the Parrett valley and the sea. The hills are dissected by numerous attractively wooded combes, where Wordsworth and Coleridge used to wander when staying at Alfoxden and Nether Stowey in the early years of the nineteenth century. In English romantic poetry the influence of this landscape can be clearly perceived. Dorothy Wordsworth especially liked its open and unfettered nature:

> Wherever we turn we have woods, smooth downs, and valleys with small brooks running down them through green meadows hardly ever intersected with hedge-rows, but scattered with trees. The hills that cradle these valleys are either covered with fern or bilberries, or oak woods—walks extend for miles over the hill-tops, the great beauty of which is their wild simplicity.[3]

Although enclosure has since taken in much of the foothill country, the Quantock hilltops still afford miles of unimpeded country for walkers.

[3] Quoted in *Murray's Handbook to Somerset*, p. 410.

West of the Vale, the Brendon Hills, outliers of Exmoor, rise sharply to their bleak windswept summits over 1,300 feet high. An ancient track runs along the crest from Elworthy to Wheddon Cross, yielding magnificent views both to north and south. The view extends over the National Trust's beautifully wooded Holnicote estate, over picturesque Minehead to the Bristol Channel and the mountains of Wales beyond. Southwards the view extends over wild moorish country to the forested Haddon Hill, with its large new reservoir. Beyond the delightfully wooded Exe valley lies Exmoor proper, rolling away to the west with range upon range of hills rising to the bleak and forbidding Chains on the western border with Devon (Plate 2). This is the legendary Doone country, with the valley of the river Barle threading its way eastwards from Simonsbath to Dulverton, through a landscape which underwent a drastic transformation in the nineteenth century. Much of central Exmoor was then reclaimed for farming by the work of the Knight family, and the roads, hedgerows, shelter-banks and stone farmsteads which we see today are of relatively recent creation. They give much of Exmoor a civilised and cared-for appearance which contrasts strongly with that of Dartmoor, but there are still extensive areas on the western side where climate and soil resisted all attempts to introduce the plough, and where the wild deer and the Exmoor ponies still hold sway.

This thumbnail sketch has given only a foretaste of the variety and attractiveness of the many landscapes included in Somerset, but it has underlined the more basic regional contrasts. In essence there are two—very different—landscapes which have been created by immense and fairly recent reclamation projects—the Levels and Exmoor, and there are two landscapes, the southern arc and the Avon – Mendip area, which have emerged very slowly over immensely long periods of time as generations of farmers have nibbled away at forest, waste and marsh, and carved a farming environment for themselves out of areas where soil and climate were much kinder than in the marshy lowlands or the rugged western uplands. This fourfold regional division has been used as the framework for this study (Fig. 1).

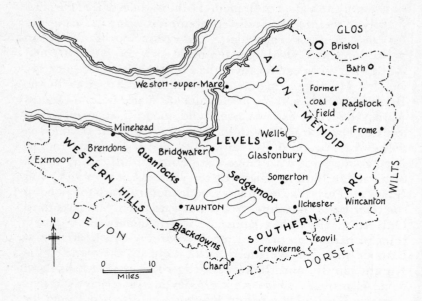

Fig. 1. The four major regional divisions of Somerset

The main phases in the evolution of the landscape

Before looking at the evolution of the landscapes of Somerset in more detail it may be helpful to attempt a brief chronological summary of the main periods of change throughout the county. The period may be broken down into shorter phases of time, based on general movements in the economy, for the direction and pace of change in the landscape was affected by movements in the national as well as the regional economy. Changes in key factors, such as population, the demand for rural and urban goods and services, the transportation network, and more generalised features still, like internal security, political stability and war and peace, all played their part. The major phases which can be identified (in broad terms) are (1) the period of original settlement, dating from the earliest imprint of man in Mesolithic times (some 10–15,000 years ago) to the Roman settlement (c.a.d. 45—410); (2) the early medieval period, stretching from the end of the Roman Empire to the first detailed survey of the landscape by William the Conqueror in 1086 (the Domesday Survey); (3) the period from 1086 to about 1320, which was a time of expanding population, production and trade, with a consequent growth in settlement in the countryside and the creation of new towns and seaports. It was also a time when castles, monasteries and parish churches were being built.

The next phase, (4), ran from about 1320 to about 1460 and was a marked contrast. This was a time which started with population growth outstripping the resources of the land, with a consequent rise in malnutrition, disease and poverty, culminating in the disastrous series of plagues which reached their height in the Black Death of 1348–9, but which continued intermittently, and with only slightly diminished destructiveness, for the next century. As a result, population was very slow to regain its lost numbers, and it has been estimated that, whereas the population of the whole of England may have been as high as five and a half millions in 1349, it was only some two millions in 1450 (though it should be emphasised that these figures are only estimates based on partial sources and hence subject to wide margins of error. The *trends* of growth and decline are not, however, in doubt—only their relative magnitude).[4] Consequently the cultivated area contracted, when settlements were deserted and some former open-field corn land was enclosed and converted to pasture for sheep-farming in order to save labour. Towns also tended to stagnate or decay, and some of the smaller ones succumbed to the competition for trade from their larger neighbours. Politically this was a mixed period. The Peasants' Revolt (1381) failed initially, but the Wars of the Roses (c. 1450–70) weakened the feudal aristocracy so that the peasants were able to improve their position economically by buying off their labour services and renting pieces of the demesne land which the lords could no longer afford to farm.

The following period, (5), from about 1460 to about 1650,

[4] M. M. Postan, *The Medieval Economy and Society* (Pelican, 1975), pp. 30–44.

was again a contrast. Population recovered slowly at first, and then, after about 1520, very rapidly, reproducing some of the strains which had occurred before 1350. It probably rose from some two million to about four and a half million. The Tudor monarchs provided stable government, the wool and cloth trades expanded rapidly, and by 1600 they were joined by many other new industries such as calamine (zinc)—and coal-mining in north Somerset, glove-making in the Yeovil area, and rope- and sail-making around Crewkerne. This period also saw the dissolution of the monasteries (1536–9) and many other religious, social and political changes which erupted into civil war in 1642—the period thus ending with unprecedented social change (the establishment of a republic in 1649) and a good deal of confusion.

The next period, (6), from about 1650 to about 1800, coincided with a steadier rate of population growth and a slower, but continuous, rate of economic and political change. From about 1700 onwards this pace increased. Many open fields were enclosed, serious work on draining the Levels began, parks and mansions were created, turnpike roads and canals improved communications, and towns were transformed (especially Bath, which became the fashion capital of the nation). The final period, (7), runs from 1800 to the present. After 1800 the pace continued to quicken with the rapid development of the coal-field around Radstock, the growth of manufacturing industries in towns like Bridgwater and Yeovil, and the spread of the railway and road network. The recent age of the automobile and the combine harvester has brought the most rapid changes of all, characterised by rural depopulation, suburban sprawl, the growth of industry and quarrying, and tourist penetration. Yet these changes are not dramatic in Somerset. The landscape still retains the major part of its historic character.

SELECT BIBLIOGRAPHY

Little, B., *Portrait of Somerset*, 3rd edn. (1974).
Dunning, R. W., *A History of Somerset* (1978).
Whitlock, R., *Somerset* (1975).
The Victoria History of the County of Somerset, Vol. I (1906), Vol. II (1911), Vol. III (1974), Vol. IV (1978).

Aston, M. and Leech, R., *Historic Towns in Somerset* (1977).
Pevsner, N., *The Buildings of England: North Somerset and Bristol* (1958) and *South and West Somerset* (1958).
Hunt, T. J. and Sellman, R. R. *Aspects of Somerset History* (1973).
Dunning, R., *Somerset and Avon* (1980).
Bettey, J. H., *The Landscape of Wessex* (1980).

2. The ancient landscape

The earliest imprint of man. Prehistoric settlements. The impact of Rome. Rural settlements. The Roman towns

The Earliest Imprint of Man

UNTIL A FEW years ago it was generally believed that the influence of the earliest settlers on the present landscape was very limited. Upland areas like Salisbury Plain, Mendip and Exmoor had their scatter of burial mounds, hill-forts and "Celtic fields" dating from the Neolithic, Bronze and Iron Ages, but it was believed that even the long period of Roman rule, from A.D. 43 to A.D. 410, did little to extend cultivation into the rich lowlands, which were thought to have been largely covered with dense virgin forest at the time of the advent of the first English settlers in the fifth, sixth, and (in Somerset) seventh centuries. In other words, it was believed that the pattern of villages, hamlets, farms, roads and hedges which we know today was essentially the work of the English settlers, who were equipped with a heavy plough capable of cutting a furrow in the soil and turning it over, thus burying stubble, grass and weeds, unlike their predecessors who had had only a light plough (called an ard), which merely scratched the surface of the field. Because of this technical superiority the English could tackle the heavy claylands of the valley bottoms, whereas the earlier settlers had been forced to cultivate the light, thin soils of the hilltops, which were all that their ards could handle.

However, recent work by archaeologists, geographers, soil scientists and historians has shown that this pattern is far too simple. No doubt it was true of the heaviest, wettest and most intractable claylands (such as those underlying the old Selwood Forest in south-east Somerset), but the trend of recent research has been to place much more emphasis on continuity of settlement, and much less on sudden breaks. It is coming to be realised that the signs of early agriculture have *survived* on hillsides and plateaux, because those areas were used only for grazing by later generations, but that the evidence for settlement in the valleys has been largely *destroyed* by subsequent farming and building operations. This has been particularly well demonstrated by Christopher Taylor in his study of the neighbouring county of Dorset, where he has shown that the landscape assumed much of its "medieval" form and pattern *before* the English conquest. Dorset, like Somerset, was a county where the English did not assume control until some 200 years after the end of the Roman Empire.[1]

The evidence of place-names can also be very deceptive. Many villages, hamlets and farms in Somerset have names derived from the Old English language. It is therefore only too easy to assume that they must have been *founded* by English settlers. Yet names can easily be changed. We do not often have direct evidence of this, but occasionally we do, such as the statement in the early charter (c.682) of West Monkton, which contains a revealing reference to Creechbarrow Hill, now on the eastern edge of Taunton, as "the hill the British call *Cructan* and we *Crycbeorh*".[2] Incidentally, *cruc* meant hill and *tan* meant fire, indicating that the hill was used for beacons. *Tan* gave its name to the river at its foot, now slightly changed to Tone, and hence also to Taunton. If a hill could have its name changed, so no doubt could a village, a hamlet, or a farm. There is a serious possibility that many of the fields of Somerset have been continuously cultivated since Neolithic times (that is, for about five thousand, or possibly even six thousand years, since archaeologists keep pushing the origins of farming farther and farther back in time). It may well be that not only the fields, but also the settlements have been continuously inhabited in many cases. If this is so (and only further archaeological research can

[1] C. Taylor, *The Making of the English Landscape: Dorset* (1970), pp. 21–83.
[2] G. B. Grundy, *The Saxon Charters and Field Names of Somerset* (Supplement to Proceedings of the Somerset Archaeological and Natural History Society, 1935), pp. 51–4.

prove it), the basic structure of the landscape as we see it today (that is, the location of settlements, roads, fields and hedges) may have been far more heavily influenced by the early pre-historic settlers than we can yet demonstrate. Their secret imprint on the landscape may be much more profound than the chance survival of barrows and hill-forts on remote and often bleak hilltops would ever suggest.[3]

However this may be (and we shall look at some more evidence later), the natural landscape into which the earliest settlers entered would also have played a significant part—for though much can be changed by men, the fundamental pattern of hills, valleys, rocks, soils and water-courses remains, and of course the influence of these factors was formerly much stronger than it is today. With their primitive stone axes and knives, and perhaps with wooden spades and ards, the earliest settlers could only clear grassland or lightly-wooded ground, and even if they made a large initial clearance by firing the vegetation, they could only prevent natural regeneration in a fairly small area at first, though once they had obtained some control over animals, grazing helped to prevent forest regeneration. What then did the natural landscape of the area later defined as Somerset look like some six thousand years ago? In the first place, the level of the Bristol Channel was lower than it is today, and the "sub-merged forests" which are marked on the maps as lying just north of the coast (there are some near Minehead) were not yet inundated. It has been estimated that seven thousand years ago the sea was ten fathoms below its present level, which meant that the whole bay between Bridgwater and Cardiff was swampy lowland. Much of this had probably filled with water by the time the first Neolithic farmers arrived, but the coastal lowlands would have been more extensive than they are now, and, as a consequence of the lower sea level, the central Levels would have been drier and less liable to flooding, though still swampy.[4] The course of the rivers was also very different. The drainage of the

[3] See P. H. Sawyer, ed., *Medieval Settlement, Continuity and Change* (1976), for much striking new evidence in support of this interpretation.

[4] L. V. Grinsell, *The Archaeology of Exmoor* (1970), pp. 15-21; Harry Godwin, "Botanical and Geological History of the Somerset Levels", *Procs. British Association for the Advancement of Science*, XII, 45 (1955), pp. 319-22.

Levels in the last three hundred years or so has led to many of them being straightened out, and in some cases being provided with totally new channels such as the Huntspill "river" for the Brue. The rivers meandered about much more than they do now, and were no doubt a rich source of fresh-water fish, since the lower tides did not then push sea-water so far up them as they did later on. In the river Parrett where there is no barrier (clyse) sea tides still cause problems.[5]

The Levels then would have presented a vast area of swampy ground, rich in grasses and bushes, but free from the dense forests of oak, alder and elm which occupied the slightly higher ground, and rose up the sides of the hills, perhaps to a height of 800 to 1,000 feet. Thus only the highest parts of Exmoor and possibly Mendip were clear of them. On these higher lands, moor grasses and lighter bushes and trees, such as birches and pines, would have grown. It is not clear whether or not Mendip was then covered by forest. The only item of environmental evidence for this period comes from the excavation of one of the Priddy Circles (Plate 5)—ceremonial monuments which seem to have been built around 2,500 B.C.—and it indicates that the area was open grassland at that date. However, Fowler points out that by then Neolithic man could have been grazing his animals on the hills for a thousand years or more, and possibly growing wheat and barley as well, so that this evidence tells us nothing about the natural landscape.[6]

However, it is clear that the earliest settled farmers would have avoided the most heavily forested areas and would have sought out locations with light, easily-worked and porous soils, which carried either grassland or only a thin cover of bushes and trees. Such areas were the less swampy parts of the Levels, the higher parts of Mendip, the Quantocks, the Brendons and Exmoor. The whole area would have been rich in wild animals suitable for hunting or trapping, such as deer, wild pig, and water-fowl, but the need to protect crops and domesticated livestock (cattle, horses, sheep, goats and pigs) from predators must also have presented serious problems. It was not just a

[5] M. Williams, *The Draining of the Somerset Levels* (1970), pp. 17–38.
[6] P. J. Fowler, "Early Mendip", in Robin Atthill, ed., *Mendip: a New Study* (1976), pp. 50–74.

question of deer trampling the crops. Wild animals such as boars and wolves still roamed the countryside (the Mells charter of 942 includes "Boar's spring" and "wolf barrow" amongst its boundary marks) so that the location of settlements had to be determined by the needs of protection as well as by water supplies and favourable soils.[7] Protection from other settlers does not seem to have been a problem at this time. The earliest Neolithic settlements were not equipped with defensive works against their fellow men, no doubt because the settlers were initially only a few, and there was land enough for all. It is only in the later Bronze Age (after c. 1,000 B.C.) and the Iron Age, that tribal warfare became a problem, and the magnificent hill-forts like Dolebury and Tedbury on the Mendips and South Cadbury and Ham Hill on the southern hills were built.

Prehistoric settlements

It is impossible to provide anything like an accurate date for the period when man first began to have an influence on the landscape. The caves of Mendip, such as Wookey Hole, provide some of the earliest evidence of men in Britain. The first of these hunters and gatherers of the old Stone Age seem to have occupied the caves as long as half a million years ago, but their occupation was succeeded by no fewer than three "Ice Ages" when southern Britain was covered by glaciers. Hence any influence they might have had on the landscape would have been obliterated. Most of the Mendip cave material is about 50,000 years old, but it was not until the re-occupation of the area after the last "Ice Age"—about 10,000 years ago—that men would have begun to make their first lasting marks upon the natural scene. Until recently it was thought that the people who lived by hunting and gathering in this last phase of the old Stone Age, (the Mesolithic period) could have had no effect on the landscape, since, being nomadic hunters, they neither built permanent settlements nor brought any land under cultivation. Recent work has, however, shown that from about 6,000 B.C.

---

[7] G. B. Grundy, *The Saxon Charters and Field Names of Somerset* (Supplement to SANHS, 1935), p. 99.

onwards these people began to develop a more complex economy, which could have had a noticeable effect on the landscape—particularly on the amount of forest cover. The analysis of pollen preserved in stratified layers in bogs enables the main features of past vegetational cover to be revealed. The best evidence comes from Hockham Mere in Norfolk, where changes in the vegetation (and the surviving bones of animals) indicate that Mesolithic men were beginning to clear woodland and to domesticate animals such as red deer about 5,500 B.C.[8] They certainly possessed stone axes and command over fire, which would have enabled them to do this, as the Australian aborigines, who had a similar economy, are now known to have done. The Somerset bogs might well reveal similar evidence, because numerous stone tools and artifacts of Mesolithic men have been found in Somerset, and Grinsell's map shows that they were well distributed over the county, occupying lowland sites such as Watchet, Shapwick and Middlezoy, as well as upland places on Exmoor and Mendip, where a Mesolithic hut site was excavated at Priddy in 1977. So it may well be that when the first groups of farmers (Neolithic men) arrived from the Continent, they did not enter an unmodified natural forest, but found a landscape where substantial clearings and thinnings had already been made by the hunting inhabitants.[9]

The points of embarkation of the first farmers and the exact dates of their arrival are still unknown, but a site at Ballynagilly in County Tyrone, Ireland, has yielded some of their characteristic pottery, the earliest of which has been dated to about 4,450 B.C. by the radio-carbon method, adjusted by the bristlecone pine calibration. Pottery of this type (to which archaeologists have given the ungainly name of Grimston Lyles Hill ware) is widely distributed throughout Britain, being found in Ireland, Scotland, Wales and England (although not, as yet, farther west than Hampshire), showing that the Ballynagilly site is not an

---

[8] R. Glasscock in Sawyer, ed., *Medieval Settlement, Continuity and Change*, pp. 191–2.

[9] L. V. Grinsell, "Somerset Archaeology, 1931–65", *SANHS*, 109 (1964–5), p. 50. For the Mesolithic hut site at Priddy see Joan Taylor's report on the excavation at Lower Pitts farm, Priddy, in *SANHS*, 122 (1978), p. 120.

isolated example.[10] As it also seems unlikely that the new-comers reached northern Ireland before England, we may tentatively suggest that their first arrival in England may have been before 4,500 B.C.

The introduction of farming was, of course, a fundamental break in the long history of mankind. Since the earliest recorded evidence of the species, about two million years ago in East Africa, men and women had led a nomadic existence dependent on the animals they hunted and the fruits, berries and nuts they could gather. The development of cereal cultivation and animal domestication meant that permanent sites could be settled, and that the associated arts and crafts of pottery, weaving, tool-making, and eventually reading and writing could be developed. Agriculture seems to have developed spontaneously in a number of centres such as China, India, Mexico and several tropical areas, but it was the centre based on the valleys of the Euphrates, Tigris and Nile in Mesopotamia and Egypt that was crucial for Europe. Gradually, either by migration or diffusion of the technique, a farming population spread westwards through Europe until it reached the British Isles. These were the first people to plant their imprint on the landscape. As we have seen, because most of the surviving evidence of their settlement is on high ground, such as long barrows on Mendip, or pottery in places like South Cadbury and Ham Hill (which later became Iron Age hill-forts) it used to be thought that they avoided the lowlands. However, some of the most dramatic new evidence for lowland settlement comes from Somerset, where the discovery of wooden trackways preserved in the peat bogs of the Levels has radically changed our ideas. These were built by the Neolithic people. The oldest track (the Sweet track) has been dated to about 3,800 B.C., and is at present the oldest known road in Europe, possibly in the world. It cannot have been built in isolation. It is necessary to assume that groups of people had already settled nearby (though no actual sites have yet been discovered), since the tracks through the swamps connect the Polden Hills with sandy islands (known locally as "burtles") a

[10] See C. Renfrew, *British Prehistory, a New Outline* (1974), for details, pp. 20–30.

few miles to their north. It also seems highly likely that more trackways lie buried in the as yet unworked peat between the burtles and Mendip, since Neolithic people occupied the caves on the south side of Mendip, like Wookey Hole. This possibility has been strengthened by the discovery in 1979 of tracks in the peat moors to the south-west of the Poldens. The tracks were no doubt used to facilitate hunting and fishing in the swamps, as well as for purposes of communication and trade (Neolithic people traded stone axes over immense distances. Examples from the Lake District and north Wales have been found in Somerset).[11]

No Neolithic settlement sites have yet been discovered in Somerset, partly because the flimsy wattle-and-daub huts they inhabited leave little trace, and more importantly because most of their sites have been obliterated by subsequent building (in villages and towns), or by repeated ploughing as the area under cultivation spread. We are, however, left with the evidence of tombs and centres of religious worship on the high ground, where stone was sometimes used in their construction. Since much of the high ground was preserved as pasture or woodland in later centuries, these features have enjoyed a much better survival rate than have the actual settlement sites. It seems that the farmers liked to settle in river valleys where there was a good water supply, and where they were not too exposed to the weather, and to bury important persons in tombs overlooking their settlements. Perhaps it was felt that the dead could keep a protective eye on their successors.

The most common tombs were the long barrows, which in Somerset have survived best on Mendip and the hills to the north of it. Some sixteen examples are known, of which the best is Stoney Littleton, near Wellow.[12] The Neolithic people also built large circular enclosures which no doubt were temples of some sort. These types of monument are called henges, after Stonehenge, their most famous exemplar, but the Somerset

[11] J. M. Coles, B. J. Orme, F. A. Hibbert, G. J. Wainwright, eds., *Somerset Levels Papers*, No. 1 (1975), No. 2 (1976); Christopher Norman and Colin F. Clements, "Prehistoric timber structures on King's Sedgemoor: some recent discoveries", *SANHS*, 123 (1979), pp. 5–18.

[12] Grinsell, "Somerset Archaeology", pp. 51–2.

examples (the Priddy Circles, and Gorsey Bigbury—again both on Mendip) have no surviving standing stones—if they ever had any. Although the four Priddy Circles (Plate 5) look very impressive from the air, having diameters of about 158 metres, they are quite difficult to spot on the ground. They were constructed around 2,500 B.C.[13]

From about 2,200 B.C. the inhabitants began to improve the tools at their disposal by substituting bronze for polished stone, and although archaeologists speak of the Bronze Age, they have drawn attention to the fact that, apart from the improvement in tools and weapons, the way of life of the people did not change. They still cultivated small patches of wheat and barley— probably moving to a new piece of land every year or so, as is still done in many parts of Africa today—and utilising the surrounding pastures, woodlands and swamps as common grazings for their cattle, sheep, goats and pigs. The importance of woodland—especially when it contained acorns and beech-mast—as a source of food for pigs, was very great.

The importance of shifting cultivation (i.e. moving the corn crops around the settlement) is something which should be noted carefully by landscape historians, for it can leave evidence of ploughing over a very much wider area than was ever culti-vated in any one year. For instance, the Quantock hills are covered with plough marks, but they have always been areas of common grazing, and so the explanation seems to be that small areas would have been cultivated as part of an "outfield" each year, later reverting to common pasture. These ploughmarks can sometimes be misleading in relation to the density of settlement. Estimates of population density derived from such data should be treated with caution. There can be no doubt, though, that the countryside was filling up during the Bronze Age, and towards its end, around 600 B.C, there is growing evidence from the multiplicity of weapons and the construction of defended sites, such as hill-forts, that competition for land was becoming a serious problem.

As with the Neolithic peoples, there is very little surviving evidence of Bronze Age settlements, and for the same reasons,

[13] P. J. Fowler, "Early Mendip", pp. 56–61.

but the evidence from barrows is much more extensive. The Bronze Age people built smaller barrows than the Neolithic ones, and they are almost invariably round in shape. Some 750 survive on the Somerset hillsides, thickly scattered on Mendip and the Quantocks especially, but quite numerous also on Exmoor. In addition, there are some circles of standing stones. The three on Exmoor, at Porlock Common, Almisworthy Common and Withypool Hill, are all rather unimpressive, with their little stones, often not more than one foot in height, half buried in the heather,[14] but the three great stone circles at Stanton Drew in the Chew valley constitute a really impressive ancient monument. Interestingly, they are not on the surrounding hills, but close to the river Chew, in the centre of an area bounded to the south by Mendip and to the north by the Avon Valley. This area has yielded quite an impressive amount of evidence of settlement, in the form of bronze implements, daggers, arrow-heads, hoards of jewellery and pottery (beakers), suggesting that it was quite densely settled. The stone circles at Stanton Drew stand in a field of several acres, and their massive size and weight must have made the construction of the temple a huge task. Some of the stones are about eight feet high and four or five feet across. The place is almost comparable with Stonehenge or Avebury, and indicates that north Somerset was an important centre of whatever religion these people practised (probably some form of sun worship). Interestingly, the parish church stands inside the area of the ancient temple, providing striking evidence of the continuity of the site as a holy place.[15]

The extent to which the natural landscape had been modified by cultivation in the Bronze Age cannot be known in detail, but the modern view is that it was much more than was hitherto believed. Indeed, in a recent book Professor Charles Thomas quotes an assertion that "between the emergence of our first British food producers (some time in the fourth millennium B.C.) and a broad stabilisation of the cultural sequence late in the Bronze Age (roughly around 1,000 B.C.), much, if not most, of Lowland Britain outside the forested zones had been carved up

[14] Grinsell, "Somerset Archaeology", pp. 53–7.
[15] L. V. Grinsell, *The Archaeology of Wessex* (1958), pp. 69–79, has a plan of the site.

or apportioned out in land-settlement terms, and indeed some favoured localities may have experienced several thousand years of sporadic cultivation."[16]

The period from about 600 B.C. to the Roman invasion of A.D. 43 is characterised as the Iron Age—again because of a change in the material used for making tools and weapons. But once more it should be emphasised that for the people living at the time no very fundamental changes occurred. New and stronger tools were available, but the ancient rhythm of corn-growing and animal-herding, supplemented no doubt by frequent hunting, trapping and fishing expeditions, continued the same as before. However, the relentless growth of population was pressing on resources all the time, and the archaeological evidence points towards increasing warfare, with numerous and elaborately defended hill-forts being built, especially after the threat of Roman invasion became serious (c.75 B.C.). The Romans wrote a certain amount about Iron Age Britain, and we have the classic accounts of Caesar and Tacitus. This evidence reveals that the Iron Age communities had been organised into kingdoms, and that trade between them (and their kinsmen in Gaul) had expanded to the point where the British kings were minting gold and silver into coins for the convenience of traders. The distribution of finds of these coins enables us to perceive in broad terms the late-Iron Age political geography of what later became Somerset. The area was broadly divided into three groups. To the north-east of a line which ran roughly along Mendip the land was occupied by a people called the *Dobunni*, whose main centre was in the Severn valley and west Midlands. Their capital (and mint) was an *oppidum* called Bagendon, a few miles to the north of Cirencester. Western and central Somerset were occupied by the *Dumnonii*, after whom Devon is named. The Somerset Levels were a frontier zone for them, and were guarded by the great Mendip hill-forts, like Dolebury and Maesbury, although these may have been built by earlier peoples. The *Dumnonii* apparently struck no coins but used iron currency-bars and cattle as a means of exchange. They

[16] Charles Thomas, "Towards the definition of the term 'field' in the light of prehistory", in Sawyer, ed., *Medieval Settlement, Continuity and Change*, pp. 15–40.

also had hill-forts on Exmoor and the Quantocks.

South and eastern Somerset formed a border zone between the *Dumnonii* and the *Durotriges*, who lived in Dorset, centred round their great hill-fort of Maiden Castle near Dorchester. The magnificent hill-forts of Ham Hill and South Cadbury in southern Somerset guarded this border zone, although it is not entirely clear which tribal group was using them by the end of the Iron Age.[17]

Very few Iron Age settlement sites survive in visible form, because they too have been overlaid by subsequent settlement and cultivation. Excavations of hill-forts like South Cadbury have revealed the remains of the post-holes made in construct-ing simple huts,[18] but the preservative qualities of the Somerset peat have enabled two settlements, at Meare and Glastonbury— the so-called "lake villages"—to be studied in great detail. Although only a few mounds are visible today, the thorough excavation of these two sites by Bulleid and Gray between 1892 and 1907, and the subsequent detailed analysis of their findings, have enabled us to form a fairly good idea of what the landscape was like and the effect which Iron Age peoples had on its development. The model of the Glastonbury settlement proposed by Clarke suggests that the village was occupied for about a hundred years during the period 200 B.C. to A.D. 1—probably from 150 B.C. to 50 B.C. At its maximum it consisted of seven clusters of round, thatched huts, each thought to have contained an extended family, or lineage, of some twenty people. The total population would thus have been about 120. The village was on a low spit of land with a lake (now drained) to its north, and a river to its east. Analysis of the pottery, loom-tools, animal bones and other finds on the site reveals that the village was linked into quite an extensive trade network, and that people probably practised partial trans-humance. They remained in the village during the summer, taking advantage of the rich growth of grass, reeds, sedges and

[17] Grinsell, "Somerset Archaeology", pp. 59–63; D. L. Clarke, "A provisional model of Iron Age society and its settlement system" in D. L. Clarke, ed., *Models in Archaeology* (1972), pp. 801–69.
[18] L. Alcock, *"By South Cadbury is that Camelot"*, *The excavations of Cadbury Castle, 1966–1970* (1972), pp. 108–13.

fruits in the marshes, and cultivating wheat and barley regularly in an "infield" close at hand, and sowing them sporadically round an "outfield" beyond. But in the winter, when the waters rose, flooding much of their land, most of the villages seem to have migrated up to Mendip with their Soay sheep, of which it is estimated that they had between 200 and 1,000. The great Mendip hill-fort of Maesbury (eight miles to the north) seems to have been the administrative (and probably religious) centre of the territory which they inhabited. They probably paid tribute to its ruler. The villagers wove cloth and made pots in the summer, and traded these for Mendip products like quern stones and lead, iron and bronze tools and ornaments.

From this semi-migratory economy it is clear that the Iron Age peoples were utilising and influencing an extensive territory. There were about three miles between the settlements of Glastonbury and Meare, and we should probably visualise the countryside as consisting of a network of settlements at about this distance from one another, surrounded by a small, continuously cultivated "infield", and a larger "outfield". The "outfield" would be only sporadically cultivated and would consist mainly of common pastures, woods and areas of sedges and reeds for roofing and weaving. There would have been related settlement areas on the hills, like the Mendips, Poldens and the Somerton uplands, for the winter, protected by hill-forts, with a network of tracks connecting all these settlements. Normal paths would have been simply of beaten earth, but, as we have seen, elaborate wooden trackways were built across the marshes. There were also smaller hamlets and single family farms, scattered between the village settlements.[19] The lake villages are of course not visible today, but the remains of Iron Age field systems may be seen on marginal lands, such as the top of Great Hill, Luccombe, near Minehead. Here the faint remains of tiny rectangular arable fields are visible, divided by banks and low ridges which were once topped by protective hedges to keep out wandering livestock, both wild and domesticated. There are also the remains of huts.

As we have seen this paucity of visible evidence gives a false

[19] D. L. Clarke, "Iron Age society and its settlement system", pp. 801–69.

impression of the influence of the Iron Age people on the development of the landscape. The evidence unearthed by the rescue archaeologists as the M5 cut its way southwards through the Levels, reveals the density of settlement. They unearthed prehistoric settlements at the rate of two per mile (on average) and many of these were hitherto unsuspected.[20] It seems likely that most of the more-easily cultivated soils were occupied in this period, and the sites of many present-day towns and villages may also date back to this time. Iron-Age coins have been found at Taunton, Yeovil, Frome, Minehead, and many other places.

It is also likely that the basic network of roads, lanes and trackways which we know today was in use in this period, and had probably already been established in the Bronze Age. Roger Leech has recently argued this case by plotting the relationship of known Romano-British settlements in the Ilchester area (Fig. 2) to the network of medieval roads (derived from the parish studies in the *Victoria County History of Somerset*, Vol. III). He concludes that there is a most striking correlation between the locations of Romano-British settlements and the positions of later medieval lanes. Of 43 certain or probable Romano-British settlements, 39 (91%) are within 100 metres (325 feet) of a later lane. This relationship is quite remarkable, and suggests very strongly that most of the present network of roads and lanes must have been in existence during Roman times. However, Leech goes further and argues that since many of the Romano-British settlements were already occupied in earlier times—often going back to the Bronze Age—there is good reason to believe that much of the road network may also derive from that era.[21]

A further interesting possibility has been raised by the work of Professor Glanville Jones, who has studied the survival of very ancient estates in Wales, which he calls "multiple estates", because of their great size and the fact that they comprise units

[20] Robert Dunning, *Somerset and Avon*, p. 6.
[21] Roger H. Leech, "Romano-British rural settlement in South Somerset and North Dorset", unpublished Ph.D. University of Bristol (1977), pp. 183–7. I am most grateful to Roger Leech for permission to quote from his thesis and for discussing the problems of the early history of the landscape with me.

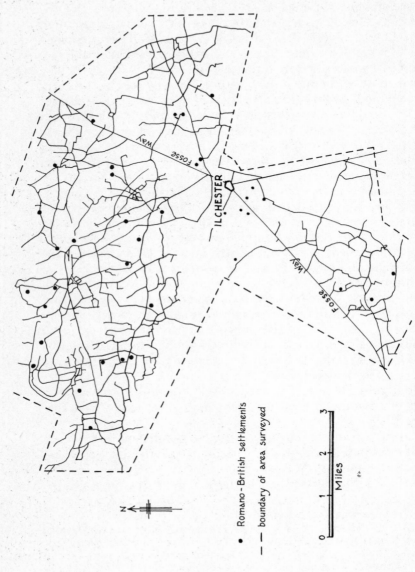

Fig. 2. Romano-British settlements and medieval roads in the Ilchester region

Romano-British settlements

boundary of area surveyed

Miles

0   1   2   3

N

ILCHESTER

FOSSE WAY

FOSSE WAY

Plate 1 The Levels in flood, near Pibsbury, east of Langport. Large areas of central Somerset looked like this each winter in the years before the comprehensive drainage schemes of the early nineteenth century. Such scenes are now less common.

Plate 2 Unreclaimed Exmoor. The stripling river Barle near Landacre bridge west of Withypool. All of Exmoor once looked like this.

Plate 3 Cadbury hill-fort, looking west with the drained Levels in the distance. Legendary site of "King Arthur's Camelot", the hill-fort commands an extensive area in south Somerset. In the foreground is the former common field of the shrunken hamlet of Witcombe, now reduced to one farm. The hamlet was situated on the right-hand edge of the field just beyond the farm.

Plate 4 Charterhouse Roman town.

Plate 5 Priddy nine-barrows. Bronze Age burial monuments on Mendip. The large number of surviving barrows in the Mendip region suggests quite a dense settlement 4,000 years ago.

of land scattered over quite a wide area (so as to utilise various environments, such as arable lowlands, hill pastures and woodlands). He maintains that these estates, which were usually controlled and organised by kings, are extremely ancient, and existed all over Britain when it was Celtic—that is, that they pre-date the Romans as well as the English. The multiple estates were of considerable size, and an account of one in the thirteenth-century *Book of Iorwerth* (an old Welsh law book) says it should comprise four vills (each consisting of sixty-four homesteads comprising four acres each). The acreages listed here no doubt referred to the arable area, not the extensive common grazings that went with it. Such a multiple estate would thus comprise 1,024 cultivated acres (by this admittedly highly schematised account) plus a very much larger area of pasture and forest.

The other marked characteristic of the multiple estate was its hierarchical and servile organisation. It existed in order to provide a surplus for kings and warrior aristocrats, and the basis of the surplus was the labour of bondmen and slaves (even the bondmen had their own slaves). Professor Jones has found evidence for the existence of ancient multiple estates in Northumbria, Yorkshire and Kent, and he believes that the south-west is an area where they were important.[22] Quoting a relevant passage from F. W. Maitland's famous *Domesday Book and Beyond* (written as long ago as 1897) Jones stresses Maitland's view of the south-west with its "scattered steads and isolated hamlets" as an area of pre-Saxon settlement. The Saxons failed to subdue the natives; they "adapted their own arrangements to the exterior framework that was provided by Celtic or Roman agriculture". Thus, "very often in the west and south-west of Britain, German kings took to themselves integral estates, the boundaries and agrarian arrangements whereof had been drawn by Romans, or rather by Celts." Maitland thought these estates and hamlets had always been worked to a considerable extent by slaves.[23]

[22] G. R. J. Jones, "Multiple estates and early settlement" in Peter H. Sawyer, ed., *Medieval Settlement, Continuity and Change*, pp. 15–40.

[23] F. W. Maitland, *Domesday Book and Beyond* (1961), pp. 112, 115 and 220.

There are twelve Somerset estates in Domesday Book which were part of the ancient demesne of the Saxon kings, such as Somerton, Cheddar, Cannington and South Petherton, which may well have been ancient multiple estates. Many were the centres of ancient hundreds. There were, too, estates of great antiquity, such as Taunton and South Cadbury, which could also qualify. South Cadbury, in particular, being a hill-fort, and having been occupied continuously from Neolithic to early Saxon times, is a strong candidate. Another contributor to the same book as Professor Jones's study has drawn attention to South Cadbury because "a number of geographically related settlement names . . . indicate the existence of a land-unit based upon South Cadbury itself, where occupation goes back beyond Roman times".[24] Apart from the villages of North and South Cadbury, the settlements of Sutton Montis, Weston Bampfylde, Little Weston, and possibly Compton Pauncefoot and Whitcomb, all appear to be related to the once-primary settlement in the hill-fort, which Alcock refers to as a town.[25] The relationship between the Glastonbury lake village and the Mendip hill-fort of Maesbury, previously referred to, would also seem to reflect a possible arrangement of the "multiple estate" type.

Much more work needs to be done on this subject, but it is quite possible that the Romanised landowners who occupied the luxurious villas which were such a notable feature of the Somerton area and the Avon valley round Bath, were former Celtic chieftains occupying estates that already existed before the Roman occupation.

The impact of Rome

The Romans invaded Britain in A.D. 43 and proceeded to conquer it fairly rapidly in the next few years. They were able to play off the rivalries between the British tribes. It seems that the *Dumnonii* surrendered early on (or perhaps became allies), but

[24] W. J. Ford, "Some settlement patterns in the central region of the Warwickshire Avon" in Sawyer, ed., *Medieval Settlement, Continuity and Change*, p. 288.
[25] Alcock, *"By South Cadbury is that Camelot"*, pp. 159–70.

the *Durotriges* and the *Dobunni* put up a vigorous resistance against the second Augusta Legion under the command of Vespasian, later to become emperor. There was fierce fighting at the *Durotrigan* hill-fort of South Cadbury and possibly at Ham Hill, near Montacute, but the Britons were no match for the highly organised and disciplined Romans. First the *Durotriges* and then the *Dobunni* were overwhelmed. Small forts were built by the Romans at South Cadbury and Ham Hill.

Initially the Romans wished to confine their conquest to the fertile south-eastern half of Britain, and decided to establish a frontier zone running roughly from Exeter in the south-west to the Humber estuary in the north-east. To control this zone they built a great road (now called the Fosse Way) in a virtually straight line from Exeter to Lincoln, to enable troops and supplies to be moved rapidly from their forts to any area under attack. It is sometimes stated that this road formed the actual frontier, but this is incorrect. It merely serviced a frontier zone, and it is quite clear that the whole of the area later to become Somerset was occupied by the Romans at the initial conquest. In fact, they were working the Mendip lead mines (well to the west of the Fosse Way) by A.D. 49.[26] The effect of these mines on the landscape is described below in relation to the mining settlement at Charterhouse.

The Romans brought to the landscape three new features which have left a permanent imprint: main roads, towns and country estates (villas and their surrounding farms) although these, as we have seen, may have pre-dated them. The impressively straight main roads are perhaps their most dramatic contribution, and several Roman roads in Somerset are still in use—some of them carrying heavy traffic, like the Fosse Way between Bath and Ilchester, the Yeovil-Ilchester road (A37) and the road which runs along the crest of the Polden Hills (A39) linking M5 (Puriton-Bridgwater exit) with Street and Glastonbury. There are also many less important Roman roads in the county. Those linking the villas to the main highways

[26] W. H. Manning, "The conquest of the West Country" in Keith Brannigan and P. J. Fowler eds., *The Roman West Country* (1976) pp. 15–41; John Wacher, *Roman Britain* (1978) pp. 30–9; and P. J. Fowler, "Early Mendip", p. 67.

remain to be traced on our modern maps, as Margary did for the Wealden ways.

Towns and urban life were the characteristic features of Roman civilisation and, although Somerset was rather far west to be involved in the mainstream of Roman Britain, it had two towns—Bath (*Aquae Sulis*) and Ilchester (*Lindinis*) which were important in Roman times, and which are still towns. It is of course not possible to prove conclusively that they were not abandoned at the end of the Roman period and then reoccupied, but the archaeological evidence from Bath (cited below) strongly suggests continuous occupation, and whilst too little excavation has been done at Ilchester to provide absolutely reliable evidence, it also points in that direction.[27] The fact that in both cases the Saxon town occupied the same area inside the walls as did the Roman town, and utilised many (though not all) of the same streets points to continuous occupation as the most plausible hypothesis. Roman towns which were totally abandoned—like *Viroconium* (Wroxeter) in Shropshire and *Calleva* (Silchester) in Hampshire—were never later re-occupied. The Saxons were superstitious about Roman ruins and do not seem to have relished settling in places where there were no longer any inhabitants.

Somerset was also the western outpost of the third feature of Roman civilisation—the villa estate. A distribution map of Roman villas (and suspected sites) shows two quite dense concentrations, and these are, not surprisingly, centred on the two main towns. Not all the thirty or so villas in the vicinity of Bath are in historic Somerset: those on the north side of the river Avon and its tributaries were in Gloucestershire, but they are now re-united with their south-bank neighbours in Avon county. Similarly, a few of the thirty-five or so villas around Ilchester are in the Sherborne area of Dorset, yet few counties can rival Somerset for the remains of Roman villas, and two of these—Low Ham and Pitney—have yielded some of the finest mosaics to be found in Britain. These are now in Taunton museum. Nor is it likely that all the villa sites have been discovered. Low Ham was only found by accident in 1938, and

[27] M. Aston and R. Leech, *Somerset Towns*, pp. 66–75.

it is quite possible that more sites will come to light in the future, especially as quite a number of suspected sites have not yet been excavated.[28]

Rural settlements

Villas may have been the most dramatic manifestations of rural life, but it is important not to get them out of proportion. Most of the inhabitants of Roman Somerset would have been peasant farmers or herdsmen, living in small villages, hamlets and isolated farms unconnected with villas. The real significance of the Roman period for the development of the landscape probably lay in the least noticeable aspect—the peaceable expansion of farming. The long Roman peace—nearly four hundred years, as long as the period from Elizabeth I to our own times—allowed agriculture to expand unhindered by the distractions of warfare and the need for defensibility, so that wide stretches of land could be brought into cultivation, and previously dangerous sites could be occupied. Alcock has suggested that people left hill-forts like South Cadbury, and settled in the plains below. We know that corn and hides were valued exports from Roman Britain (along with slaves), and although we cannot know how much of the county had been brought into cultivation in Roman times, we can deduce from the distribution (and size) of villas and other farm sites that it must have been fairly extensive. For instance, Fig. 3 shows the distribution of villas and large farms in the vicinity of Ilchester. This shows that the low hills to the north and south of the town—which were then no doubt islands in the surrounding wetlands—were intensively settled. The magnificence of the villas—with their lines of rooms around courtyards, their heated baths and their elaborate mosaics—would in itself suggest the production of a considerable surplus for their maintenance. The careful study of the associated farm buildings by Professor Shimon Applebaum—especially of Pitney—enables us to gain an even more detailed picture of their economy.

[28] Leech, "Romano-British rural settlement . . .", pp. 121–6.

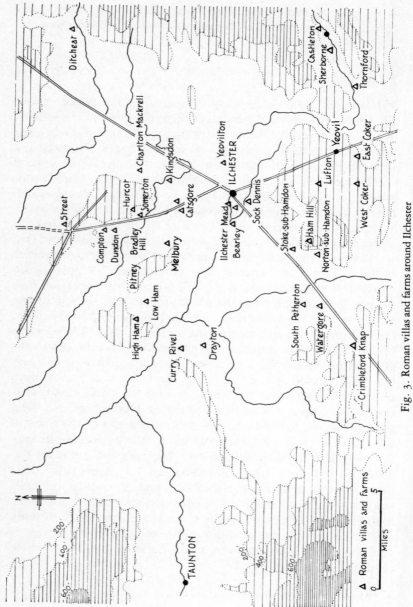

Fig. 3. Roman villas and farms around Ilchester

At Pitney grain production and pig-fattening seem to have been specialities. From the capacity of one granary Applebaum estimated that some 300 acres of arable land would be needed to fill it (assuming that half this area lay fallow each year), but he notes that other granaries probably existed, and that the total area under cultivation was probably much larger. Two rooms which are believed to have been pigsties were found, and it seems that some of the grain produced may have been used for feeding pigs in the winter to provide ham and lard for urban markets such as Ilchester, and also possibly for the legionary garrison at Caerleon in South Wales. A road ran along the Poldens to the Roman port at Combwich on the Parrett estuary, from which boats could easily cross to Caerleon. Wherever the markets may have been, it is clear that the villas were engaged in specialised production—no doubt relying on slave labour.[29]

Although there is some evidence that the Somerset villas may have been built in the late third and fourth centuries by Gaulish landowners seeking safety from the raids and revolts which were occurring with increasing regularity across the Channel, Tacitus makes it clear, rather scornfully, that the native British chiefs were anxious to adopt Roman ways soon after the conquest. Describing the policy of Agricola, who was his father-in-law and who governed Britain from A.D. 77 to 83, he states that:

> To induce a people, hitherto scattered, uncivilised and therefore prone to fight, to grow pleasantly inured to peace and ease, Agricola gave private encouragement and official assistance to the building of temples, public squares and private mansions . . . he trained the sons of the chiefs in the liberal arts. . . . The result was that in place of distaste for the Latin language came a passion to command it. In the same way, our national dress came into favour and the toga was everywhere to be seen. And so the Britons were gradually led on to the amenities that make vice agreeable—arcades, baths, and sumptuous banquets. They spoke of such

[29] S. Applebaum, in *The Agrarian History of England and Wales*, 1 (1972) ed. H. P. R. Finberg, pp. 179–87.

novelties as 'civilization', when really they were only a feature of enslavement.[30]

Roger Leech's recent work bears this out. He shows that at least eleven of the villas in the Ilchester region were built in the second century or earlier, and suggests that one of the reasons why the early villas have not always been noticed in excavations was that they were frequently built of timber—so that the only visible evidence for their existence would be the slight discolouration of the soil left by post-holes. This evidence is notoriously difficult to identify and interpret, and would not have been noticed by many of the earlier excavators, who were not trained to recognise it. A very good example of such an early timber villa was found in East Devon, not far south of Somerset at Holcombe near Lyme Regis, about nine miles south of Chard.[31] Probably similar sites in Somerset have not yet been discovered.

Villas, of course, could not exist in isolation. They were usually worked by slaves, who were perhaps resident near the villa, and by tenants (of varying degrees of servility) who lived in villages and hamlets nearby. The villa at Catsgore, about two and a quarter miles south-east of Somerton, is a good example. About half a mile to its north-west was a small village situated on the road from Somerton to Ilchester. This settlement has been partially excavated, and is one of the most important sites in England for the understanding of Romano-British settlement. The remains of a number of buildings connected with farming and crafts were found, and the village appears to have covered about ten acres. It was apparently founded about A.D. 80, and was twice expanded and rebuilt, first around A.D. 150, and again sometime near A.D. 300. The first two-thirds of the fourth century were a time of prosperity in rural Somerset, when many villas were built or extended, and when the elaborately-heated bath-houses and mosaics were installed. However, conditions deteriorated with the increasing disunity and confusion at the heart of the Roman Empire. Usurpations (such as

---

[30] *Tacitus on Britain and Germany* (Penguin Books, 1948), p. 72.
[31] Leech, "Romano-British rural settlement", pp. 87–105.

that of Magnentius, a barbarian who seized the imperial throne in 350), inflation and ever-increased taxes to support the expanding civil service and barbarian mercenaries in the army, made the Empire both unpopular and vulnerable to outside attack.[32] In 367 there was a vast conspiracy of Picts, Scots, Franks and Saxons, who raided widely, and many settlements, such as Catsgore, seem to have been abandoned at this time, judging by surviving coin evidence, but there is no evidence that they were destroyed. One theory is that the people migrated to escape from the raiders; another is that they were dispersed as a punishment for collaborating with the enemy. If this last suggestion is accurate, it implies that the cause of the Roman decline was more internal than external: that barbarian invaders (initially German mercenaries) were, so to speak, sucked into a vacuum, rather than being the prime, active agents of destruction. This evidence would certainly fit the case of many of the villas in Somerset, which seem to have gradually declined, rather than to have been violently destroyed. The Roman villa economy depended ultimately on the vitality of the towns as a market for its surplus agricultural produce, and as a source of supply for its manufactured luxuries, like pottery, silver, glass and tiles. The army must also have been an important market for the villas. Once the towns began to decline, and the army to be withdrawn by usurping contenders for the Empire (many of whom, like Constantine I, were stationed initially in Britain), the villa economy ceased to be viable, and the Catsgore evidence suggests also that this weakness may have been exacerbated by revolts of the slaves and servile tenants. Whatever the reasons, the villa economy seems to have been in advanced decline some considerable period before the final withdrawal of the legions in 410, so that the Celtic kingdoms which succeeded the Romans were based to some extent on a reversion to the subsistence agricultural economy of earlier times, although the kings and chieftains must have been able to command at least a food-rent in order to survive.[33]

[32] See J. Wacher, *Roman Britain* (1978), pp. 54–61.
[33] R. H. Leech, "Larger agricultural settlements" in *The Roman West Country*, p. 145.

The Roman towns

Bath (*Aquae Sulis*) was the most important Roman town to be included in Somerset, and it still has the most impressive visible remains in Britain even if they are much restored. Archaeological excavation has revealed a great deal about the Roman city, but much more could be discovered if it were not buried beneath the magnificent medieval abbey and the excellent Georgian buildings. Bath centred on a temple which was adjacent to the hot springs and dedicated to the Celtic goddess Sul and the Roman goddess Minerva, which suggests that it was already a place of some significance before the Romans came. They, however, could hardly be expected to resist a natural spring which delivers nearly two and a quarter million litres of mineral water a day at a temperature of about 50°C. Bath quickly became a centre for Roman leisure, and was well served by the expanding road system. The Fosse Way crossed the Avon at Bath, and roads also radiated to London and the seaport of *Abonae* (Sea Mills, near Avonmouth) and Hamworthy on the south coast (now a suburb of Poole).

Next to the temple the elaborate baths were built with their range of hot and cold pools, using both natural and artificial heating. The great bath still retains its lead flooring, no doubt derived from the Roman lead-mining centre at Charterhouse-on-Mendip, now visible only as crop marks on aerial photographs (and by gentle humps and undulations in the ground). Quite a number of stamped pigs of lead from it have survived, however, so that there can be no doubt of its former importance.

Bath attracted pilgrims and tourists from all over the Roman Empire and some forty of these have left their names and inscriptions on altars and gravestones. So quite a large town must have grown up around the baths, with numerous hotels, lodgings and shops, but it has not been possible to establish the Roman street plan by excavation. Bath had walls in medieval times, and if these followed the same course as the Roman walls, as at London, Exeter and many other towns (though this has not been definitely established at Bath), the area enclosed was quite small—only nine hectares compared with forty hectares for the average Roman country town. There were graveyards lining all the roads into Bath, and it seems likely that there were extensive suburbs outside the walls. Perhaps only the sacred precinct was enclosed.

Like other Roman towns, Bath entered into decline long before it was occupied by the West Saxons; this, we know from the Anglo-Saxon Chronicle, was not until after their great victory over the Britons at nearby Dyrham in 577. That it was still occupied in 577 we know not only from that record, but also from recent archaeological excavation beneath the Pump Room cellars in the area of the temple precinct, but this evidence reveals that the baths themselves had long been abandoned and had been overwhelmed by flooding, which had apparently begun sometime in the fourth century. It has been suggested that there was a rise in the level of the Bristol Channel and of the water table generally, but this has recently been disputed.[34] In any case, Bath has always been liable to flooding and still is. The baths may always have been dependent on constant maintenance and drainage operations. Initially, attempts were made to raise the hypocaust basement floors, but after a while these were abandoned and the whole area became filled with mud—eventually to a depth of forty centimetres. It is because this mud was filled with household rubbish, animal bones and broken pottery that we know that people were still inhabiting parts of the town and using the abandoned baths as a refuse tip.[35]

Ilchester ("the fort or town on the river Ivel or Yeo") was called *Lindinis* by the Romans (meaning "Little Marsh"), and became the capital of a sub-region of the Durotrigan tribal area, probably not before the third century. The town began as a Roman fort, probably enclosing about thirty acres (twelve hectares) and built c. A.D. 50. Soon a civilian town grew up around the fort, which was not defended until the late second or early third century, when a clay rampart was erected enclosing

---

[34] A "marine transgression" of the Somerset Levels, c. AD 250, was proposed by Harry Godwin, "Botanical and Geological History of the Somerset Levels", *loc. cit.*, pp. 321–2, but has been disputed by A. S. Hawkins, "Sea level changes around Southwest England", in D. J. Blackman, ed., *Marine Archaeology, Colston Papers* (1973), pp. 67–88.

[35] B. Cunliffe, *Aquae Sulis* (1971), pp. 31–2.

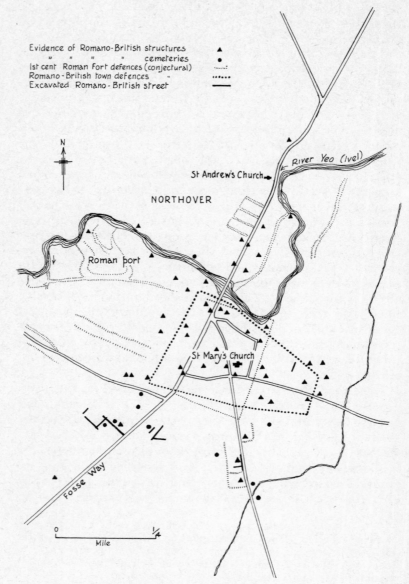

Evidence of Romano-British structures
     "   "   "   cemeteries
1st cent Roman fort defences (conjectural)
Romano-British town defences   "
Excavated Romano-British street

N

River Yeo (Ivel)

St Andrew's Church

NORTHOVER

Roman fort

St Mary's Church

Fosse Way

0   ¼
Mile

Fig. 4. Ilchester, the Romano-British town

an area of about twenty-five acres (ten hectares). In the fourth century massive stone walls with gates were built on the same lines, but the town was always much larger than the walled area, especially on its south and west sides (Fig. 4). There seems to have been a river port to the west of the town, and remains of Roman quays have been found, as well as considerable suburban development along the roads leading to Dorchester and Exeter. Because the recent excavations carried out in connection with by-pass construction were confined to the edges of the town, detailed knowledge of its central area is still sparse, but the town is believed to have had a population of about 2,000 at its peak of prosperity. It is thought that the houses were originally wattle-and-daub huts, which were replaced by rectangular stone buildings before the end of the first century. Ilchester may have extended north of the river Yeo to include what later became the parish of Northover. The church of St Andrew there was an important Saxon minster, which possibly stands on the site of a Roman building, and may have been placed there in association with a late Roman cemetery nearby; this was almost certainly Christian. There is quite a reasonable case for con-tinuity of occupation in Ilchester since Roman times. Roger Leech points out that Ilchester was certainly not "a poor and unimportant village" in late Roman times, as was once believed (Haverfield in *Victoria County History of Somerset*, 1906), but was an important town. It already covered about twenty hectares (fifty acres) in the second century, and was a *civitas* capital in the third century. The excavations of 1974 produced Saxon pottery from a range of dates, while the town was a mint in 973 and a burh in 1086.[36]

The significance of the smaller Roman towns (*vici*) and ports, which have hitherto been rather neglected, has also been emphasised by Leech, to show that Roman Somerset was more urbanised (and hence probably more densely settled) than we have realised (Fig. 5). Camerton on the Fosse Way, about six miles south of Bath, has long been known as the site of a small town, but there is now reason to believe that there was another at Shepton Mallet, which is half-way between Ilchester and

[36] Aston and Leech, *Somerset Towns*, pp. 66–75.

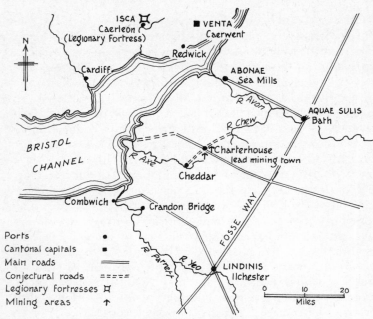

Fig. 5. Roman ports and towns in the Bristol Channel region

Bath. The remains at Westland, on the Roman road to the west of Yeovil, were previously thought to be those of a villa, but now they seem more likely to relate to a small town there. Similarly the thirty acres of ruins at Littleton, north of Somerton, which Colt Hoare described in 1832 as containing walls, bricks, tiles, coins and fragments of mosaic, seem too extensive for a villa. There is also reasonable evidence for the existence of ports (as we have seen) at Cheddar, Combwich and Crandon Bridge near the south-western end of the Poldens, on a site which is now inland but which formerly stood on a meander of the river Parrett (which was cut off and filled up in 1677).

Finally there was the important lead-mining town of Charterhouse-on-Mendip, the remains of whose gridiron of streets are visible on aerial photographs (Plate 4). The site is also surrounded by much "gruffy" ground, the remains of open-cast mining. Some of this was originally Roman, but it has been extended by subsequent reworking of the site by Victorian miners, who re-smelted the old slag heaps to obtain some lead still left in them. The Roman settlement at Charterhouse was large and important, for desire for lead was one of Claudius's reasons for invading Britain. The remains of an amphitheatre and a Roman fort survive, and also of the roads connecting the mines to the ports of export. One road led eastwards along the Mendip hilltop to Salisbury and Southampton Water. Others were shorter. One ran northwards to the river Chew, where the "pigs" of lead were shipped to *Abonae* (Sea Mills) on the Avon for transhipment overseas. Another road led southwards to Cheddar, where there was a small port on the river Axe.[37]

SELECT BIBLIOGRAPHY

Grinsell, L. V., "Somerset Archaeology, 1931–65", *SANHS*, Vol. 109 (1964–5), pp. 47–77.

Grinsell, L. V., *The Archaeology of Exmoor* (1970).

Dobson, D. P., *The Archaeology of Somerset* (1931).

Atthill, R., ed., *Mendip, a New Study* (1976).

Alcock, L., *"By South Cadbury is that Camelot" The Excavation of Cadbury Castle, 1966–70* (1972).

Branigan, K., and Fowler, P. J., eds., *The Roman West Country* (1976).

[37] Leech, "Romano-British settlements", pp. 14–28.

3. The evolution of settlement from the English invasions to the Domesday Survey (1086)

The English settlement—continuity or a new beginning? Settlement patterns. The landscape in 1086

The English settlement—continuity or a new beginning?

WE HAVE SEEN that ideas about the importance of the Saxons in the history of settlement have been undergoing radical revision, and that the significance to be attached to the fact that the majority of today's place-names are English rather than British has been questioned. This reappraisal was recently well summarised by Margaret Gelling, a leading place-name scholar who wrote:

> one theory which is very much implied, but not quite stated, in many history books . . . is that when you get a place-name like Edgbaston you can visualise a band of Anglo-Saxon pioneers being led through the forest by a man called Edgbeald, arriving at the site, and the leader deciding to put a *tun* there. The other possibility however, is that Edgbeald did not found or farm the settlement and that the place only acquired the name after the institution of some sort of incipient manorial system.[1]

This interpretation of place-names turns the previously accepted version of the Saxon Conquest upside down, and implies that it was something much more akin to the Norman

---

[1] M. Gelling, cited by Robin Glasscock in Peter Sawyer, ed., *Medieval Settlement, Continuity and Change* (1976), p. 193.

Conquest, in which the leading landholders and officials were replaced, but that British peasants and labourers continued to work the land as they had always done. Since the Saxon conquest of Somerset was relatively late in date, such an interpretation seems more fitting for Somerset than for some other counties. Nevertheless, the replacement of the British language by English, and the form of the earliest Wessex laws (those of King Ine, written c. 694) suggest that the pattern was more complex than that outlined above: that what occurred was a merging of peoples. The Saxon invaders included peasants (and their own slaves) as well as lords and chieftains. On the other hand, many of the previous British estates survived. Some of the earliest Saxon land grants, made soon after the conquest, have boundary features which indicate that they were not recently created out of an empty land.

The evidence for continuity in the Ilchester area, which we have already noted in Chapter 2, is amplified by Dr Dunning in a recent study. Settlements around the town, like Bearley, Sock Dennis and Northover, whose boundaries run along the Fosse Way, and which have yielded Roman remains, are probably estates with a continuous history (see Fig. 5 on p. 70). He concludes that

> at least some of the parishes near Ilchester whose boundaries are governed by the Fosse, owe something directly to the boundaries chosen by Romano-British farmers; and that Bearley, the two parts of Sock and probably Northover, surrounding Romano-British farm complexes or suburbs found or only suspected, are contributions to the growing body of evidence for the continuity of landscape features over two thousand years.[2]

There are many other examples of continuity. A recent study of the history of British woodland by Oliver Rackham reveals that there is "no hint of the massive return of secondary forest invading the good arable land, which we would expect to follow severe depopulation", if the Saxon invaders had really

---

[2] R. W. Dunning, "Ilchester: A Study in Continuity", *SANHS*, 119 (1975), p. 48.

caused it.[3] As we have seen, Roger Leech's study of *known* Romano-British settlement sites (and of course many may have escaped notice, since their identification depends largely on chance finds) has shown a close relationship to the existing road pattern. Not surprisingly, he also found a similar relationship with later medieval settlements. The Romano-British settlement pattern consisted of hamlets and individual farms, rather than the compact villages of later Saxon settlement, but these latter tend to be either on, or close to, the Romano-British settlements (not usually more than 500 to 1,000 metres away). In the central Somerset area around Somerton where, as we have seen, there was fairly dense settlement in late Roman times, there appears to have been considerable continuity of occupation. Examples of medieval sites overlying Roman ones are Pawlett, Crandon, Slape, Chedzoy, Wearne, Melbury, Upper Hayes Farm, Littleton, Somerton Randolph, Hazelgrove and Sparkford. These all come from quite a small area, and the list could be considerably extended by other examples elsewhere in Somerset.

In 1924 Haverfield and MacDonald argued that Roman Britain had nothing to do with modern Britain "racially, topographically, culturally". Recent research has shown that such a judgment is a long way wide of the mark, and that there was in fact very considerable continuity in all three spheres—topographically in settlement sites, racially through inter-marriage between Saxon and Romano-British, and culturally through the survival of Christianity in places like Glastonbury, where Radford's excavations in 1955 uncovered Romano-British pottery at the west end of the nave of the abbey.

Significant though such continuity was, it is important not to go too far in the opposite direction and to suggest that the Saxon Conquest was unimportant for the landscape. For Leech shows that one half of all the settlements in Somerset known to have been in existence in the fourth century had been abandoned between the fifth and seventh centuries (dispersed settlements often being replaced by villages), so that the arrival of the

[3] O. Rackham, *Trees and Woodland in the British Landscape* (1976), pp. 51–2.

74

Saxons had a very real impact on the evolution of the landscape and the settlement pattern as we know it today. The British population had been decimated by plague (mentioned by their writer Gildas about 540) and there had also been a large emigration to Brittany (which abandoned its old name of Armorica and took this new one as a result). Consequently there must have been a fair amount of disused land—both cleared and uncleared—when the first Saxons arrived. Even if they did not found every place which now bears an English name, they certainly founded many settlements, and expanded others, although the idea that the dispersed settlements are "Celtic" in origin and that villages are English is now discredited. It is clear that there was a very gradual evolution from one to another, which was still in progress in 1086. Nevertheless, the Saxons founded new settlements as well as expanding old ones. They cleared a great number of our present arable fields and meadows, and they developed and extended the basic network of roads, lanes and pathways. Finally, a great many towns in Somerset owe their origins to them.[4]

In view of their importance, it is frustrating to be unsure of their date of arrival. It has already been said that this was of late date, which means essentially in the seventh century rather than the sixth, but there is still considerable uncertainty as to whether it was late or early in the seventh century. Unfortunately, the surviving documentary evidence (mainly contained in the Anglo-Saxon Chronicle) is extremely sparse, and is capable of differing interpretations. Nor can the surviving archaeological evidence be sufficiently closely dated to solve the problem. The result is that we have several interpretations which have not as yet been reconciled. There seems to be fairly general agreement that the initial incursions of the Saxon mercenaries who revolted against Vortigern, the British ruler who succeeded the Romans, did not reach Somerset. This revolt occurred around the year 460 and was followed by a rallying of the British, who won a great victory at a place called *Mons Badonicus*, sometime between 490 and 518. The British leader in this battle was subsequently identified as "King" Arthur and

---

[4] Leech, "Romano-British rural settlement", pp. 168–210.

historians have been disputing about his existence ever since. The Arthurian legends are strong in Somerset, both Glastonbury and South Cadbury being closely associated with his life. Powerful arguments for Arthur's historical reality have been recently marshalled by John Morris and Leslie Alcock, but dissent is still rife (although unlikely to be successful in Somerset).[5]

Various sites have been suggested for this famous battle, of which two of the most convincing—Badbury Rings in Dorset, and Bath—would have kept the Saxons out of Somerset. The argument for Bath rests not only on the similarity between their names, but also on an interpolation in one of the manuscript versions of the celebrated book, *Concerning the Ruin and Conquest of Britain*, written by the British monk Gildas about 540, which speaks of the victory at Badon "which happened near the mouth of the Severn" (*qui prope Sabrinum ostium habetur*).[6] If this interpolation were based on real knowledge, it would greatly strengthen the case for a site near Bath as the scene for the battle. John Morris favoured Little Solsbury Hill, just north of Bath, where there is a magnificent—and strongly fortified—hill-fort, which commands the lower Avon valley.[7]

The battle at Badon was not mentioned in the Anglo-Saxon Chronicle, but this is not surprising, considering that the English were not in the habit of celebrating their defeats. The Chronicle is, however, silent on affairs in western Britain during this long period, and does not record a significant victory until the year 552, when the West Saxons, advancing north-westwards from the Southampton area, captured the hill-fort of Old Sarum, the ancient Salisbury. In 556 they recorded another victory at Barbury Castle, north of Marlborough. Their advance then seems to have swung northwards from Salisbury, and there

---

[5] See. J. Morris, *The Age of Arthur: A History of the British Isles from 350 to 650* (1973) and Leslie Alcock, *Arthur's Britain, History and Archaeology, 376–634* (1971). For a strong counter-attack against Arthur's existence, see David Dumville, "Sub-Roman Britain: History and Legend", *History*, Vol. 62 (June, 1977), pp. 173–92.

[6] H. P. R. Finberg, *Lucerna: Studies of some problems in the Early History of England* (1964), p. 53.

[7] Morris, *The Age of Arthur*, pp. 112–15.

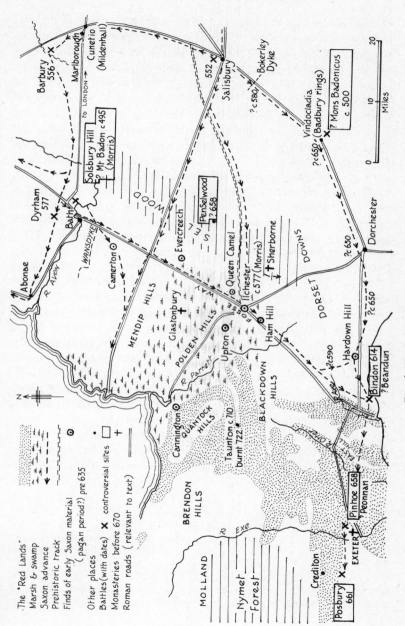

Fig. 6. The Saxon advance into Somerset

The 'Red Lands'
Marsh & swamp
Saxon advance
Prehistoric track
Finds of early Saxon material
  (pagan period?) pre 635

Other places   ⊙
Battles (with dates)   ×   controversial sites
Monasteries before 670   □   +
Roman roads (relevant to text)

N

Miles
0   10   20

Barbury 556 ×
Marlborough
Cunetio (Mildenhall)
to LONDON
552 × Salisbury
Bokerley Dyke
? c.580
Vindocladia
? c.650 (Badbury rings)
× ? Mons Badonicus c.500

Solsbury Hill
? Mt Badon c.495 (Morris)
Dyrham 577 ×
Bath ×
WANSDYKE
Abonae
R. Avon
Camerton ⊙
MENDIP HILLS
⊙ Evercreech
Penselwood
? c.658
S   M

DOOM WOOD
FOSSE WAY
⊙ Queen Camel
Ilchester
c.577 (Morris)
+ Sherborne
Dorchester
? c.650
? c.650

Glastonbury +
POLDEN HILLS
Upton ⊙
Ham Hill
DORSET DOWNS

Cannington ⊙
QUANTOCK HILLS
R. Parratt
BLACKDOWN HILLS
? c.590
Hardown Hill ⊙
? c.650
Bindon 614
? Beandun
? c.650

BRENDON HILLS
Taunton c.710 burnt 722 •

MOLLAND
Nymet Forest
R. Exe
Crediton • ×
EXETER ×
Pinhoe 658
? Peonnan
Posbury 661 ×
R. Otter
? c.682
EAST HILL

is no evidence that they moved westwards along the Roman road leading to Mendip or the ancient trackway which led to Ilchester. Their advance to the south-west into Dorset was blocked by the British defences at Bokerley Dyke on the border between Dorset and Wiltshire.[8] (Fig. 6). The western edges of the Wiltshire Downs are bleak and inhospitable, while beyond them lay the huge impenetrable forest of Selwood (called the *Coit Maur*, the "great forest", by the British) which stretched from Chippenham in the north southwards to the Vale of Blackmoor in north Dorset. None of this area would have been attractive to settlers in search of new land.

After the victory at Barbury Castle in 556, there was a gap of twenty-one years until 577, when the West Saxons broke into the Avon valley and won the great victory at Dyrham which gave them control of Gloucester, Cirencester and Bath. This enabled them to drive a wedge between the Britons in the south-west and their allies in Wales. From this point the picture becomes unclear. The generally accepted view was that the West Saxons occupied north Somerset as far as Mendip, though a variant of this view holds that they were confined to the Avon valley, and that the frontier was formed by the long earthwork known as the Western Wansdyke, which runs from the hills south of Bath westwards to the great hill-fort of Maes Knoll on the Dundry Hills. This earthwork faces northwards and could have been constructed by the British to mark the boundary with the Saxons, but it was not a defensive work since it frequently follows a lowland course across indefensible places. Alternatively it could have been built by the West Saxons themselves around the year 628, when the English conquerors of the west Midlands (the Mercians) occupied the Avon valley and there was need for a frontier with them.[9]

[8] See C. Taylor, *The Making of the English Landscape: Dorset* (1970), pp. 42–3.

[9] See A. and C. Fox "Wansdyke Reconsidered", *Archaeological Journal*, CXV (1958), pp. 1–48 for the view that Wansdyke was built by the West Saxons, and J. N. L. Myres, "Wansdyke and the origin of Wessex", in H. R. Trevor-Roper, ed., *Essays in British History* (1964), pp. 1–27, for a more sceptical approach, in which the view that it was built by the Romano-British is not ruled out.

Whether the Saxon frontier was along the Wansdyke or along Mendip is perhaps not very important: what was generally agreed until fairly recently was that the Saxons did not make any significant advances into Somerset until their great victory at *Peonnan* in 658. Unfortunately, this battle, like so many others in the Anglo-Saxon Chronicle, is not precisely located. The name *Peonnan* is derived from the British word *Pen*, meaning hilltop—of which of course there are large numbers in the south-west. The battle has been traditionally located at PenSelwood—the Pen above Selwood, which stands on the eastern border of Somerset near Mere (Wiltshire). The Chronicle entry is as follows:

> 658 In this year Cenwealh fought against the Britons at Peonnan, and put them to flight as far as the Parrett.[10]

This carries the implication that the British fled a long way, so that a site like PenSelwood, twenty-one miles east of the Parrett, would seem plausible, but as Albany Major pointed out many years ago, there are quite a number of other *Pens* with equally good claims: Pennard Hill, Pen Hill in Yeovil, and Pendomer are examples. It was then assumed that the Parrett became the frontier for a period until further victories under King Centwine (676–85) carried the West Saxons into Devon.[11]

However, in 1960 Professor Hoskins published a major re-interpretation of the westward expansion of Wessex, in which he rejected the entire chronology previously accepted. For him the placing of the battle of *Peonnan* in 658 at PenSelwood (or anywhere else east of the Parrett) involved very great difficulties in interpreting the English settlement of Devon, where place-names and other evidence suggested that the English were settled on the fertile redlands of mid-Devon around Exeter and Crediton very shortly after the victory of 658, and consequently that the battle must have been much farther

[10] *Anglo-Saxon Chronicle* in D. Whitelock, ed., *English Historical Documents, c. 500–1042*, Vol. 1 (1955), p. 152.
[11] A. Major, *Early Wars of Wessex* (1913), pp. 44–81.

west than PenSelwood. He suggested a hilltop in east Devon, possibly Pinhoe, just east of Exeter, and resolved the difficulty over the British retreat to the Parrett by suggesting that they fled north-eastwards, back towards their settlements around the Quantocks, and possibly to their religious centre at Glastonbury, which may still have been retained by the British on its island site till around 670.[12]

There has been some reluctance to agree with Professor Hoskins' siting of the battle of *Peonnan*, but much of the evidence with which he supported it has been accepted, particularly his suggestion that the previously unlocated English victory at *Beandun* in 614 occurred at Bindon near Axmouth in east Devon. This was the prelude to the West Saxon advance into east Devon, culminating in the victory of *Peonnan* and the occupation of Exeter around 658. If the West Saxons were as far west as Axmouth in 614, it is difficult to see how their victory at *Peonnan* can have been so far east as PenSelwood. Alternatively, the Saxons could have invaded south Devon by sea, and advanced *eastwards* to Axmouth, leaving west Somerset as a British "island" between Saxons in Devon and east Somerset.

Another way out of this conundrum was offered by John Morris in his book *The Age of Arthur*. He accepts Hoskins' contention that the victory at Dyrham was followed by an advance down the Fosse Way and by the occupation of Ilchester. This is shown by the discovery of Saxon graves dating from before the Saxons' conversion to Christianity about 635. Morris notes that six small graveyards surrounded Ilchester,

the furthest four miles to the northwest, at Pitney, by Somerton. They are known from chance finds, but from several of them chance has preserved grave goods fashionable well before the end of the century, earlier than any others known so far west of the old centres; and the unimportant little village of Somerton gave its name to a distinct people, the *Sumorsaete*, whose expanded territory is still known as Somerset. The seizure of Ilchester was clearly a deliberate

[12] W. G. Hoskins, *The Westward Expansion of Wessex* (1960), pp. 1–22.

military decision. The town was the strategic focus of the region, where several Roman roads converged . . . at Ilchester the English of Somerset constituted a garrison. They were needed, for in the marshes ten miles to the north Glastonbury is reported to have remained in British hands for several generations to come, and at the mouth of the Parrett the large British population who used the cemetery at Cannington endured as long.

Morris further accepts Hoskins' siting of *Beandun* at Bindon, but he also accepts the traditional location of *Peonnan* at PenSelwood, despite the fact that there is no positive evidence for it, and he explains the fact that the English were fighting so far behind their settled areas by asserting that the victory at *Peonnan* was gained against an invading force of Britons. He believes the Britons who were still in north Somerset joined forces with an invading army sent by King Morcant of Glevissig (Glamorgan) which cut deep into Wessex, before being repulsed at PenSelwood.[13]

The most recent review of the archaeological evidence, however, by Rahtz and Fowler, casts some doubts on the early date for the Saxon graves, noting that it is difficult to date graves accurately and that pagan burial customs could have continued long after the "official" conversion of the kingdom. Additionally, they doubt whether there are enough early burials to indicate a definite occupation: they suggest that the graves may be those of defeated warriors from raiding parties, or alternatively those of Saxon settlers who were allowed to settle peaceably amongst the British.[14]

A recent student of the period, Ian Burrow, has pointed out that there may be no relationship between battles, Saxon political control, and Saxon land-taking. Germanic mercenaries could have settled in Somerset while it was still under British political control, and, conversely, English political control need

---

[13] J. Morris, *The Age of Arthur, A History of the British Isles from 350 to 650* (1973), pp. 230, 293–6.

[14] P. A. Rahtz and P. J. Fowler, "Somerset, 400–700" in Peter J. Fowler, ed., *Archaeology and the Landscape. Essays for L. V. Grinsell* (1972), pp. 187–217.

not have been accompanied by land-taking and settlement until much later.[15] Nor is the situation made any easier by the enigmatic entry in the Chronicle under the year 722 that Queen Aethelburg (wife of Ine, King of Wessex) had "demolished Taunton, which Ine had built". Ine reigned from 688 to 726 and is known to have fought against the British in Devon and Cornwall. Why then did he need to fortify Taunton so far to the east? The answer seems to be that when the West Saxons occupied central Devon and began to move into Cornwall, they left the inhospitable uplands of Exmoor and the Brendons in British hands. We know that the immediate reason for Queen Aethelburg's demolition of Taunton was to prevent it falling into the hands of one Ealdberht, who had revolted against Ine, but the underlying implication is that Ealdberht had British allies in north-west Somerset, who might occupy Taunton and would be difficult to dislodge unless the fortifications were destroyed.[16]

With so much disagreement amongst the authorities it is not possible to present a satisfactory account of the Saxon occupation of Somerset. It is clear that the later the Saxon occupation, the less would have been its influence on the pattern of settlement and the shape of the landscape. Whether the Saxons occupied the east and south-east of the country after 577, or whether they made no important advances until 658, it seems probable that the centre and west of the county remained British throughout most of the seventh century. In fact, we have no absolutely incontrovertible evidence of Saxon occupation anywhere in Somerset until 670–2, when the first land charter shows King Cenwalh giving a property at Meare and two small islands (believed to be Westhay and Godney) with fisheries, woods and "all other appurtenances" to Abbot Beohrtwald of Glastonbury, but the implication is that some years of

---

[15] See I. Burrow, "Aspects of Hillfort and Hill-Top Settlement in Somerset in the First to the Eighth Centuries AD" (Unpublished PhD, University of Birmingham, 1979), pp. 20–1. I am most grateful to Dr Burrow for help with various aspects of the prehistory and archaeology of Somerset.

[16] Major, *Early Wars of Wessex*, p. 88.

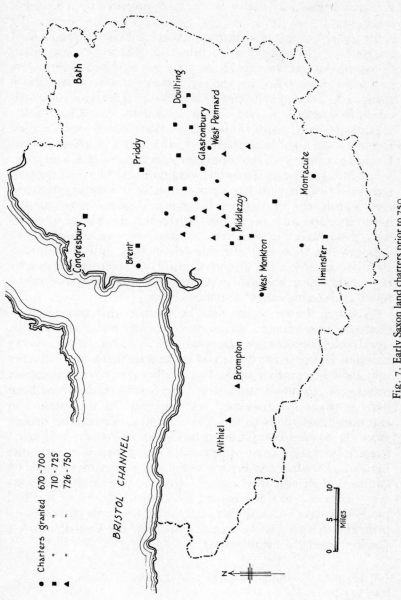

Fig. 7. Early Saxon land charters prior to 750

settlement and pacification would have preceded the making of land grants.

From 670 onwards the kings of Wessex issued a spate of land charters to the abbeys and churches of Somerset, of which Glastonbury and possibly Exeter were the main beneficiaries. As can be seen from Fig. 7, the early grants around Glastonbury itself were followed shortly afterwards by grants in the north (Bath in 675 or 676, and Congresbury between 688 and 726). Grants in the south followed at Montacute—then called *Logworesbeorh*—(between 676 and 726), and Isle Abbots (693). Grants in the west of the county were far fewer and of later date. West Monkton, near Taunton, was granted in 682, but lands in the western hills were not involved until the second quarter of the eighth century when Brompton (Ralph) was granted between 729 and 744, as was Withiel in Brompton Regis in 737.[17] So far as it goes, the charter evidence thus tends to support the view that the infertile western hills remained a British redoubt in the seventh century, and were only taken by the English after they had occupied the more fertile areas in the south and in the Vale of Taunton Deane.

Another source which may be used in this connection is place-name evidence. As we have already seen, this can be unreliable, because names were changed, but where names based on British roots do survive it suggests that Saxon influence may have been rather weak. Practically every river in Somerset retains its original British name. The Saxons seem to have been particularly unimaginative in naming rivers, as, for instance, in the numerous rivers called Avon which is simply the British word for river. Information in E. Ekwall's *Dictionary of English Place Names*, shows many places with purely British names, like Lydeard, Dowlish and Priddy and places with names formed by combining British and English elements, like Compton (*Cwm-tun*—or *comb-tun*) Congresbury (St Congar's *burh*—or fortified place—Congar was a Welsh saint) and Crewkerne (*Cruc-aera*—from the British *cruc*—a spur of a hill, and the English *aera*—a house, especially a storehouse).

[17] H. P. R. Finberg, ed., *The Early Charters of Wessex* (1964), pp. 109–54.

One interesting aspect of British place-names is their even distribution across the county. There is not a greater density in the west, as might have been expected, and, if anything, there are more British survivals in the area around the Fosse Way (which was probably the first to be occupied) than elsewhere.

In addition, Ian Burrow has shown that British names are just as numerous in areas of fertile soil as they are elsewhere. This tends to confirm the views of those who see the Saxon occupation of Somerset as more of a merging of peoples than an expropriating conquest.[18]

Place-names can throw out some hints about both continuity of settlement and the characteristics of the ancient landscape. A particularly intriguing example of possible continuity of settlement since Roman times is provided by the name Ubley, a village beneath the northern slope of Mendip, whose southern boundary ran up on to the plateau, and abutted on the ancient parish of Charterhouse-on-Mendip where the old Roman lead-mines lay. The first recorded mention of Ubley was in a charter of King Edgar (959–75), where it was recorded as *Hubbanlege*. Ekwall says it derives from Ubba's ley (Ubba's clearing in the woods), but a pig of Roman lead was recently discovered, bearing the inscription BRIT. EX. ARG. VEB, meaning "British (lead) from the VEB . . . lead-silver works'. *Veb.* was probably an abbreviation of the Roman name for Charterhouse, and since V and U are interchangeable in Latin, it is quite possible that Ubley derives from Veb-ley, and was originally a settlement where Romano-British lead-miners lived.[19]

Another example of a descriptive place-name is Rimpton (the settlement on the rim or border). Rimpton lies near the Somerset-Dorset border and was first recorded in 938, though that does not mean that it was not in existence before that date. Runnington in Langford Budville parish, one mile north-west of Wellington, also has an interesting name. The Old English word *run* meant "secret council" or "secret discussion", and this was perhaps a place where council meetings were held, or else it

[18] Burrow, PhD thesis, pp. 87–9.
[19] See J. Campbell, et al., *The Mendip Hills in Prehistoric and Roman Times* (1970), p. 29.

belonged to an important counsellor who gave confidential advice to the king.

Settlement patterns

One of the earliest descriptions we have of the Somerset landscape is given in the boundaries in the charter of West Pennard (Plate 8) which was given to Glastonbury Abbey in 681 (Fig. 8), though it is probable that in these early days the kings did not actually give away the land itself, but rather the services of the tenants who occupied it—especially as they often reserved some of the services to themselves. Primitive peoples seldom recognise absolute private ownership of land. These boundaries were described in relation to prominent landmarks, so that the new owners could be sure of their territory.[20] Many of these landmarks refer to streams and hills, and so are not very informative, but some of them refer to human activity. Two of the landmarks are leas—that is, clearings in woodland—which were held by named persons. Thus the charter begins by saying that the boundary runs "from Cobba's Lea up along the brook to Tota's Lea". Grundy identifies this brook as Coxbridge Brook, but we do not know whether Cobba and Tota had established homesteads in their leas or whether they lived in West Pennard village and merely cultivated their clearings. Certainly these would not appear to be part of any common-field system such as characterised much of Saxon farming. The boundary then ran eastwards up a stream to *Cullanbyrig*— Colla's fortified place or camp, which was on the crest of Pennard Hill on the 400-foot contour, commanding fine views over Glastonbury and the surrounding hillside. The boundary then made a detour to include a stone quarry, before continuing over Pennard Hill along an ancient trackway, which is still used

[20] G. B. Grundy, *The Saxon Charters and Field Names of Somerset* (1935), pp. 74–7. It is not clear whether the survey is exactly contemporary with the Charter, but Grundy describes it as "certainly of Saxon age".

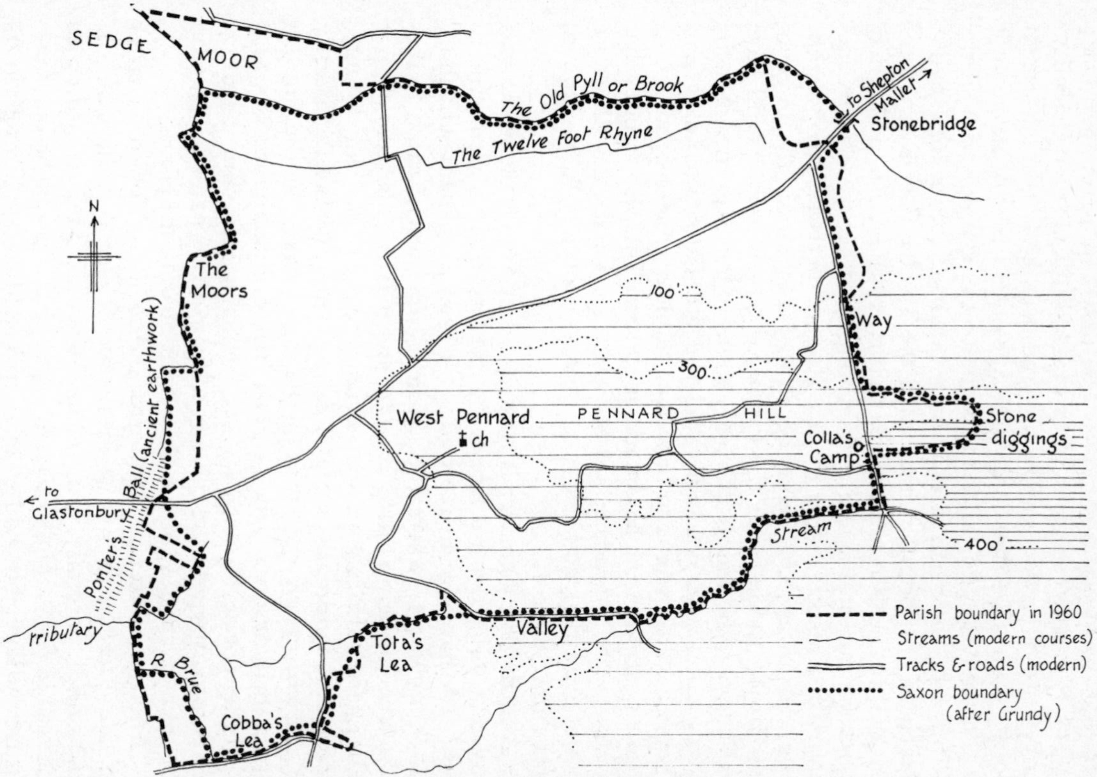
SEDGE
MOOR
The Old Pyll or Brook
The Twelve Foot Rhyne
to Shepton Mallet
Stonebridge
N
The Moors
100'
Way
300'
West Pennard
ch
PENNARD
HILL
Colla's Camp
Stone diggings
Ball (ancient earthwork)
to Glastonbury
Ponter's
Stream
400'
tributary
Valley
Tota's Lea
R Brue
Cobba's Lea
Parish boundary in 1960
Streams (modern courses)
Tracks & roads (modern)
Saxon boundary (after Grundy)

Fig. 8. West Pennard Saxon charter (681) in relation to the modern parish boundary

as a road. It then descended Pennard Hill to a stone bridge across a brook described as "the old pyll" (now the Whitelake river). It is interesting to find a bridge built of stone at such an early date, and what can be the significance of calling a stream "old"? Can it be that some drainage of this part of Sedgemoor had already begun, and that some of the excess waters of the Whitelake river had already been canalised into a "new pyll"? Today an important rhyne called the Twelve Foot Rhyne runs parallel to the Whitelake river slightly to the south, and it may be that some drainage ditches (though not necessarily this one) had already been dug in the Roman period. The western boundary was left vague because it ran along the edge of undrained moors, and the extent of the swamps would have varied with the seasons. Grundy seems to have assumed that the Saxon boundaries coincided with the later parish boundary, and there certainly seems to be a remarkable correspondence, if his identification of the landmarks is correct. This also implies that many parish boundaries in Somerset are identical with estate boundaries that go back to pre-Saxon times, as West Pennard must have done.

Another early charter is that for West Monkton, which was given to Glastonbury Abbey by the Saxon King Centwine in 682. We have already referred to the example of name-changing in this charter, where the landmark of Creechbarrow Hill is described as being called *Cructan* "in the British language", but this charter also has another reference to the British inhabitants. One of its landmarks is the *Wealaford* (now Walford). Literally *Wealaford* meant the "ford of the foreigners"—as the English arrogantly described the original British inhabitants. *Weala* is also the root of the word "Welsh" which has the same meaning. This ford is where the main road from Bridgwater to Taunton (A38) now crosses the brook in front of Walford House.

Another interesting landmark in the West Monkton charter is *Haegstealdcumbe* (now Hestercombe)—the valley of the *Haegstalds*. Literally, this means "warriors", but according to Ekwall, a *haegstald* was usually a younger son who had no share in the village, but had to take up a holding for himself on its edges. The Old German *hagastalt* formed a definite class in the community. Certainly the hamlet of Hestercombe would fit well into this description, since it lay about a mile and a half from West Monkton village in a wooded combe in the foothills of the Quantocks. The hamlet later disappeared to make way for Hestercombe House and Park. Another prominent landmark was the ancient ridgeway which ran along the crest of the Quantocks, and formed the northern boundary of West Monkton in the charter (though the modern boundary runs along the brook slightly to the south). This ridgeway is still a road, and the charter shows that it has been in existence for at least 1,300 years (and probably much longer).

Other varied aspects of the Saxon landscape are revealed in the charter landmarks. References to open or common field strips of arable land are fairly numerous. At Ruishton, in 854, one part of the boundary was formed by a projecting piece of ploughland. At Middle Stolford, near Pitminster, in 938, the boundary ran along the balk of a ploughland (i.e. an unploughed section used to separate two strips in separate ownership, and in this case in separate estates). In 702 at Pilton the boundary was demarcated by "the old triangular piece of ploughland". This was probably where the boundary between Pilton and North Wootton forms an angle a little to the south-east of North Wootton village. One of the most interesting references occurred at Wrington where, in the charter of 904, the boundary runs along the east side of the *wynter acres*—a reference to the land where the winter-sown crops of wheat and rye were grown.

References to the actual crops also occur. At West Bradley in 842 there was a wheat lea; at Long Sutton in 878 an "enclosure where beans grow"; at Henstridge in 956 there was a "hay enclosure"; and at Bishops Lydeard a "lea where flax grows" (975–8). Most of the common types of tree like ashes, alders, oaks and willows are mentioned, but occasionally fruit-trees occur, like the pear-tree at High Ham in 973. A more unusual reference was to the "enclosure where ferns grow" at Wrington in 902. Was this a piece of land which had reverted to scrub, or were the ferns actually cultivated as a floor covering for houses, like rushes?

Livestock are also mentioned in the charters by their habitat, such as the "oakwood where swine are pastured" at Pitminster in 938; the "dairy farm" at Weston near Bath, in 946; the "cattleshed with a house attached" in the same place. This is an early reference to a form of the "long house" shared by cattle and people, which was common in the Middle Ages. Wild animals are also referred to, as in the "wolf barrow" and "wolf brook" at Mells in 942, and in references to enclosed game-parks where deer were kept for hunting. One is mentioned in the West Bradley charter of 842.

Occasionally more unusual features of the landscape are illustrated. In the Bishop Lydeard charter of 905–8 there is a reference to the "moot lea", or open-air meeting place, on the boundary between Bishops Lydeard and Cothelstone which lay over 800 feet up on the Quantocks in what is now a wooded valley between Cothelstone Hill and Gib Hill. It is also mentioned in the Cothelstone section of the Taunton charter of 854, and remains of a hedged enclosure may still be seen in the woods. It would seem a strangely remote place for meetings, except that it is on one of the great Quantock ridgeways, and was probably open pasture land in Saxon times.

Another ancient earthwork, Wansdyke, appears in the Marksbury charter of 936, where it is described as "Wooden's dyke". An even more ancient survival was the ruined Roman villa mentioned in the Drayton charter (made between 924 and 940). It is referred to as a *stankestlas* (stone castle) and stood near the present Stanchester House at the east end of Curry Rivel village, near the entrance to Midelney Place. A more mundane reference is to "Lutt's quarries" in the North Stoke charter of 808—one of several references to quarrying, which was clearly an important occupation in Somerset over a thousand years ago, just as it is today.

Finally we may leave the charters with two brief references to settlements. It is clear that, although many Saxon farmers cultivated their land—or at least the arable parts of it—in open fields where everyone grew the same crop and where only furrows separated one man's land from another's, this was not the only form of settlement. Isolated individual farms also existed, known as "worths". These were often carved out of the common woodlands or rough pastures on the edges of the village land, and so sometimes appear as boundary marks in the charters. One such worth was recorded in the charter for North

Wootton in 946. The reference is to a "farmsteading on the Humber", a stream which Grundy identifies as the Redlake river which flows through North Wootton village. The boundary crosses it at a farm on the north-east of the village which is now a vineyard. This successor to the ancient Saxon worth is now called North Town House.[21]

The last reference is to a church. The Saxons were great builders in timber, and their churches were no exception to this rule (though there is some Saxon stonework visible in the churches of Shepton Mallet, Milborne Port and Wilton, on the outskirts of Taunton), but the most famous church in Somerset—the old church at Glastonbury Abbey—was built of timber, as witnessed by King Cnut's charter of 1032, where the Danish king confirmed the abbey's privileges in a charter "written and promulgated in the wooden church at Glastonbury, in the king's presence'.[22]

Apart from land charters, there are one or two other sources which describe the Saxon landscape. The laws of King Ine of Wessex (c.694) throw some light on the situation in the years when the West Saxons were moving into the lands to the west of Selwood. The general atmosphere of insecurity and the oppressiveness of the great forests are vividly revealed in the law which states that "if a man from afar, or a stranger, travels through a wood off the highway and neither shouts nor blows a horn, he shall be assumed to be a thief, and as such may be either slain or put to ransom."[23]

On the other hand the wanton destruction of forest was discouraged by heavy fines, especially the destruction of forests by fire "because fire is a thief", while the penalties for the unauthorised felling of trees by an axe (presumably in common woodlands) were much lower because "the axe is an informer and not a thief." However, there were certain exceptions to this: "if anyone cuts down a tree that can shelter thirty swine, and it becomes known, he shall pay 60 shillings."[24] This shows that

[21] Grundy, *Saxon Charters*, pp. 1–144.
[22] H. P. R. Finberg, *The Early Charters of Wessex* (1964), pp. 149–50.
[23] F. L. Attenborough, ed., *The Laws of the Earliest English Kings* (1922), p. 42.
[24] Ibid., *Laws*, p. 51.

the keeping of swine in forests was an important source of
income; in this case, the pigs were probably living off the acorns
of a large oak. The phrase about it "becoming known" also
illustrates what must have been the relatively lawless conditions
in the early days of settlement, but the laws are also interesting
because they offer definite protection to the British inhabitants.
The fine for killing a Briton who possessed a hide of land was
120 shillings (probably one pound of silver). If he had half a hide
it was 80 shillings and if he had no land it was 60 shillings. The
idea that the British were all dispossessed is refuted by these
laws, and other laws refer to Britons who were obviously men of
some substance, such as those who held five hides, and those
who were in the king's service and could "ride on his errands".[25]

Since most of the land was common woodland or common
pasture, it was necessary to fence crops against straying animals,
and there were laws which reveal that some kind of rudimentary
common-field farming existed, by providing for penalties for
any farmers who failed to fence his share of the common arable
field. This does not, of course, imply that the crops were
commonly owned, but that each farmer had some strips of
cropland in a field. Since in the law this land is referred to as
partible, it is possible that strips were interchanged by the
farmers from year to year, as "doles" of meadow land frequently
were in later centuries.

Some idea of the produce of the land may be obtained from
the law which specifies the annual food-rent which was due to
the king. Interestingly, this is set out in terms of what was owed
from each ten hides, suggesting that the kinship group of ten
men (the tithing) was the basic unit of settlement, and that they
were collectively responsible for delivery. The rent consisted
of:[26]

Produce	*From 10 hides*		
Vats of honey	10	Ambers of clear ale	30
Loaves	300	cows or wethers	10
Ambers* of British ale	12	geese	10

*this measurement was four bushels in the thirteenth century, but it is not known
whether it was the same in the seventh century.

[25] Ibid., *Laws*, pp. 45–7.   [26] Ibid., *Laws*, pp. 49–51, 59.

hens	20	salmon	5
cheeses	10	pounds of fodder	20
ambers of butter	1	eels	100

The inclusion of salmon and eels shows the importance of fishing in the economy, and this must have been especially so in the vast areas of undrained swamp and marshland in central Somerset. Perhaps this tax was not too onerous on an annual basis, especially as in Bishop Asser's opinion Somerset formed part of a rich kingdom. At any rate, when Alfred founded his monastery at Athelney he had to import foreign monks because no West Saxons were interested. Asser, a poor Welshman from St David's, believed the reason was "the nation's too great abundance of riches of every kind".[27]

The Levels were described in sombre tones by Asser in his *Life of King Alfred* in connection with the famous campaign against the Danes in 878, when Alfred was forced to take refuge on what was then the island of Athelney, (Plate 16) in order to escape from the Danish invaders (it was here that later legend asserts that he burnt the cakes—Asser includes no such romantic episode). He describes how Alfred journeyed with a small force "in difficulties through the woods and fen-fastnesses" to Athelney, "which is surrounded on all sides by very great swampy and impassable marshes, so that no one can approach it by any means except in punts"[28] (Fig. 9). Alfred's subsequent great victory over the Danes occurred in May 878 at a place called *Ethandun*; this saved England from a heathen conquest. *Ethandun* is usually located at Edington in Wiltshire, but Albany Major's contention that the battle occurred at Edington on the Poldens might merit further research. The Somerset Edington is close to Wedmore, where the peace was signed, and to Aller, where the Danish king, Guthrum, was baptised. Major also believed that Alfred's victory was so complete because the Danes were driven westwards after their defeat, and

[27] "Asser's Life of Alfred" in D. Whitelock, ed., *English Historical Documents, c. 500–1042* (1955), p. 273.

[28] Asser, *Life of Alfred*, p. 273.

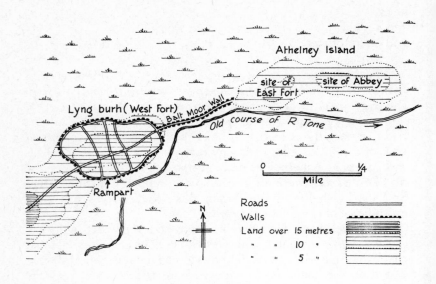

Fig. 9. Lyng and Athelney, c. 890

were trapped in a fort at Dunball on the western end of the
Polden Hills, from which they were unable to escape because it
was surrounded by swamps. Hence their total surrender.[29]
However that may be, Alfred founded a monastery at Athelney
to commemorate the victory. Athelney was at that time connected to dry land "by a bridge which has been made with
laborious skill between two fortresses. At the western end of this
bridge a very strong fort has been placed of most beautiful
workmanship by the king's command."[30] This fort (or *burh* in
Old English) was Lyng (now the village of East Lyng). The
bridge which linked it to Athelney is probably represented by
the ancient causeway which still carries the modern road be-

[29] Major, *Early Wars of Wessex*, pp. 145–207. See also D. Whitelock,
"The importance of the battle of Edington, AD 878" (a lecture given to the
friends of Edington Priory Church, Wiltshire, 1977).
[30] Asser, *Life of Alfred*, p. 273.

94

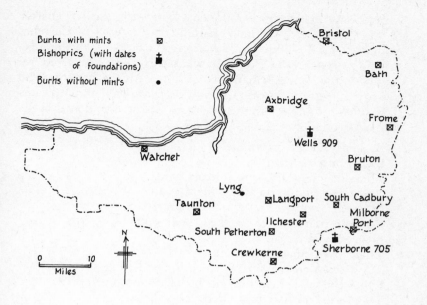

Fig. 10. Burhs and bishoprics, c. 700–c. 1000

tween the two places for part of its route (though the causeway
was no doubt reinforced in later times).

East Lyng is a particularly interesting place because it is a
Saxon *burh* which never grew into an important town like so
many others (Fig. 10), and hence its modern plan preserves the
ancient one in fossilised form. Of course, the ancient buildings
have all been replaced, but the remains of the earthen ramparts
may still be seen, and the modern property boundaries are based
on the ancient "burgage tenements" (though no doubt amalga-
mations and minor changes have taken place).

We have seen that both the Roman towns of Bath and
Ilchester reappeared as Saxon *burhs* within the area of their
Roman walls. Bath must still have been a fortified stronghold in
577, when the West Saxons occupied it after their victory at
nearby Dyrham, and referred to it as a "chester" (i.e. *castra*, or
fortified place). Almost a century later (in 676) Osric, the
under-king of the *Hwicce* (who occupied much of Gloucester-

95

shire and Worcestershire) founded a convent in Bath by charter
to the Abbess Bertana which granted 100 *manentes* (i.e. the rents
from 100 servile holdings) "adjoining the city" for the foundation of a nunnery.[31] Precisely what this "city" involved we
cannot know, but a remarkable Saxon poem (dating from the
seventh or eighth century) can only refer to Bath, and indicates
that substantial and impressive ruins of the abandoned baths
were still visible:

> Bright were the buildings
> Bath houses many . . .
> Therefore these halls are a dreary ruin
> And these pictured gables, the tiles are tumbling
> From the roof with its crown of rafters;
> Ruinous masses have wrecked the pavement,
> Heaved it in heaps.
> There stood arcades of stone,
> The stream hotly issued with eddies widening
> Up to the wall encircling all the bright-bosomed pool.
> There the baths were hot with inward heat:
> Nature's bounty that
> So they caused to flow
> Into a sea of stone the hot streams[32]

However, ruins cannot be the whole story. It is inconceivable,
as Edward Hutton has remarked, that Osric would have placed a
nunnery in the city unless the place was reasonably safe and well
ordered, and not a devastated shambles.[33]

The landscape in 1086

William I's great Domesday Survey of 1086 provides the first
reasonably detailed account of the English landscape. It enables
us to obtain a general picture of its main features and of the
variations between the regions. The survey was a remarkable
administrative achievement for the eleventh century (there is
nothing like it anywhere else in Europe), but it can still be a

[31] Finberg, *West Saxon Charters*, p. 109.
[32] D. P. Dobson (also catalogued as Mrs Dobson Hinton), *The Archaeology of Somerset* (1931), pp. 163–4.
[33] E. Hutton, *Highways and Byways in Somerset* (1924), p. 20.

deceptive document. It purports to list every husbandman and townsman, and to provide details of the amount of ploughland, pasture, meadow and woodland, and even to count the numbers of livestock, on the lords' demesne farms. Yet there is reason to believe that there are a good many omissions and rough estimates masquerading as precise figures, so that attempts to work out such important matters as the density of population and the area of land which had been brought under cultivation are not so easy as would appear at first sight. Even so, the amount of detail which the survey contains is staggering, and enables contrasts to be made between different regions, which are likely to reflect real differences, even if the precise figures are suspect.

The settlements mentioned in the survey (612 of them) have been mapped by Welldon Finn and Wheatley, and this map reveals an interesting contrast between east and west Somerset, divided roughly by the river Parrett. The east was, by and large, a land of compact villages and hamlets with not much dispersed settlement between them, while the west was a land of small hamlets and isolated farmsteads, reflecting its predominantly upland and pastoral character. For instance, in the east, Glastonbury Abbey's manor of Ditcheat, near Castle Cary, contained thirty-six families consisting of thirteen *villani* (villagers, probably holding virgate farms of about thirty acres each by some form of servile tenure); eighteen *bordarii* (smallholders holding four or five acres by servile tenure—possibly some of it on newly-settled lands on the borders of the original settlement); three cottagers (similar to the bordars), and two slaves, who probably worked the Glastonbury Abbey's demesne farm. There was said to be land for thirty plough-teams, though only ten and a half were recorded (a complete plough-team contained eight oxen, and half a team had four). This was an open-field village working its lands in the semi-co-operative fashion of such communities (it was not finally enclosed till 1844), and it was surrounded by common pastures, meadows and woods.

In contrast, the western settlement of Enmore, at the foot of the Quantocks to the west of Bridgwater, was only a small hamlet where three *villani*, three bordars and two slaves had only one plough-team between them. A mile to the east there

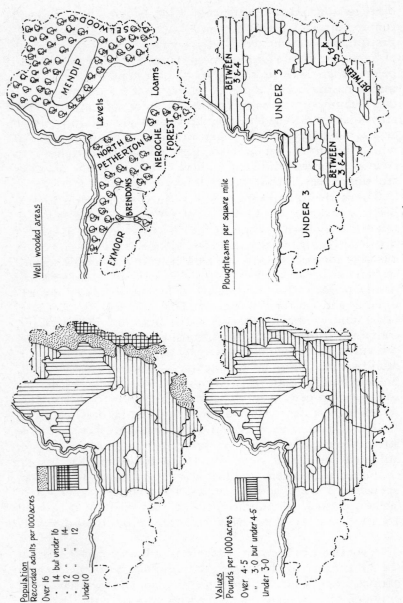

Population
Recorded adults per 1000 acres

Over 16
" 14 but under 16
" 12 " " 14
" 10 " " 12
Under 10

Values
Pounds per 1000 acres

Over 4·5
" 3·0 but under 4·5
" under 3·0

Well wooded areas

EXMOOR
BRENDONS
NORTH PETHERTON
MENDIP
SELWOOD
Levels
NEROCHE FOREST
Loams

Ploughteams per square mile

UNDER 3
BETWEEN 3 & 4
BETWEEN 3 & 4
UNDER 3
BETWEEN 3 & 4

Fig. 11. Some Domesday statistics, 1086

were three similar little hamlets around Lexworthy (probably
represented today by the farms of Lexworthy, Trokes and Stone
Hall), while a mile to the west up a Quantock combe at an
altitude of 550 feet stood Blaxhold, where three *villani*, two
bordars and a slave had two plough-teams.[34] Today it is a single
farm.

Paradoxically, the west appears to have been more densely
settled than the east since it had more settlements, but because
of their smaller size its actual density of population was far
smaller than that of the east. It is difficult to quantify these
densities because the Domesday population figures are the most
frustrating part of the survey. They hint at important omissions
(particularly amongst the urban population) which lead us to
suspect that the recorded population is too low, but they do not
provide much assistance to enable us to estimate how large the
omitted section was. However, by comparing the recorded
population with the amount of land which was under arable
cultivation, it is possible to arrive at estimates which seem
consistent and reasonable.

The recorded population of Somerset (using the county
boundary as it was between 1895 and 1974, which was slightly
different from the Domesday boundary) may be tabulated as
follows:[35]

Description	Numbers	Percentage
Villani (villagers)	5,234	39
Bordarii (borderers)	4,743	35.6
Servi (slaves)	2,106	15.7
Cottarii (cottagers)	390	2.9
Coliberti (landless but free, labourers)	208	1.5
Porcarii, fabri, etc (swineherds, smiths etc)	172	1.3
Burgenses, homines (burgesses, men)	541	4
TOTALS	13,399	100

[34] *VCH*, Somerset, 1, pp. 465, 472 and 490.
[35] Adapted from R. Welldon Finn and P. Wheatley in H. C. Darby and
R. Welldon Finn, eds., *The Domesday Geography of Southwest England* (1967),
p. 162. I have added the 22 *homines in paragio* living in Yeovil to their totals.

It will be seen at once that the survey lists only working heads of families. No women and children appear (and elderly people are probably also omitted), so that the listed population has to be multiplied by some unknown factor to account for these missing people. A factor of five is usually considered reasonable, and this raises the total to 66,995, but this can hardly be accepted as an adequate total for the county. It omits all landowners, whether they were barons, knights or freeholders, and this absence of freeholders in puzzling, since we know that the *ceorl*, or freeholding farmer, was an important person in Saxon times, and it seems very unlikely that he can have altogether died out. Further doubts are raised when we consider that the Domesday Survey of the eastern counties records freeholders in quite large numbers (for example, in Lincolnshire 45 per cent of the recorded population were *sokemen*—a type of freeman—and in Suffolk 35 per cent were freemen and another 5 per cent were *sokemen*). A new interpretation of this contrast has recently been suggested by Sally Harvey, who points out that the fundamental aim of the survey was to obtain new, accurate valuations for taxation, and that where small freeholders were responsible for taxes (as in East Anglia) they were minutely recorded, but that if lords were responsible for the payment of taxes (including those of freeholders in their manors, by whom they would be reimbursed) there would be no need for the survey to record the existence of the freeholders. She says that rent-paying freeholders on the lands of Burton Abbey in Staffordshire (known to exist from the abbey's records) are not listed in the survey, but she believes that their existence is indicated in the number of plough-uplands entered for the manors in which they resided. We shall return to this question of the significance of ploughlands later on, but here the point to note is that the failure of the survey to list freeholders for Somerset is not conclusive proof that they did not exist, though we have no way of knowing how important they might have been numerically.[36]

Another important omission from Domesday Book may be

[36] S. Harvey, "Evidence for settlement study: Domesday Book" in P. Sawyer, ed., *Medieval Settlement*, pp. 195–6.

suspected—that of the borough population. Somerset had eight towns which were definitely boroughs, and three more which probably were, but in all cases the only inhabitants listed were burgesses. Whereas in the survey of East Anglia Norwich had 480 bordars listed as well as its 665 burgesses, and Dunwich had, very significantly, 178 poor men (though curiously no burgesses). It has always seemed improbable that the borough population could have consisted solely of burgesses. Surely they must have had servants and employees such as the poor men listed at Dunwich? Again, we have no way of knowing how many urban poor there were, but it is very difficult to believe they were not more numerous than the relatively prosperous burgesses, if the later history of medieval towns is any guide.

In addition to the urban poor, the survey also omits the bailiffs, who must have managed the numerous manors held by great absentee landlords like the king himself, the Count of Mortain, Roger de Corcelle, the abbeys of Glastonbury, Muchelney, and Bath, and the bishops of Wells and Winchester. Churchmen of all types, whether bishops and canons or priests and monks, are almost entirely omitted. It might not be unreasonable to add 4,000 or 5,000 more families to the 13,399 recorded in the survey, to give about 17,400 to 18,400 families; this when multiplied by five, would yield 87,000 to 92,000 people. To this, perhaps about 1,000 unmarried churchmen would need to be added to give a total population in the region of 88,000 to 93,000. Figures such as these do not mean very much taken in isolation, but when compared with later figures (such as the population in the first census in 1801, of 274,000), or the area of land recorded in Domesday as being under cultivation, they become more meaningful.

The survey recorded 3,886 plough-teams, and it is generally assumed that each team would plough around 100 to 120 acres a year. This gives us a ploughed area of something between 388,600 and 466,320 acres—of which, of course, about half would have been fallow land—so that it might be reasonable to assume that there were about 200,000 acres of crops and the same quantity of fallow. So with a population in the region of 90,000 there would be, on average, slightly over two acres of crops per head of population. This seems about right, considering that much of the oats, barley, beans and peas which were grown would have been fed to livestock, and that there was probably not much more than one acre of breadcorn per head of population, if that. Since yields are known to have been very low (often only a fourfold return on the seed grown, compared with twenty- to thirty-fold today), the relationship between the estimated population and the area of crops seems satisfactory. There would seem to be rather too much arable land for the *recorded* population of only 13,399 families (about 66,000 people).

The recorded plough-teams can also be used to work out a rough estimate of the proportion of the county which had been brought under arable cultivation. Somerset contained 1,032,320 acres (before 1974). If about 200,000 acres were under crops and the same amount was ploughed fallow, this accounts for about 40 per cent of the county, leaving 60 per cent for common meadows, pastures, woodlands, moors and marshes. Considering how extensive the moors like Exmoor were, and how huge an area the undrained Levels covered, it would appear that the farmers of 1086 and their forebears had brought a quite respectable proportion of the cultivable land into use (Fig. 11).

One of the most intractable problems of Domesday is the discrepancy between the number of plough-teams recorded and the number of plough-lands—an excess of lands of about 20 per cent. Curiously, some places (about 14 per cent) had more teams than they had plough-lands, while 35 per cent had the same number, and 51 per cent of the settlements had more land than teams. Various explanations have been put forward to account for these discrepancies. Where there were too many plough-teams, it looks as though the juries who provided the evidence were trying to say in an oblique way that the lords had granted too many tenancies to small farmers, and that holdings had become uneconomic. Where there were too many plough-lands, Maitland suggested that the juries were not trying to make an estimate of new land which might be brought under cultivation, but were saying (again in an oblique way) how much land had been under cultivation in 1066—which was one of the questions Domesday sought to answer. By this explanation it would appear that about one acre in five had slipped out of cultivation by 1086, but recently Sally Harvey has suggested a quite different explanation, as we have already hinted. She suggests that, when the survey says there is land for five ploughs but there are only four teams, what it is *trying* to say is that, in addition to the four teams held by the servile tenants, there is another team held by unrecorded freemen. If this explanation is correct, then the real arable acreage was not that ploughed by the 3,886 servile teams, but the 4,855 recorded plough-lands. This would push the arable area up to nearly 500,000 acres—or fifty per cent of the county. Since Somerset was not like Yorkshire, a county devastated in revenge for revolt against the Normans, this explanation perhaps seems more reasonable than one which would imply that one acre in five had been lost to cultivation in the twenty-one years of Norman rule.

Another problem which we can look at more closely in the later regional chapters, is the question of the eighty or so modern settlements which are not mentioned in the survey. This does not by any means indicate that they did not exist in 1086: some like Binegar, Dinder and Wookey were mentioned in Saxon charters, but many were dependent settlements which were recorded under the head manor, like the fifteen unnamed settlements around Taunton recorded under that place, and the many other unnamed manors recorded under Cannington, Williton and Carhampton.[37] Absence from Domesday may, of course, indicate that a settlement was founded in the expansion of cultivation between 1087 and around 1348 (the peak reached before the Black Death), but each case needs to be carefully examined in relation to all available documentary and field evidence before this can be definitely accepted.

Despite the attack upon the woodlands which had been going on since the origins of farming, the county was still relatively densely wooded compared with today (Fig. 11). It was not an open landscape dotted with occasional woods, but a well-wooded landscape broken by numerous patches of cultivation. Domesday shows that most places had some woodland (except

[37] Finn and Wheatley, *Somerset Domesday*, p. 141, and *VCH*, Somerset, passim.

in the uplands like Exmoor and Mendip, and in the Levels), and it is probable that many villages (and most hamlets) were still separated from their neighbours by belts of forest, as they are in many African countries today.

Domesday also gives the impression of an overwhelmingly rural landscape with towns sparsely scattered over the countryside, and minuscule in size. As we have seen, this is partly an illusion, caused by the almost certain under-recording of the poorer townsmen, and partly a result of the survey's feudal nature, for it only indicated that a settlement was urban if it was a borough and its inhabitants held their land by the burgage tenure (a favourable and relatively free tenure which safeguarded its holder from most of the more unpleasant aspects of feudal dependence). The Domesday boroughs in order of size (by recorded burgesses) were Bath, Ilchester, Milborne Port, Taunton, Langport, Axbridge and Bruton. Frome, Milverton and Watchet also seem to have been boroughs, although they had no recorded burgesses (only *villani*, bordars, etc.), while Yeovil had in 1066 twenty-two men holding *in paragio* (equally), who were attached to the manor by 1806. They seem to have been townsmen holding under some form of tenure akin to burgage.

Bath was far and away the largest borough. It had 192 recorded burgesses, giving it a burghal population of about 1,000 and a possible actual population (allowing for unrecorded poor inhabitants) of 2,000 or 3,000. Ilchester followed, with 107 recorded burgesses and perhaps 1,000 to 1,500 inhabitants in all. Milborne Port (69 recorded burgesses) and Taunton (64) came next with possibly a population of 600 to 1,000. The other three were much smaller places. Langport had only 39 recorded burgesses, Axbridge 32 and Bruton a mere 17. Langport and Axbridge thus probably had about 400 to 500 inhabitants each, and Bruton about 250.

It is noticeable that nearly all the boroughs lay in the east or centre of the county. There was no borough west of Taunton (though Milverton and Watchet had been boroughs, and may possibly have retained some urban characteristics). Crewkerne and Ilminster had markets, but such prominent modern towns as Bridgwater, Wells, Glastonbury, Chard and Weston-super-

Mare seem to have been scarcely more than villages—although the survey's inability to distinguish townsmen, unless they held by burgage tenure, may conceal urban development which was more important than we realise.[38]

SELECT BIBLIOGRAPHY

Morris, J., *The Age of Arthur: A History of the British Isles from 350 to 650* (1973).

Alcock, L., *Arthur's Britain, History and Archaeology, 376–634* (1971).

Rahtz, P. A. and Fowler, P. J., 'Somerset, 400–700' in Peter J. Fowler, ed., *Archaeology and the Landscape. Essays for L. V. Grinsell* (1972).

Grundy, G. B., *The Saxon Charters and Field Names of Somerset* (1935).

Hoskins, W. G., *The Westward Expansion of Wessex* (1960).

Finberg, H. P. R., *The Early Charters of Wessex* (1964).

Victoria County History of Somerset, Vol. I (1906).

Finn, R. Welldon, and Wheatley, P., 'Somerset' in H. C. Darby and R. Welldon Finn, eds., *The Domesday Geography of Southwest England* (1967).

Thorn, C. F. (ed.), *Domesday Book: Somerset* (1980).

[38] Finn and Wheatley, *Somerset Domesday*, passim.

4. The medieval landscape

Expanding settlement, 1086–1320. Crisis and decline, 1320–1460.

DURING THE PERIOD between the Domesday Survey and the Renaissance, the Somerset landscape underwent a great transformation, based on expanding rural settlement and the rapid growth of towns, both old and new, up to about 1320. This was followed by a century and a half of contraction and decline. The reasons for this later crisis are not fully known, but they are associated with persistent plagues, shrinking populations, and decaying trade. Inevitably the settled area was reduced as towns and villages declined. Some of the smaller villages and hamlets even disappeared altogether, and sheep grazed where once houses had stood and streets had been thronged with chattering people. But before surveying this troubled period, we must turn our attention to the remarkable time of growth which preceded it.

Expanding settlement, 1086–1320

This was a period when village lands were increased at the expense of scrub pastures and forests, and when town growth was also rapid. Successful villages grew into towns, and lords of manors vied with one another to found completely new urban settlements on green field sites.[1] The whole movement was based on a quickly growing population, and, although we do not have fully accurate figures for the population of the county as a whole in the Middle Ages, the surviving manorial records show that the rate of expansion of population and cultivated land was very rapid. For instance, the population of the Bishop of Winchester's extensive Taunton manor increased two and a

[1] See W. G. Hoskins, *The Making of the English Landscape* (1955), pp. 61–91, and M. W. Beresford, *New Towns of the Middle Ages* (1967).

half times between 1209 and 1311, and the records of Glastonbury Abbey indicate a similar situation, though they are not
quite so full as those of Taunton.[2] This increasing population
must have pressed on the common pastures and woodlands, and
much new land must have been brought into cultivation by the
process of field-by-field reclamation (known at the time as
assarting from the Old French *essarter*, 'to grub up trees'). There
is also evidence which strongly suggests that reclamation of
marshland was occurring, especially on the salt marshes along
the coast. For instance, the twenty hides at *Brentmerse* (in South
Brent) were valued at £54. 10s. in the Domesday Survey in
1086, but they had been worth only £15 in 1066. Such a steep
rise in so short a period is difficult to account for without
reclamation. It also seems probable that new settlements,
especially farms and hamlets, if not villages, were established in
formerly unoccupied places. This, however, is not quite so easy
to demonstrate as was once thought, for although the names of
many farms and hamlets, which were not mentioned in the
Domesday Survey, appear in the twelfth and thirteenth
centuries in the records of lay and ecclesiastical landowners, it
cannot always be assumed that they represent new settlements.
In Professor Hoskins' study of the 'Highland Zone of Western
Britain in the Domesday Survey', he showed that many places in
Devon, Cornwall and Somerset, whose names appeared for the
first time after Domesday, were in existence by 1086. Although
not named they were in fact held by people listed in the Survey
(usually *villani*). Thus the pattern of post-Domesday settlement
seems to have been not so much the establishment of entirely
new settlements as the considerable *expansion* of those that
already existed.[3]

We may take as an example the large and populous village of
Martock, which lies just north of the main road (A303) between
Ilchester and Ilminster. It had only one entry in the Domesday
Survey, while, in the succeeding centuries, manorial records list
the names of no fewer than nine dependent settlements—Bower
Hinton, Hurst, Newton, Coat, Stapleton, Ash, Witcombe,

---

[2] M. M. Postan, *Medieval Economy and Society* (Pelican, 1975), p. 36.
[3] W. G. Hoskins, *Provincial England* (1963), pp. 15–52.

Milton and Long Load. It would be tempting to suggest that these were all new settlements established in response to land hunger after 1086, but when one examines the Domesday entry for Martock this begins to seem unlikely; for in addition to a demesne farm containing three ploughs (and being worked by six slaves and fourteen *coliberts*), there were no fewer than sixty-five villagers and twenty-four bordars with twenty-eight ploughs between them. It is most unlikely that these eighty-nine tenants all lived and farmed in Martock village. It is far more probable that they were distributed amongst the dependent settlements as well, as clearly happened in the huge entry for Taunton, where all the many settlements included in the later manor of Taunton Deane were included under the heading of Taunton. However it is clear that the Martock settlements must have expanded in size in the succeeding centuries, for by 1302 the eighty-nine tenants had increased to more than two hundred. There were a hundred and twenty-five in Martock, Bower Hinton, Hurst, Newton and Coat, and, although we do not have contemporary records for the other five settlements, they probably contained at least another hundred farms, judging from later records (e.g. thirty-seven tenants in Stapleton in 1308, thirty-four in Long Load in 1440, and eight in Ash between 1309 and 1432—Witcombe and Milton not yielding records of this period). Most of the dependent settlements had their own open-field systems, and this suggests that they were of ancient origin. As wasteland was reclaimed it was added to the open fields furlong by furlong, so that while these settlements were probably all in existence in 1086, they were greatly expanded in the following 250 years.[4]

In hillier parts of the county, these assarts tended to be enclosed into small paddocks suitable for livestock, and this can be seen in the small fields on the scarp of the Mendips in parishes like East and West Harptree, where the old open fields lay in the plain and the common pastures lay on the hilltop, so that medieval expansion forced farmers to reclaim woodland which lay on the scarp between. Similar crofts at Frome, which were free of common grazing rights in 1218, were probably assarts

[4] *VCH*, IV, pp. 78–97.

from the neighbouring Selwood Forest, while the Bishop of
Wells obtained licences to assart 120 acres from the woods of
Cheddar on three separate occasions in the thirteenth century.[5]

In the south of the county at Knowle St Giles on the slopes of
Windwhistle Hill reclamation from the woodland produced a
freehold estate called Wood (now Woodhouse Farm) held by
John of Wood in the early thirteenth century (though it is
always possible that one of the five *villani* and four *bordarii*
recorded in Domesday had a small-holding there in 1086).[6]
Reclamation was no doubt more extensive in the western uplands, where the Domesday population was small and the
available land plentiful. It is probable that the higher of the
thirty-four farms which eventually emerged in the remote upland parish of Luxborough in the Brendon Hills were created in
this period, though even here some caution is necessary because,
although there were only seventeen *villani* recorded in 1086,
there were also two demesne farms and fourteen bordars.[7] If the
bordars held small-holdings in what were the centres of later
farms, that would account for thirty-three farms—leaving only
one farmstead for post-Domesday creation. Careful fieldwork in
the area might solve some of these problems for the upland
parishes of west Somerset, where settlement was based on
hamlets and individual farms, making the identification of
Domesday holdings easier than in open-field villages.

However, the region where medieval reclamation from the
waste was at its most dramatic and significant was in the central Levels. In the thirteenth century especially, the great
ecclesiastical landowners like Glastonbury, Muchelney and
Athelney Abbeys, and the bishops of Bath and Wells, who
owned most of the Levels, set about a systematic policy of land
reclamation. They worked outwards from the fertile "islands"
in the levels, like "Sowy" (or Zoy, where Westonzoyland,
Middlezoy and Othery are located) and Athelney (Plate 16),
gradually reclaiming the nearest marshes, protecting them by

[5] F. Neale, "Saxon and medieval landscapes", in *Mendip, a New Study*, pp.
89–90.
[6] *VCH*, IV, p. 160.
[7] E. F. Williams, ed., *Parish Surveys in Somerset, Luxborough* (1978), pp. 5,
6, and 27; *VCH*, I, pp. 501 and 503.

walls, like the wall which accompanies the winding Haymoor
Old Rhyne in North Curry, the low remains of which can still
be seen in the midst of the reclaimed meadows. It was built
around 1316. Most of the reclaimed land was turned into rich
water meadows for haymaking, but some was used for growing
corn. In addition to wall-building, existing watercourses were
deepened and straightened and new irrigation ditches were dug.
In his excellent study of the draining of the Levels, Michael
Williams has some maps showing the extent and location of
medieval reclamation. Most progress was made on the western
side of "Sowy" between Westonzoyland and Athelney, where
some 970 acres had been reclaimed by Glastonbury Abbey by
1240, and many more by 1311 (when floods inundated 1,350
acres of reclaimed land where crops of barley, beans, oats and
peas had been growing). By the same date, another 886 acres
had been reclaimed in the moors to the south of Athelney in the
Tone valley between Lyng and North Curry (in Hay Moor—
then called "Boterlake"—Curry Moor and Stan Moor). Another
centre of activity was the moorland to the west of Glastonbury
around Godney and Beckery. Although exact computations are
impossible, it is clear that several thousand acres were reclaimed
and greatly raised in value.[8]

Impressive though the reclamation was, it was dwarfed by
even more ambitious schemes for altering the courses of rivers
(Fig. 12). The main reason for this, initially, was probably to
improve river transport in the Levels, and especially to enable
the officials of Glastonbury Abbey to move produce from the
outlying estates to the abbey itself (which, it has to be re-
membered, was still an island except in the summer, and was
valuable and fertile land, even though always liable to sudden
floods). The river Brue, which flows to the south of Glastonbury
and now goes westward to join the sea at Highbridge, was the
main river involved. Prior to the thirteenth century its course
partially encircled Glastonbury from the south, around the
western side (through Beckery) and then northwards through the
Panborough-Bleadney gap in the Wedmore-Wookey Hills, to
join the river Axe just north of Bleadney. This was a tortuous

[8] M. Williams, *The Draining of the Somerset Levels* (1970), pp. 50, 55, 57,
62–3, and 75–81.

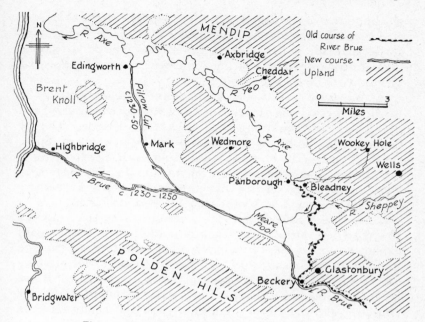

Fig. 12. The new courses of the River Brue, c. 1230–50

and unsatisfactory channel, and when the Axe valley was flooded
(as it frequently was) the waters dammed up and flowed back,
causing widespread flooding around Glastonbury. So a new
course had to be made for the Brue. This seems to have been
done sometime between 1230 and 1250. It was led westwards
into Meare Pool (an extensive lake which used to exist to the
north of Meare village), and then further westwards to Mark
Moor, where it apparently divided into two channels. One was
an artificial cut called Pilrow Cut, which flowed northwards
through Mark to join the river Axe near Edingworth. The other
was a new course for the Brue, directly westwards to the sea at
Highbridge, which was made by diverting it into the course of a
much smaller stream which already existed, and which the
waters of the Brue then widened by erosive action. Other minor
alterations were also made in the courses of the Tone near
Athelney and the Axe near Axbridge.

Although the area of land reclaimed was small in relation to the huge size of the Levels, and the alterations to the courses of rivers were minor compared with later works, a very important start was made in draining the Levels. Some of the directions taken (especially the re-routing of the Brue) formed the essential groundwork for all later progress.[9]

As we have seen, another important development in the medieval period was the expansion of towns, which grew and developed their marketing function as trade expanded. The list of Domesday boroughs was soon joined by new towns. Some sprang up naturally on trade routes, such as Bridgwater, which was the lowest convenient place for crossing the river Parrett, or were deliberately created by enterprising lords as money-making concerns, like Wellington, Wells and Chard.

Only three of the Domesday *burhs* grew into large modern towns. These were Bath, Taunton and Yeovil. Bath's main expansion, of course, came in the eighteenth century, but the foundation of Bath Abbey in 758 (to replace the nunnery founded in 676) and the adoption of the city as the episcopal seat by Bishop John de Villula in 1091, when he rebuilt the abbey church, gave the city a significant role. Its merchants were important enough to have formed a gild to whom Richard I granted a charter in 1189. It granted freedom from outside tolls and all their customs freely "as have our citizens of Winchester and their Merchant Gild". From at least 1220 Bath had its own mayor, and it was clearly an important market town although it expanded very little outside its original (probably Roman) walls, which were rebuilt and strengthened.[10]

Taunton belonged to the Bishop of Winchester and was the administrative centre for his very large manor, as well as being the market centre for the rich Vale of Taunton Deane. It received an important charter from King Stephen about 1136, giving its burgesses the immunities and privileges of those of London and Winchester. A castle was built in 1138, and by the thirteenth century the town was involved in the cloth industry. A fulling mill was built in 1219—the earliest known in the

[9] Ibid., *The Draining of the Somerset Levels*, pp. 65–74.

[10] M. Aston and R. Leech, *Somerset Towns*, pp. 13–19, 143–6, 147–54, and 31–4; Sir W. Savage, "Somerset Towns", *SANHS* (1954–5), p. 49; E. Hutton, *Highways and Byways in Somerset* (1924), pp. 21–34.

west of England—and another was added at nearby Bishop's Hull in 1246.[11] Taunton's excellent location in the valley between the Blackdown and Quantock Hills on the main route to Exeter, and the absence of important competitors, enabled Taunton to grow steadily.

Yeovil which, as we have seen, was not a borough in a legal sense in 1086, also developed in this period, but only slowly. It was given a charter by King John around 1205, but this has been lost, and its details are unknown; however, it probably granted some form of free burgage tenure, since later documents refer to the "Free Borough of Yeovil", which was in existence before 1310. Yet there were only twelve burgesses at that date, and so, although the town had achieved some measure of legal independence since 1086, it was still a fairly small place and had not yet established its supremacy over its nearby rival, Stoford. This place, which is now a mere hamlet in Barwick parish, was at the "Stoneford" over the Yeo where the road to Dorchester crossed into Dorset. A document of 1273 records seventy-four burgage holdings there, which, if they were all occupied, suggests that Stoford was a much more important place than Yeovil. Yet by 1569 it had decayed so much that a military muster of that year recorded only eleven names. The reasons for Yeovil's later rise at Stoford's expense are not fully known, but it is clear that in this period Yeovil was still quietly laying the foundations for its later growth.[12]

To the dozen or so Domesday boroughs were added in this period over twenty new towns, some of which, like Bridgwater, Wells and Chard, took root and flourished, and others, like Stoford, Downend (in Puriton parish) and Newport (in North Curry parish) either quickly shrivelled and died, or else gradually faded out after a promising start. Bridgwater, with its strategic site on the lowest crossing of the Parrett, was the most successful of the new creations—called merely Bridge in the Domesday Survey, it had belonged to Walter de Douai, from whom its modern name is derived (Bridge Walter or Walter's Bridge). A later lord, William Brewer, obtained a charter from

[11] R. Bush, *The Book of Taunton* (1977), pp. 21–56.
[12] L. Brook, *The Book of Yeovil* (1978), pp. 13–55; Aston and Leech, *Somerset Towns*, pp. 163–6, 126–30.

King John and built a castle. Sea-borne trade was important from the first, and the town advanced rapidly. By 1312 it had evidently overtaken Bath and Taunton, for in the Exchequer Subsidy for that year it was assessed for more than they were. Bridgwater paid £11.11s.5d, while Bath paid £8.4s.7d, and Taunton £7.3s. Wells was also a successful new town which had been encouraged by the bishops to grow around the cathedral. It had a market by 1136, two charters from the bishops (1166–91), and by 1312 it also had overtaken Bath and Taunton (being assessed at £10.6s). Chard was another of the bishops' towns. Like Yeovil it benefited from being on a main road from London to Exeter, and having good communications with south-coast ports like Axmouth and Lyme Regis. It had a charter from King John (now lost) and one from the bishop in 1234, which delimited the town and laid out burgage holdings in one-acre lots at a rent of twelve pence per year.[13]

Castles also became a feature of the landscape in this period, although Somerset did not have as many as some counties. The de Mohun's dramatic fortress at Dunster was (and is) one of the most impressive, but its early rival, the Count of Mortain's stronghold at Montacute, seems to have been destroyed after the failure of his rebellion against William the Conqueror in 1087. Farleigh Hungerford, near Frome, (an impressive ruin) and Taunton (restored) still survive, at least in part, but most of the more famous medieval castles, like Nether Stowey, Bridgwater, Richmont (in East Harptree), Stogursey and Castle Cary no longer stand.

The once great monasteries have suffered a similar fate, although the evocative ruins of Glastonbury, Muchelney and Cleeve Abbey (near Watchet) (Plate 10) still give some impression of the grandeur and magnificence which they exhibited in their prime. Their effect on the landscape which, as we have seen, was at its most profound in the Levels, will be illustrated in the regional chapters.[14]

---

[13] Aston and Leech, *Somerset Towns*, pp. 13–19, 31–4, 147–54.
[14] Hunt and Sellman, *Aspects of Somerset History*, pp. 19–20, 23–5.

Crisis and decline, 1320–1460

A great variety of evidence attests to the decline of the population in this period, even though we do not have reliable figures to enable us to make exact measurements. There is good national evidence (some of it derived from Taunton manor) that yields of grain had been declining in the late thirteenth and early fourteenth centuries, with the result that hunger and malnutrition were weakening the population. The years 1315–17 were made miserable by disastrous harvest failures, and some evidence suggests that the population was already beginning to fall before the catastrophic visitation of the bubonic plague (the Black Death) in 1347–8. The ravages of the plague left an indelible mark on contemporaries (perhaps because the clergy were so hard hit, and it was they who wrote chronicles). There are no reliable figures, but modern estimates range from the conservative one that 20 per cent of the population perished, to disastrous assessments which put it as high as 40 to 50 per cent.[15]

The over-crowded and insanitary towns probably suffered much more than the countryside. In Taunton "market tolls were slashed to a mere 5s.4d that year. The fulling mill was closed down for want of cloth workers, there were defaults of rent, and the disease probably carried off, among others, the town priest, Walter de Foxcote."[16] Recent excavations near the church in the village of North Petherton, near Bridgwater, have shown that the churchyard was temporarily extended to take excess burials in the mid-fourteenth century, as it also was in many towns such as Bristol, Poole, Winchester and Worcester.[17] Plague returned again in the early 1360s, the mid-1370s, and sporadically throughout the fifteenth century, so that the population did not begin to grow again until around 1475, and not very noticeably until the 1520s.

The effects of this long period of economic decline on the countryside were profound, because the smaller population had

---

[15] Postan, *Medieval Economy and Society*, pp. 39–44.

[16] Bush, The *Book of Taunton*, p. 131.

[17] P. J. Leach et al., "Excavations at North Petherton, Somerset 1975", *SANHS*, 121 (1977), p. 21.

a reduced demand for all products—whether agricultural or industrial. However, the economic recession did not affect all classes alike. If landlords had to abandon their demesnes and let them out to peasants, and if the great merchants involved in exporting wool and cloth had to cut back on their operations, the peasants and the wage-labourers (or more accurately their survivors) generally gained. Rents fell, labour services were commuted, and peasants were able to enlarge the size of their farms, both by taking over the holdings of the deceased and by renting parts of the demesnes. Sometimes the demesnes struggled on at a reduced level, as at Lopen near Crewkerne, where in the 1370s the demesne work-force was cut from nine to four (only one of these a ploughman). However, in the early fifteenth century the demesne was divided up and let out in small parcels to the tenants. This was particularly common in places like Lopen, where there was no resident Lord.[18] It was not only peasants who gained. For those who lived by wages (they were probably not more than 10 or 15 per cent of the population, and many were small-holders who were only part-time wage earners), there was a double gain: money wages rose, and the price of food, fuel, clothing and other necessities fell. In addition, many who had previously been landless were probably able to rent small-holdings. This is not to say that peasants and workers were prosperous—merely that the extreme pressures of poverty and servitude were relaxed.

The most noticeable way in which these changes affected the landscape was in the retreat of the corn crops from the margins of cultivation to which they had been carried, and the conversion of much of the land to grass. The hillside ridges, known as strip lynchets, which are so noticeable in parishes like Yarlington (Plate 7) and West Chinnock, no longer bore waving strips of corn, but were covered with grass grazed by the ubiquitous sheep. Landlords were trying to cut costs by substituting shepherds for ploughmen, and were adjusting their farming to the new markets for wool and mutton. All over Somerset, as the cornlands shrank, and the more remote settlements were abandoned, sheep replaced men. In 1395 Somerset

[18] *VCH*, IV, p. 166.

led all English counties in the production of woollen cloth, being the only one to produce over 10,000 cloths, followed by Wiltshire with between 5,000 and 10,000. No other county produced more than 5,000.[19]

The surviving records provide only a few glimpses of the thousands of sheep who grazed the country at this time. Already in 1330 Glastonbury Abbey had 1,504 sheep grazing on its Mendip manors of Doulting, Wrington, Marksbury, Mells, Batcombe and Pilton. Mendip at this time was still quite unenclosed, and was one huge sheep-walk with springing pasture stretching for more than twenty miles from Batcombe on the south-eastern edge to Bleadon Hill above Weston overlooking the Bristol Channel. Sheep were equally prominent elsewhere in the county. Sir Hugh Luttrell had 668 grazing at East Quantoxhead near Watchet in 1419.[20] Not only arable land was being enclosed (usually in small pieces) and converted to pasture, but settlements also were shrinking. If few villages disappeared totally, as was quite common in the Midland counties, many shrank into hamlets, while scores of hamlets were abandoned or were reduced to single farmsteads; and some of the more remote farms, especially those high up on Exmoor, were also given up. Bagley, near Stoke Pero, and North Colly Hill in Luxborough are good examples. A recent survey, by no means complete, based on aerial photographs, has identified about 500 places where some evidence of shrunken settlement occurs, ranging from villages and hamlets to single farmsteads. The 500 sites also date from all ages, so that not all the evidence for shrinkage relates to this period. Even so, the evidence for decay is far greater than had existed only a few years ago, when the last national survey of deserted settlements was made. It is also clear that, in the majority of cases, decline occurred in the fifteenth or sixteenth century, and the check to growth which settlements received after 1348 was often the initial shock which set in motion a slow process of decay from which they never recovered. Settlements were seldom aban-

[19] R. A. Pelham, "Fourteenth century England" in H. C. Darby, ed., *An Historical Geography of England before 1800* (1951), pp. 250–2.

[20] R. W. Dunning, *History of Somerset*, pp. 16–17.

doned because all the inhabitants actually died of plague. A more common pattern was for those which were situated on infertile or difficult soils to be given up as their inhabitants moved to farms which became available in more favoured areas.[21]

The whole process can be seen in microcosm in the parish of Mudford just to the north of Yeovil (Fig. 13). As its name implies, this parish is situated in a low-lying area (in the valley of the river Yeo) where there is a good deal of heavy clay. It once contained no fewer than seven hamlets, of which two have completely disappeared (Nether Adber and Mudford Terry), and three are much shrunken (Hinton, West Mudford and Up Mudford) as can be seen from Fig. 13. Aerial photography reveals Nether Adber as one of the most sharply defined deserted settlement sites in Somerset, with the remains of its former arable fields clearly visible in the surrounding ridge and furrow, and the site of the hamlet revealing the former streets and the plots of the buildings. There is a tradition that the Black Death caused the desertion, about 1349, and it may have been partly responsible, for later records show that only one family—the Huntleys—lived there. In 1633 Thomas Gerard, of nearby Trent, wrote that the "Huntley family flourished in Nether Adber even until our grandfathers' days when all of a sudden it sunk." This suggests a final abandonment sometime in the reign of Queen Elizabeth I.[22]

Another sign of the stagnation at this time was the virtual stoppage of reclamation work in the Levels. Dr Williams notes that very few drainage works can be attributed to this period. With the fall in rents consequent upon the reduced demand for farms, it was no longer worth while for abbeys like Glastonbury to incur the heavy costs of drainage and land reclamation. In fact, the evidence suggests that there was considerable difficulty in maintaining existing works, particularly sea-walls. The lands of Cannington Priory, north-west of Bridgwater, were severely flooded in 1425, and fifty years later the sea-wall at Bleadon was broken up and destroyed by the unusual "violence and ferocity

[21] Information kindly supplied by M. Aston of the Department of Extra-Mural Studies, University of Bristol.

[22] M. A. Aston, "Deserted settlements in Mudford Parish, Yeovil", *SANHS*, 121 (1977), pp. 41–53.

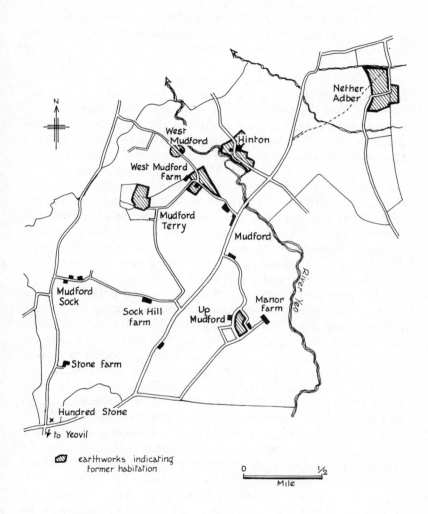

Fig. 13. Former settlement sites in Mudford parish, near Yeovil

of the wind and sea".[23] A century of reduced manpower for maintenance may also have played its part.

Generally speaking, this was a period when the towns either stagnated or decayed, although concentration on the wool trade and wool exports may have enabled a few towns to counteract the trend. Yeovil in particular seems to have benefited to some extent from Ilchester's decline, which was grievous. In 1276 it had been a thriving place with no fewer than six separate parishes, but decline set in a little before 1300, and was then continuous. In 1361 the Crown was persuaded to move the county's law courts from Somerton to Ilchester "for the relief of the town greatly impoverished and distressed by divers adversities". In 1377 it was reported that the "greater number" of the inhabitants had left the town, and in 1502 the only three remaining parishes were amalgamated into one. No wonder that when John Leland, the king's travelling antiquary and reporter on the state of local castles and defences, visited Ilchester about 1540 he remarked on its "wonderful decay".[24] The physical shrinkage of Ilchester must have been very considerable, and even today it is still a small place.

Somerton also suffered in this period, and declined after a burst of expansion in the late thirteenth century, when the present market-place was built to the south of the church, and new streets were laid out. The county courts and gaol were moved to Somerton in 1278, and a bright period of expansion seemed to lie ahead, but rivalry with Ilchester was endemic, and when Ilchester secured the courts in 1366, it merely increased Somerton's problems. The town grew very little between 1290 and the suburban development of the twentieth century.[25]

Yeovil, by contrast, seems to have benefited to some extent by its neighbours' misfortunes. Detailed information on its topography is lacking, but between 1380 and 1400 it continued to build its magnificent church—known as the "lantern of the west" because it contains so much glass. It is a very large church, 146 feet long and 50 feet wide, and having a massive

---

[23] M. Williams, *The Draining of the Somerset Levels*, pp. 82–3.
[24] *VCH*, III, pp. 187–8.
[25] *VCH*, III, pp. 129–53.

Plate 6 The village of Greinton on the south slope of the Polden Hills near Street. The former common arable fields may be seen in the foreground, and the former common meadows on the Levels in the background. Note the post-enclosure farmsteads on the Levels. Enclosure of the surrounding fields took place under the Sedgemoor Enclosure Act of 1791.

Plate 7 Lynchets at Yarlington, near Wincanton. Usually medieval in date, lynchets were extensions of arable strips from the common fields on to adjacent hillsides. They are particularly extensive at Yarlington.

Plate 8 This lane on Stickleball Hill divides the parishes of East and West Pennard, east of Glastonbury. It is an ancient Saxon estate boundary, mentioned in a charter of 681 (see chapter 3).

Plate 9 The remains of Woodspring (or Worspring) Priory, near Weston-super-Mare. The Priory was founded in the 1220s by Reginald FitzUrse, a grandson of one of the murderers of St. Thomas Becket, as an act of penance. Surviving monastic churches are rare. This one only escaped destruction because it was turned into a private house.

Plate 10 The gatehouse of Cleeve Abbey, near Watchet. The Abbey was founded by William de Roumare in 1198 and its surviving buildings are amongst the best monastic remains in Somerset. This attractive gatehouse was rebuilt in the early sixteenth century.

Plate 11 The ruins of Nunney Castle, near Frome. Built by Sir John Delamare in 1373, it was not really defensible, despite its moat (visible on the left beneath the church). It's an early example of the castle built more for residential comfort than military strength. It was never rebuilt after its destruction in the Civil War (1642-6).

Plate 12 A planned medieval street at Mells, near Frome, seen from the church tower. Mells belonged to Glastonbury Abbey and Abbot John Selwood (1455-92) decided to rebuild it in the form of a cross. The street, still known as New Street, was the only one completed.

tower at the west end 90 feet high. It is built from local limestone, but the exterior and interior dressings are made from the beautiful golden Ham stone. The twenty huge windows were its special feature. They contained five lights each, and those in the aisles were twenty feet high, and nine feet at the base. Unfortunately, none of the ancient painted glass remains.

How could Yeovil afford this huge church in a time of depression? Good fortune played its part. Yeovil was able to draw upon the accumulated savings of the past, because, owing to an accident of manorial history, its rector was also lord of the town, and in 1219, in a dispute with the neighbouring Maltravers family (who claimed the lordship), it was agreed that the rector should keep it but should not benefit personally. Each year he collected the rents from the borough, but he had to use them for the benefit of the church, so that a large fund accumulated, which was eventually available for building. Nevertheless, it seems doubtful whether Yeovil would have embarked upon this extensive building project if the town had not been reasonably prosperous and optimistic about its future.[26]

This lengthy period of population decline and economic hardship was prolonged by the murderous conflict between rival factions of the aristocracy, known as the Wars of the Roses, which lasted from about 1450 to 1470. But from about 1460 there were distinct signs of a recovery in economic activity and the spread of settlement. Exports of wool to the expanding economies of Renaissance Italy and Flanders grew rapidly, and Somerset merchants and farmers were in the forefront. It was in this period of revival that many of the glorious church towers for which the county is so famous were built. In fact some of the best, like Chewton Mendip, were not completed until the sixteenth century, so that this aspect of the Somerset landscape, which is usually considered to be specifically fifteenth century, is best left for the next chapter, where we examine the effects of a new period of economic expansion in the late fifteenth and sixteenth centuries.

[26] J. Goodchild, *The Borough of Yeovil* (1954), pp. 103–7.

SELECT BIBLIOGRAPHY

Aston, M. and Leech, R., *Historic Towns in Somerset* (1977).
Hunt, T. J. and Sellman, R. R., *Aspects of Somerset History* (1973).
Dunning, R. W., *A History of Somerset* (1978).
Williams, M., *The Draining of the Somerset Levels* (1970).

5. The emergence of the modern landscape

Economic recovery, 1460–1650

FOR REASONS WHICH are still not entirely clear, economic conditions began to improve in the 1460s. The virulence of the plague seems to have diminished, and the population slowly began to increase again, with a beneficial effect on the demand for all commodities. Overseas demand for wool and woollen cloth was particularly strong, and this was soon reflected in the landscape by a persistent conversion of arable land to meadow and pasture for the ever-expanding sheep flocks. In many parishes (but by no means all) this involved the enclosure of the open fields (and sometimes the common pastures as well), thus bringing to an end the ancient type of rural economy and life. Small hedged fields replaced the extensive open cornlands, and the pattern of settlement was also affected. When common rights existed on land, no one could build on it—with the result that houses and farms tended to be crowded together in the villages and hamlets. With enclosure and the ending of common grazing rights, farmers could move their steadings out of the villages and on to sites more convenient for their fields. Likewise small-holders and farm workers could build cottages on what had formerly been common rough grazings. All this was, of course, confined to the old area of open fields in the east and south of the county, but even there sixty-seven villages retained at least some of their open fields until the era of enclosure by Act of Parliament (roughly 1796 to 1847 in Somerset's case).[1]

[1] See W. E. Tate, *Somerset Enclosure Acts and Awards* (1948).

Towns began to expand again with the growth of trade, and throughout the period this growth was internal as well as external. Not only new industries, but also a new regional specialisation in agricultural production widened the trading network, so that there was a need to improve and extend the roads. Rivers also had to be widened and deepened; new bridges had to be built and old ones improved. The face of the landscape was changing quite rapidly in the reigns of Henry VIII, Elizabeth I, James I and Charles I: the uncomfortable medieval castles were increasingly abandoned and replaced by country houses, frequently surrounded by the extensive parks of the new gentry such as the Phelips at Montacute and the Pouletts at Hinton St George. These were the two most influential families in the county in Charles I's reign.[2]

Although the strong overseas demand for wool and cloth was initially beneficial and helped to revive the stagnant economy, it began to exercise a less healthy effect after about 1550, when the rapidly increasing population required more cornland to feed it; yet the profits from conversion to pasture for sheep (derived ultimately from abroad) still made this more attractive than corn production to landlords and farmers. It was only in the 1580s and 1590s, when corn prices rose to disastrous levels and famine threatened, that there was some slackening of the pressure for enclosure.[3] Of course, enclosed land could always be used for corn production (and increasingly was), but villagers felt that there was no guarantee that it would be (as there was in the old, traditional rotations of the open fields), and this helps to explain why there was so much popular opposition to enclosure. It was not just a blind and obstinate refusal to adopt improved methods of farming, but was based on a genuine fear of the shortage of bread in an age when corn could not be imported. The fact that enclosure was often used by large landlords and farmers as an opportunity to get rid of small

[2] T. G. Barnes, *Somerset, 1625–1640: A County's Government during the "Personal Rule"* (1961).

[3] See W. G. Hoskins, "Harvest Fluctuations and English Economic History", *Agric. Hist. Rev.*, XII (1964), pp. 28–46, reprinted in W. E. Minchinton (ed.) *Essays in Agrarian History*, I (1968), pp. 93–115.

farmers (if they were tenants) or to buy them out (if they were freeholders) did not increase its popularity, either. Neither were customary rights to graze livestock on the commons and to cut firewood and turf always compensated for in enclosure agreements.

These developments were occurring all over the county. At Aller, on the edge of the Levels, near Somerton, the open fields remained unenclosed until 1797, but the more valuable meadows were mostly enclosed by 1577. Between 1614 and 1616 there was a struggle between the lord, Sir John Davis (who had recently purchased the manor) and the tenants over attempts to enclose the remaining forty-seven acres of common meadows. The lord believed that enclosure would double their value (and hence the rent he could charge), and he erected hedges and gates, but in 1615 the tenants broke these down and put their cattle into the meadows. The manorial steward suggested that the lord should convert the tenants' ancient customary tenures into leaseholds for a term of years, "and then their custom will never be worth a button", but this scheme seems to have failed. In 1623 Sir John Davis sold the manor to John Stawell of Cothelstone and the meadows remained open for common grazing until 1797. The tenants at Aller also had extensive common grazing rights on the still unenclosed and undrained marshes of Sedgemoor.[4]

At Charlton Adam, on the gently rising ground a few miles to the north of Ilchester, matters proceeded more peaceably. Pressure on the cornfields was initially eased in the sixteenth century by a division of the two medieval fields, the North Field and the South Field. Each was divided into two parts, and presumably the rotations were altered in such a way that, instead of one whole field lying fallow each year (i.e. half the arable land), only one of the four new fields was fallowed, reducing the total fallow to one quarter. This measure may have raised productivity sufficiently to allay the demand for enclosure, because the cornfields were not enclosed till the eighteenth century (and not completely then), but the lord was able to enclose the common meadows and pastures by agree-

---

[4] *VCH*, III, pp. 63, 67–8.

ment with the tenants. In 1565 a deed reveals "enclosure being already begun, shall proceed further next year"; while in 1634 the lord reached an agreement with thirteen customary tenants to enclose and divide up 132½ acres of common pasture. A further 53½ acres were similarly allotted to two freeholders. Thus the landscape at Charlton Adam became a patchwork quilt of small, hedged closes scattered about amongst the common fields, with the closes always increasing in number. A map of 1810 shows a mainly enclosed landscape, but with little patches of open field still surviving all over the parish.[5]

A contrast to Charlton Adam is provided by Hinton St George on the low limestone ridge in the south of the county between Ilminster and Crewkerne. Here the lords Poulett were extending their large house and fine park, and replacing the open landscape of arable fields by pastures, woods, avenues of trees and decorative vistas. By the 1560s the three open arable fields had been almost completely enclosed, and two estates of seventy-four and eighty-six acres, based on the hamlet of Craft (now disappeared) to the south of Hinton, had been purchased. The park spread out over the former west and south Fields, and the Pouletts consolidated their estate by exchanges of land. One tenant in Craft was licensed to enclose his holding, but another had to be given pasturage for his oxen and cows in the park, because no other suitable arrangement could be made. In 1569 the park contained deer, and was said to be four miles in compass. Work in the 1650s included taking in and hedging fields, laying old hedges, and planting hawthorn around the perimeter. Cherry trees for the orchard were also purchased from London in 1652.[6]

Over in the west, on Exmoor, the search for more and improved pasture took the form of overstocking the commons with agisted livestock (i.e. animals belonging to farmers too far from the moor to possess common rights, who paid those with such rights to let them graze their sheep and cattle on the moor). This led to extensive quarrels and disputes about how many livestock the commoners could put on the moor and how much

---

[5] *VCH*, III, pp. 83, 89–90.
[6] *VCH*, IV, pp. 38–40, 44–5.

the Foresters (officials who rented Exmoor from the Crown) could charge for agisted stock. There were also complaints of illegal enclosures by the Exmoor farmers, especially the fifty-two "free suitors" who occupied holdings in the parishes of Withypool and Hawkridge in the valley of the river Barle. A witness in a court case in 1608 (himself a free suitor) declared that, "He thinketh that the common grounds belonging to the tenements of the said defendents and the residue of the said 52 suitors cannot maintain so many sheep, cattle and widge beasts (horses) as the said defendents and the rest of the 52 suitors do usually keep of their own and other mens upon the said commons." He also alleged that a piece of ground of about eight acres near the moor pound in Withypool, "about 5 or 6 years past", was illegally "enclosed and tilled" by several of the free suitors. In another case, in 1617, it was alleged that the sub-lessees of the Forest had profitably stocked it with "30,000 sheep and great numbers of cattle, horse beasts and hogs unringed of strangers and borderers".[7]

It is not surprising that Charles I turned his mind to enclosing and "improving" Exmoor, Dartmoor, Neroche, Mendip and other royal forests in 1629, after he had decided to rule without Parliament and had thus become desperately short of money. (Forests, incidentally, were royal hunting grounds and did not necessarily contain any trees. Certainly Exmoor had hardly any.) A memorandum amongst the state papers for 1630 shows that the king's advisers were thinking in very grandiose terms, and clearly had no conception of the realities of farming on Exmoor and Dartmoor:

> Note of the King's Intention to improve the Forests of Exmoor and Dartmoor.
>
> In the counties of Somerset and Devon are the two great forests of Exmoor and Dartmoor, containing at least 150,000 acres, the inheritance of the Crown.
>
> In Somerset are many great Moors and Commons containing at least 40,000 acres worth every acre 20 shillings per annum.

[7] E. T. MacDermot, *A History of Exmoor Forest* (1973 ed.), pp. 247, 249, and 257.

And in Somerset, Devon and Cornwall are many hundred thousand acres of other commons and Wast ground which never yieldeth any benefit to the Crown and little good to the Commonwealth, and his Majestie hath tithe to much of it.

His Majesties intendments are to drawe all such unnecessary Forests and Waste Lands to improvement, whereof many are already lately accomplished. And it is without question that out of theis three Counties there may in short space be raised in present money to his Majesties use at least £100,000 in Fines, and a great yearly rent reserved to the Crown. For in such affairs one third or fourth part is reserved in Demesne to the Crown, which to be leased for years or lives will raise the Fines and Rents aforesaid.

If some great person were authorised by his Majestie to undergo the weight of it, the business would proceed happily; but without such assistant, those works are not to be dealt in.

Needless to say, no "great person" was prepared to "undergo the weight" of this project, which would have required a vast investment in hedging, liming and reseeding without any real prospect that the litigious Exmoor tenants could be coerced into surrendering their common grazing rights, or be persuaded to pay any of the proposed fines and rents.[8]

A final example of the piecemeal enclosure of the common fields may be taken from the north-east of the county where, in the prosperous wool village of Norton St Philip on the eastern edge of Mendip, the open fields had been reduced to mere remnants by 1606. A large area in the North Field known as "goddes piece" had recently been converted to enclosed pasture. A fairly typical farm was that held by Alicia Aprise, who had twenty-two acres of enclosed land and only eight and a half acres lying in the open fields (five acres in the North and three and a half acres in the South Field). Of her enclosed land six acres had been taken from the South Field.[9]

As mentioned in the previous chapter, the years of expanding

[8] Ibid., *Exmoor Forest*, pp. 266–7.
[9] H. L. Gray, *English Field Systems* (1959 ed.), pp. 99 and 526.

population and renewed economic growth after 1460 heralded the golden age of church building in Somerset, which lasted until the Protestant reformation of the 1530s. Somerset church builders adopted their own version of the prevailing Perpendicular style, and placed their main emphasis on the construction of magnificent lofty towers, richly decorated and sculptured. They are considered to be amongst the finest in England, and are usually placed at the west end of the church. This was an innovation, for earlier church styles, such as those of North Curry and Stoke St Gregory, favoured octagonal central towers. There are three regional types of Perpendicular tower—the southern, or Taunton, and two northern types, the Bristol and the Wrington. The Taunton type is distinguished by having a staircase turret at one corner, and double buttresses at the others. All its pinnacles are of equal height and the towers are divided into stages by string courses. The churches of St Mary Magdalene (a Victorian copy of the original) and St James, Taunton are good examples, as are the towers at Isle Abbots, Bishops Lydeard (in beautiful red sandstone) and Huish Episcopi, near Langport.[10]

The Bristol type is distinguished by a prominent turret crowned by a single spirelet rising above the rest. Outside Bristol it may be seen at Banwell and Cheddar in the north, and at Yeovil in the south. The Wrington type lacks the staircase turret and the horizontal divisions, and is panelled, with two enormously lofty belfry windows, with pinnacled turrets of the same height. In addition to Wrington itself, examples may be seen at St Cuthbert's in Wells, St John's in Glastonbury and North Petherton. By contrast, spires are rare in Somerset, but there are good examples at Congresbury, Croscombe and Castle Cary.

In 1539, Somerset, like the rest of England, was shaken by the dissolution of the monasteries, bringing to an end an institutional ideal which had lasted for almost a thousand years. The effects were more profound in Somerset than in many other counties because of the large proportion of the land which belonged to the abbeys—particularly in the Levels and on

[10] Murray's *Handbook to Somerset*, p. lii.

Mendip. The main effects of the dissolution on the landscape occurred not so much in the immediate vicinity of the abbeys themselves as in their outlying properties, where resident gentry were for the first time enabled to establish themselves. This led to the building of many impressive new manor houses with their associated gardens, parks, lakes and ornamental woods, of which some examples will be given below.

The other principal effect concerned the draining of the Levels, where the passing of the wealthy abbeys with their centralised funds and administrative systems made reclamation projects more difficult to organise and finance. On the other hand, land shortage and agricultural profitability restored incentive, so that, to a limited extent, the new owners of the manors flanking the Levels encouraged reclamation, as we have seen in the case of Aller.

As to the monastery buildings, surprisingly few were converted into great houses, and of those few only a handful remains. The Berkeleys converted Bruton Priory into their seat, and the Hoptons did the same for Witham Priory, but both are now demolished. Cannington Nunnery, which was made into a residence by the Rogers, is the most notable survival. It is now the Somerset College of Agriculture and Horticulture. Other abbeys crumbled away. At Glastonbury it is only the impressive abbey ruin which attracts so many tourists each year. At Muchelney some of the buildings have been restored by the National Trust. (Plate 23) The ruins of Cleeve Abbey near Watchet (Plate 10) may also be visited, and still give a good idea of what a monastery was like in its prime. Athelney, by contrast, has disappeared completely, and no traces of it are visible in the farm which now stands on its site. Woodspring (Plate 9) (or Worspring), lying remote amongst reclaimed marshes to the north of Weston-super-Mare, has also been converted into a farm, but some of the buildings still survive. The chapel, which is embedded in the farmhouse, has recently been restored and opened to the public. It is surprisingly small, and reminds us that the great monasteries like Glastonbury were not typical. Little houses of ten or so monks, as at Woodspring, were equally representative.

Enclosure, reclamation and industrial growth

Between about 1650 and 1850 the rural landscape gradually came to assume its modern form, as village after village enclosed the remnants of its open fields, and a patchwork quilt of pastures, orchards and meadows mingled with the cornfields— all neatly enclosed by quickthorn hedges in the southern lowlands and by stone walls on Exmoor and Mendip. The great work of reclaiming and enclosing the Levels took place between about 1770 and 1840, to produce the thousands of regular drainage ditches (rhynes) which form such a prominent feature of the modern landscape, though it should be emphasised that this initial division and enclosure of the Levels did not solve the problem of winter flooding, which was not brought under control until the 1940s—and even then it was not totally eliminated, since the cost was considered to be greater than any advantage that would be gained thereby. Carefully controlled winter flooding does no serious damage to pastures, provided it does not last for more than two weeks at a time.

For the half century following 1650 the population increased only slowly, so that pressure from that source did not lead to rapid or dramatic changes, but from about 1700 onwards the rate of population growth began to accelerate, and although Somerset escaped the dramatic increases associated with industrialisation in the north and the Midlands, the steadily rising numbers began to make their mark, especially in the towns. The urban landscape began to change, as brick, stone and tiles replaced timber and thatch as building materials, and as the streets were adequately paved, drained and lighted. The expansion of trade necessitated a drastic face-lift for the communications network. Firmly gravelled turnpike roads replaced muddy and twisting lanes in the later eighteenth century, and the heavier goods began to travel by canal, and after 1840 by railway (especially coal imported from South Wales or produced in the burgeoning coalfield between Pensford and Radstock). Competition from the railways caused a deterioration of the roads after about 1870, and the turnpike trusts gradually became insolvent, but with the advent of motorcars in the twentieth century the balance tipped again, and road improvements, culminating in the M5 motorway (opened 1974–5) became one of the most significant agents of landscape change.

The gentle nature of population growth in Somerset can best be appreciated if it is compared with a rapidly industrialising county like Lancashire.

Although population figures for periods before the first census in 1801 are only estimates based on a miscellany of baptismal, burial, taxation and military records, there is general agreement that the population of both counties was not significantly different in 1700 (between 200,000 and 250,000 people). However, as industrial growth began to take hold in Lancashire, it started to pull ahead at a constantly increasing rate. At the first census in 1801, Somerset had advanced to 274,000 people, but Lancashire was nearly three times as populous with 673,000. By 1951 this gap had become a yawning chasm. Lancashire (with 5,118,000 people) was ten times as populous as Somerset with 551,000. This contrast was not just achieved by a greater migration of industrial workers into Lancashire than into Somerset: there is evidence that by out-migration Somerset was losing people who were born in the county, especially in the early nineteenth century, when the population was increasing more rapidly than a still largely rural county could absorb.[11]

There was a tendency for the rate of migration to slow down after 1830, and this was probably due to the expansion of Bristol southwards into Somerset, and the development of the Mendip coalfield. Somerset people should, however, perhaps be grateful that the opportunities for migration afforded by industrialisation in other parts of England and Wales transferred out of the county some of the potential landscape devastation associated with nineteenth-century industry and population growth.

We may now briefly survey the main ways in which changes in farming, industry and communications have affected the landscape since 1650. The enclosure of the open fields of the north, east and south of the county had been proceeding gradu-

[11] See P. Deane and W. A. Cole, *British Economic Growth, 1686–1959* (1964), pp. 98–135. Some of the population estimates used are subject to revision, but the general trends are not in doubt.

ally by a piecemeal process for a long time, as we have seen, but the process speeded up appreciably in the latter half of the eighteenth century. A parish like Shepton Beauchamp, in the south of the county between Ilminster and Ilchester, still had about half its land lying in unenclosed strips, according to a map of 1755, but enclosure by private agreement began in 1807 and was largely completed by 1850.[12] Many other parishes were undergoing the same process, but since it required the consent of every landowner, Parliamentary Acts were increasingly used to coerce reluctant minorities.

There were 67 places where enclosure of open-field arable was regulated by Parliamentary Act and Award (all occurring between 1796 and 1847). There were also about 160 places which had common meadows and pastures enclosed by the same procedure, mainly in the Levels and on uplands like Exmoor, Mendip and the Blackdown Hills. (The replacement of ancient ecclesiastical parishes by modern civil ones leads to small variations in the totals.) Fig. 14 shows the distribution of the places affected by Parliamentary enclosure, but it should be emphasised that the area of open-field arable affected by these Acts was often quite small. For instance, the total amount of land enclosed, including common meadows, pastures and woods, was only 210 acres at Lilstock in 1811, and 300 acres at Berkley and Standerwick in 1818. However, there were a few Acts which covered much larger areas, such as the 4,400 acres at Cheddar in 1801, the 1,025 acres at Martock in 1810, and the 1,100 acres at Middlezoy in 1800.[13]

All these enclosures of the remnants of the open fields were of minor significance, however, compared with the major attack which was made on the wetlands between 1770 and 1840. With the population of the country continually rising, Britain had ceased to be a food exporter (about 1760) and became dependent on imports. When France and Spain started to assist the revolt of the American colonies in 1778, Britain faced the prospect of her supplies being cut off. Prices rose rapidly, and local improvers like John Billingsley of Ashwick Park, near Shepton

[12] Hunt and Sellman, *Somerset History*, pp. 35–8; *VCH*, IV, p. 215.
[13] W. E. Tate, *Somerset Enclosure Acts and Awards*, passim.

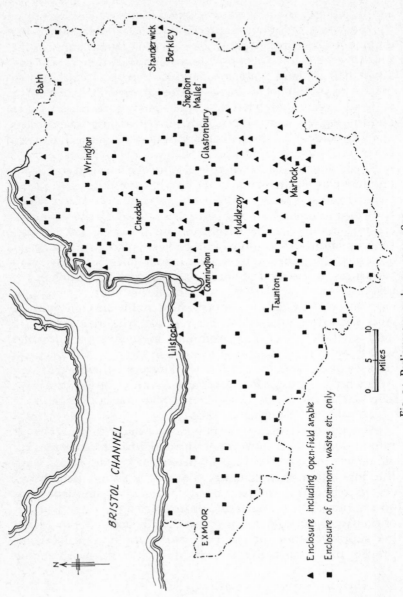

Fig. 14. Parliamentary enclosure, 1751–1879

▲ Enclosure including open-field arable

■ Enclosure of commons, wastes etc. only

Mallet, and Richard Locke of Burnham, began to be listened to with increasing seriousness when they urged that the moors should be drained, enclosed and put to more productive use. Some 45,000 acres of unimproved common grazings still survived, often under water for half the year. People with common grazing rights tended to over-stock them. The flooded herbage provided little nourishment, while the stagnant waters helped to spread animal diseases, like foot-rot and liver fluke in sheep.

Division of the land into privately-owned plots was in itself of some help, because, when the land was allotted, a network of drainage ditches (rhynes) was dug to divide the new properties. These carried off much of the surface water, and helped to move it towards the rivers (though drainage ditches could, of course, have been dug without division and private ownership, if the commoners had been prepared to co-operate in their maintenance). It was the rivers themselves which were the root of the problem. Since the coastal clay belt was slightly higher than the Levels, the rivers had only a few places where they could flow through it. Consequently, when heavy rainfall on the surrounding hills filled the rivers rapidly, these narrow channels through the clay belt could not accommodate the additional water, which flooded back. This was, however, only part of the problem, and not the most serious, for, as we noted in chapter 1, when the high tides characteristic of the Bristol Channel were flowing in, the sea-water entered the rivers and caused the waters to back up and overflow into extensive floods. The tides could reach as far inland as Ilchester, Langport and Taunton, unless stopped by clyses at the river mouths. These prevented salt-water floods, but still could not prevent fresh-water inundation when the rivers were suffering "tide-lock" (i.e. the high tides had closed the clyse gates). All the rivers flowing into the Bristol Channel now have such clyses except the Parrett, where navigational needs and technical difficulties have prevented construction of a clyse. Most of the clyses were built (or reinforced) in the period between 1770–1840. Nor were clyses enough. Rivers tended to silt up if they were allowed to meander and flow slowly. Straight cuts could speed the flow and improve the scouring action along the bed.[14]

[14] M. Williams, *The Draining of the Somerset Levels*, pp. 1–17.

The river Brue and its valley, between the Poldens and Wedmore, was the first to be tackled. The enclosures took place between 1774 and 1797, and a new channel was dug for the Brue, and provided with a new clyse between 1802 and 1806, but the work was badly done and, although the moors were much improved, the anti-flooding measures were less effective than had been hoped. The enclosing activity spread into the Axe valley between Wedmore and Mendip in the 1790s. This was the smallest area of wetlands (only eighty-one square miles), and a new course and clyse for the Axe, completed in 1810, proved highly successful. The same period saw enclosure carried out in King's Sedgemoor between Zoyland and the Poldens, and in the Cary valley to the east. An Act of 1791 secured the enclosure, which followed the digging of a twelve-miles-long new course for the river Cary, called the King's Sedgemoor Drain (Plate 20). This river had previously flowed into the Parrett at Burrowbridge, accentuating flooding problems around Athelney. The new course led it directly westwards and into the Parrett estuary at Dunball, through a new clyse. But here again the work was poorly planned and executed, and flooding was by no means stopped. Low bridges placed over narrow banks were bottlenecks which prevented flood-waters getting away, and added to the problems.

Work in the northern Levels, (the moors lying between the western edge of Mendip and the Failand ridge) and in the Weston valley between Clevedon and Portishead, was delayed until 1800. Much enclosure took place between 1800 and 1810, but although John Rennie's scheme (1819–27) for improvements to the Congresbury Yeo (and a new clyse) was very successful, the Kenn moors and the Weston valley were still subject to extensive flooding, despite expensive but ineffective drainage works.

The southern Levels—the valleys of the Parrett and its tributaries, the Tone, Isle and Yeo—were the last to be tackled (between 1810 and 1840), and because of the decision not to build a clyse at the mouth of the Parrett, the benefits of enclosure and drainage ditches were much reduced. Extensive flooding can (and does) still occur in this part of the Levels.

In summary, although the landscape of the Levels was totally transformed between 1770 and 1840, and their agricultural contribution much increased, control over flooding was not achieved. It was not until 1940, when a new channel (called the Huntspill river) was dug for the Brue, that effective control was secured for all the wetlands to the east and north of the Parrett. But the southern and western moors still await a really comprehensive drainage scheme.[15]

However, if flooding was not totally eliminated by 1840, the appearance of the landscape had altered beyond all recognition. A gridiron of neat green pastures, divided by rectangular drainage ditches, had replaced the former rough marshland, and the overgrown thickets of woodland had been replaced by rows of pollarded willows which ran along the edges of the many newly-constructed roads. These willows give a characteristic charm to the drained wetlands, but their purpose was purely utilitarian: from their numerous branches (withies) an extensive trade in baskets, panniers, fish-traps and screens was maintained, and although it has declined much in recent years, in the country round Athelney and Curry Rivel withies can still be seen soaking in numerous rhynes, and drying in rows. The soil in this area has just the right degree of moisture and alkalinity for withies. They are also grown as a field crop in several places. They are planted in February in rows about two feet apart and with about eighteen inches between the withies (known as a set). They are harvested by hand in the autumn, when they are about six feet high (Plate 47). The fields full of withies, rustling in the wind, are a sight almost unique to the Somerset Levels.

During the same period as that in which the Levels were drained (1770–1840), the vast common pastures on top of Mendip were also enclosed by Parliamentary Act, and divided up by stone walls and hedges. New roads were made and new farms were created, transforming the landscape of this formerly isolated and bleak range of hills.[16]

The great upland waste of Exmoor was an altogether more daunting problem, but it too was enclosed by Parliamentary

[15] Ibid., *Somerset Levels*, pp. 126–260.
[16] M. Williams, "The enclosure and reclamation of the Mendip hills, 1770–1870", *Agric. Hist. Rev.*, 19 (1971), pp. 65–81.

Act in 1815, and purchased by John Knight, a Worcestershire ironmaster with a passion for agricultural improvement. He and his son, Frederic, were engaged in building roads, farms, fences and windbreaks of timber for a period of about seventy years, beginning in 1820. They built the village of Simonsbath with its church and post office, and laboriously carved about sixteen farms out of the stubborn moorlands. Financially their vast work was disappointing (which was hardly surprising), but they had the satisfaction of seeing much of Somerset's last great wilderness transformed, at least partially, into a landscape with a human face.[17]

With the increasing wealth brought by improved agriculture and expanding trade, a change began to take place in the character of dwelling-houses, both in town and country. This had started as early as the 1570s, and was very noticeable in the period up to 1640, which Professor Hoskins (who first drew attention to it) has characterised as the period of the "great rebuilding". However, it continued strongly after 1640, and a recent study of the livestock region around Yetminster, in north Dorset just over the Somerset border, has shown that in many pastoral regions the period 1688–1730 was equally important.[18] Similarly detailed analyses of Somerset villages have not yet been undertaken, yet in many pastoral parts of the county it would seem likely that conditions were analogous to those in north Dorset. There are some suggestive Somerset examples. For instance, in Tintinhull, near Montacute, a family of successful yeomen, the Nappers, rose into the gentry in the seventeenth century, substantially improved two farmhouses and built a third between about 1670 and 1722. The house known as Tintinhull Court was a medieval farm which was extensively rebuilt about 1673, when a new stone façade was added with mullioned and transomed stone windows, surmounted by hood moulds. About 1687 a new house (the Dower House) was built, again of stone in the symmetrical classical style. Finally an old farmhouse, dated 1630, was substantially altered about 1722,

[17] See C. S. Orwin and R. J. Sellick, *The Reclamation of Exmoor Forest* (1970).
[18] W. G. Hoskins, "The rebuilding of rural England, 1570–1640", *Past and Present*, 4 (1953); R. Machin, *The Houses of Yetminster* (1978).

when a new classical west wing was added in Ham stone ashlar. This building is now called Tintinhull House and is owned by the National Trust. It is considered to be an unusually perfect example of its size and period. No doubt there are in Somerset many other examples of rebuilding in this period. More research on this aspect of vernacular architecture could profitably be undertaken.[19]

The rebuilding transformed not only the manor houses of the rich, but also quite humble farmhouses and cottages, as well as innumerable town houses. One of its chief characteristics was the replacement of vulnerable cob walls and thatched roofs by stone or brick construction and tiled roofs. This was especially the case in towns, which had been constantly wracked by disastrous fires before these changes were made. Many towns have a distinctly Georgian look today as a result of wholesale rebuilding after some such disaster. For instance, there were big fires at Wellington in 1731, Wincanton in 1747, Minehead in 1791, and Merriott in 1811.[20]

A prominent housing alteration was the ceiling-over of the open halls which had characterised so many houses, and the creation of bedrooms upstairs. This involved the insertion not only of a staircase, but also of a separate hearth and chimney to replace the open fires which had formerly burned in the centre of the hall. Houses had thus been filled with smoke, which could escape only through small holes under the roof eaves. These inserted chimneys (often placed outside on the end of the house) and new windows, associated with the addition of upper storeys to the old halls, may be seen all over Somerset in countless farms and village streets. Another new development of the eighteenth century was the building of cottages for farm labourers as distinct purpose-built homes, rather than as converted farmhouses or barns. One early example occurs in Somerset at West Mudford in 1728 (significantly an area of early enclosures). Here

[19] *VCH*, III, pp. 256–9.
[20] See W. G. Willis Watson, *A Chronological History of Somerset* (1925). I owe this reference to the kindness of Prof. E. L. Jones, who is making a special study of the impact of fires on the development of townscapes. See also E. L. Jones and M. E. Falkus, "Urban improvement and the English economy in the seventeenth and eighteenth centuries" in *Research in Economic History*, 4 (1979), pp. 193–233.

a pair of semi-detached cottages was built of lias limestone with lofty mullioned windows in Ham stone. The cottages share a central chimney stack and each has a hall-kitchen in front and a scullery behind.[21]

Industrialisation was not a prominent cause of landscape change except in the northern coalfield and the Mendip quarries, but even in the coalfield the profusion of small, scattered mines meant that the whole area around Radstock (which was the centre) retained a much more rural aspect than was the case in the great northern and Midland coalfields. Some of the older handicraft and domestic industries of Somerset were declining, as we have seen. Frome and Wellington (at either end of the county) retained their cloth industries on a factory basis, but many other towns, like Shepton Mallet, Bruton and Taunton, saw them wither away, and even in Frome and Wellington it was a question of survival and stabilisation—not of the hectic growth of northern industrial towns like Bradford and Halifax. However, Bridgwater expanded on the basis of its brick industry, while tourism led to the rapid growth of seaside resort towns like Weston-super-Mare, Clevedon, Portishead and Minehead in the nineteenth century.[22]

Communications improved noticeably after about 1750, when the new turnpike trusts began to straighten highways and to lay properly bedded stone and gravel surfaces. These were known as Macadamised roads after their inventor, John Macadam, who perfected his methods while working for the Bristol Trust. He flourished between 1816 and 1836, and during this time worked for six other Somerset Trusts: Bath, Frome, Minehead, Yeovil, Shepton Mallet and Bridgwater.[23] The reclamation of the Levels led to a great network of new roads across them, and the same thing happened on uplands like Mendip and Exmoor, though to a much lesser extent.

Canals came late to Somerset and never had a very significant effect on the landscape. The first to be built was the short but

[21] M. W. Barley, *The English Farmhouse and Cottage* (1961), pp. 250–1.

[22] M. A. Havinden, "The Southwest; a case of de-industrialisation?" in Marilyn Palmer ed., *The Onset of Industrialisation* (1977), pp. 5–11.

[23] Hunt and Sellman, *Somerset History*, p. 40.

dramatic Somerset Coal Canal in 1805, which carried coal barges from Paulton down to the Avon at Midford, south-east of Bath. The fall of 154 feet required no fewer than twenty-two locks. Railway competition ruined it in the 1850s, but it staggered on till 1898. A railway (now also abandoned) was built on part of its route. The Kennet and Avon Canal from London reached Bath in 1810, but its Somerset section was very short. The Bridgwater and Taunton Canal, opened in 1827, is the only survivor in the county, but it is now used mainly as a drainage relief channel to prevent flooding in the Levels. Some picturesque deserted canals are the Glastonbury to Highbridge (1834–53); the Grand Western (Plate 52), which connected Taunton to Tiverton in Devon (1838–67); the Westport (1840–78), which connected the navigable part of the river Parrett near Langport to a new canal port at Westport (about five miles north of Ilminster), where some sturdy old warehouses survive; and the Chard canal (1842–67), which linked Chard to the Bridgwater and Taunton canal at Creech St Michael, near Taunton.[24] Many of these canals involved tunnels, inclined planes and lifts which have left their marks in remote corners of the county and which will be discussed in more detail in the regional chapters.

The railway network began to take shape after 1843, when the Bristol and Exeter Company's broad-gauge (7 foot ¼ inch) main line was completed. (Fig. 15) This was, of course, a part of the Great Western Railway system. It ran through Yatton, Highbridge, Bridgwater, Taunton and Wellington. The modern route to London from Taunton through Castle Cary and Westbury was not opened until 1906. Competition from the standard-gauge railways (4 foot 8½ inches) did not come till 1860, when the London and South-Western Railway completed its main line from Exeter to Waterloo, which passed through Crewkerne, Sherborne and Templecombe. However, this line barely touched the southern fringe of Somerset. In 1892 the Great Western system finally agreed to convert its lines to the standard gauge, but in the meanwhile both systems had been extending branch lines in all directions, so that by 1910 (when

[24] Ibid., *Somerset History*, pp. 43–6.

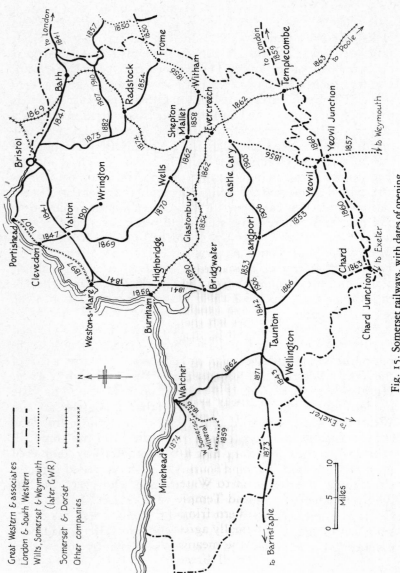

Fig. 15. Somerset railways, with dates of opening

the last line was built) there were very few parts of Somerset that were not within a few miles of a railway.[25]

Somerset did, however, have one other rather unusual main line—the Somerset and Dorset railway (the S. & D.), known affectionately to its customers as the "Slow and Dirty". This line was unusual because it never had any extension to London. It was opened in 1863, from Burnham-on-Sea to the port of Poole in Dorset, with the idea that passengers from Cardiff would take ship to Burnham, proceed by rail to Poole, and then cross the English Channel to Cherbourg. Not surprisingly, hardly any traffic materialised for this route, and so in 1874 the Somerset & Dorset linked up with the Midland railway system at Bath by extending a link northwards from Evercreech Junction across the Mendips. Where this line went over the summit at Maesbury it produced one of Somerset's most dramatic pieces of railway engineering. The "Pines Expresses" from towns in the north of England and the Midlands to Bournemouth were introduced on this route in 1910 and ran until the 1950s. The whole of the Somerset and Dorset system was closed down in the 1960s, along with all the branch lines in Somerset.[26] The only railway lines still remaining are the main lines. The most important is the Paddington to Exeter line via Castle Cary and Taunton. There is also the old Great Western line from Paddington via Bath, Bristol, Weston-super-Mare and Bridgwater to Taunton. The former Southern Railway line from Waterloo to Exeter still passes through south Somerset, with stations at Yeovil Junction, Crewkerne and Chard Junction, but the only link it retains with the other lines in Somerset is the short connection from Yeovil Junction to Yeovil (Pen Mill station), which serves the Castle Cary-Yeovil-Dorchester-Weymouth line. The only other important cross-country service is the Bristol-Bath-Westbury-Salisbury line.

With the revived enthusiasm for steam trains as holiday attractions, some of the old branch lines are enjoying a resurrection. The picturesque West Somerset line has been re-opened as a private company, and in the summer runs steam trains from

[25] See D. St John Thomas, *A Regional History of the Railways of Great Britain*, I, *The West Country* (3rd ed. 1966).
[26] See R. Atthill, *The Somerset and Dorset Railway* (1967).

Minehead towards Taunton. The former East Somerset line also has plans for a passenger service between Shepton Mallet and Witham.[27]

The twentieth-century changes in the landscape are discussed in the regional chapters which follow, but their general impact may be briefly noted here. Although new industries have been founded, like aircraft production at Yeovil, and old ones expanded (shoe-making at Street, Radstock, Shepton Mallet and elsewhere), the influence of industry on the landscape has probably declined in general. This is because so many of the old industries have closed down. The most notable of these is the coalfield around Radstock, which had been declining since 1920, and whose last mines ceased work in 1973. With the mines went the network of feeder canals and railways, and many of the associated industries like iron founding, but the region still retains an important industrial component, since light industries such as printing, textiles, electronics and shoe-making thrive in the area. Parts of the former coalfield have now become so rural in appearance that it is difficult to believe that the area was ever industrial. This is partly the result of landscape reclamation, which was carried on not only by the National Coal Board but also by some of the pre-war coal companies.

Quarrying for Mendip limestone is, however, one activity which has not declined. Indeed, the need for roadstone for the ever-advancing road network has caused a boom. The resultant huge quarries on the south face of Mendip are jagged scars on the otherwise smoothly rounded face of the ancient limestone ridge.

Another ancient extractive industry which has enjoyed a recent revival is peat-digging in the Levels between the Poldens and Mendip, especially around Shapwick (Plate 15). During the nineteenth century local villagers were given small allotments of peat for fuel, but this use gradually declined, as coal, gas and electricity became more cheaply available. However, in recent years a new demand for peat has emerged as a soil additive for market gardens and nurseries; so the old diggings are active again, with huge machines gouging out the peat and creating ponds and lakes as the holes fill with water. The long rows of

[27] See Colin G. Maggs, *The East Somerset Railway, 1858–1972* (1977).

black peat drying in the sun give the landscape a strangely surrealistic aspect.

Somerset has not suffered so much as many other counties from suburban sprawl, but the southern extension of Bristol, and to a lesser extent the spread of Bath, Weston-super-Mare, Yeovil and Taunton, have covered acres of fields with houses, schools and, above all, roads. The southern suburbs of Bristol stretch for several miles south of the city. The demands of motor traffic have taken two forms. Old towns with narrow streets, like Shepton Mallet and Keynsham, have been extensively hacked about to allow modern traffic to pass through (and, less destructively, around) the towns, and new trunk roads have been driven through the county, of which much the most important is M5, the great motorway which runs from Avonmouth southwards through the Levels, around Bridgwater, Taunton and Wellington, to cross the Blackdowns into Devon. Since motorways are much wider than railways, their impact on the landscape is even more dramatic, and M5 not only provides a giant causeway through the western wetlands, but also provides engineering sculpture on an impressive scale where it cuts through the Failand ridge between Clevedon and Avonmouth.

Finally, we may note the modern development of reservoirs to supply the growing urban population. Bristol was the first in the field with the little reservoir at Barrow Gurney (1852), but this was soon inadequate. By 1905 the river Yeo had been dammed to create the Blagdon Lake, and in the 1950s the even larger Chew Valley Lake drowned an extensive area (1,200 acres) between Chew Stoke and Bishop's Sutton. Cheddar has a small reservoir, and Yeovil a very attractive one at Sutton Bingham, much used for boating. Bridgwater has a reservoir to its west at Durleigh, and Taunton a most dramatic one in the Brendon Hills at Clatworthy (built in the 1950s). Finally, the Exeter, Tiverton, Taunton and Bridgwater districts are served by the large new reservoir at Wimbleball, created by damming the Haddeo, a tributary of the Exe. Wimbleball is in the Brendon Hills between Wiveliscombe and Dulverton. Special care has been taken to preserve amenity, and the environs have been designed by Dame Sylvia Crowe, a leading landscape architect. Although opinions may differ as to the effects of

145

reservoirs on a landscape, their influence in Somerset has not been unduly obtrusive, and several of them are undeniably attractive.

SELECT BIBLIOGRAPHY

Dunning, R. W., *A History of Somerset* (1978).
Hunt, T. J. and Sellman, R. R., *Aspects of Somerset History* (1973).
MacDermot, E. T., *A History of Exmoor Forest* (1973 edn.).
Orwin, C. S. and Sellick, R. J., *The Reclamation of Exmoor Forest* (1970).
Tate, W. E., *Somerset Enclosure Acts and Awards* (1948).
Williams, Michael, *The Draining of the Somerset Levels* (1970).

TWO

Regional Studies

6. The reclamation of the wetlands

The causes of flooding. Early attempts at reclamation. The drive for comprehensive reclamation, 1770–1840. Problems of the new landscape. Communications and the growth of towns.

The causes of flooding

OF THE TWO distinct, but related, reasons which used to turn the central plain of Somerset into a vast lake from autumn to spring, the sea-flooding from unusually high tides in the Bristol Channel was the more damaging (because salt harmed the land), but the river-flooding, caused by the excess of water resulting from very high rainfall in the surrounding hills, was the more widespread. The two would come together when high tides flowed up the rivers and met the excess fresh water flowing down. In the almost flat basin of central Somerset, only a few feet above sea-level, this collision would break the river banks, sending the waters far and wide. Even when much work had been done and the region was ostensibly drained, freak tides and rains could cause devastating floods, such as those of the winter of 1872–3 when over 107 square miles were under water from October to March.[1]

River flooding has always been the more frequent of the two causes, because the more difficult to control. The sea is to some extent held back by the belt of slightly elevated land, about three miles wide, which runs down the coast, and by the clyses in the mouths of all rivers flowing into the Bristol Channel except the Parrett. Most of the existing clyses have replaced earlier ones. Fig. 16 shows how the old clyse at Highbridge (built before 1485) was replaced in 1803 in connection with the drainage of the Brue valley marshes between the Polden Hills and the Wedmore

[1] Williams, *Somerset Levels*, p. 13.

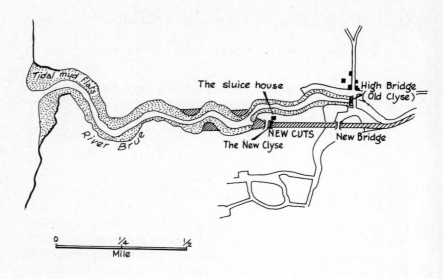

Fig. 16. The new course of the lower river Brue at Highbridge, from a plan of 1803

"island" (Plate 14). The river Brue was made wider and straighter near its mouth, and the new clyse was built farther downstream than the old one.[2]

River-flooding is particularly difficult to control for several reasons. The flat terrain means that the rivers tended to meander about the countryside and to flow very slowly, depositing silt in their beds, thus further slowing their flow. Deposition at the river mouths was specially troublesome. This problem was accentuated by the suddenness with which tremendous extra loads of water could be deposited into the rivers by heavy rainfall on the surrounding hills, which are some of the wettest in England. For instance, the nine highest recorded rainfalls in England between 1865 and 1956 in twenty-four-hour periods all occurred in these hills. Two of these were associated with sizeable flood damage in the Levels—the 9.56 inches of rain recorded at Bruton, near the source of the Brue, on 28th June,

[2] SRO, "A plan of the Brue drainage, 1803", by Wm. White.

1917, and the 9.40 inches recorded at Cannington in the lower Parrett valley near Bridgwater on 18th August, 1924.[3] The significance of these falls can be gauged when it is realised that the average rainfall in England is only about thirty-five inches a year.

It can thus be seen that the problems of draining the Levels were severe. Cuts straightening the rivers would increase their flow marginally, but they still had trouble flowing through the higher clay belt near the sea, and then could not enter it at high tides. Drainage ditches which were dug so as to carry surface water off the surrounding moors into the rivers were not always successful for the same reasons: the rivers could be higher than the ditches which were trying to deposit water in them. The only solution to this problem was to have pumps available to lift the flood waters into the rivers. This is the modern solution, where powerful diesel and electric pumps do the work. In the nineteenth century steam engines were used, and these could have been used even earlier, except that the eighteenth-century Newcomen steam engines (invented about 1710) were extravagant in their use of coal, and would probably have cost more than the improved value of drained land. Another possible solution was to use windmills. These were widely employed in the Fens of East Anglia, where a traveller in 1748 "riding very lately from Ramsey to Holme, about six miles across the Fens, counted forty in my view". But for some reason which is not clear, very few were used in Somerset. Only two examples have been recorded: one in 1613 at Bleadon near the mouth of the river Axe, where a sea-wall had been built to prevent flooding in the Axe estuary and the sea was "kept out from overflowing the same by a windmill built at the time of the said enclosure for that purpose".[4] It would appear that any sea-water which managed to lap over the wall was pumped back again into the sea. The other example was in 1722 at Common Moor, about a mile north of Glastonbury, where the pumping was described by a contemporary observer, Dr Claver Morris, in 1723: "Mr Chancellor Bridge and I returned home through Glastonbury,

[3] Williams, *Somerset Levels*, pp. 11–14.
[4] H. C. Darby, *Historical Geography of England before AD 1800* (1951), p. 462; Williams, *Somerset Levels*, pp. 94–5.

Mr Nicholls accompanying us from Kennard Moor, and we went and saw Mr Nicholls Engine to throw water into all the Dictches of Common-moor, and he set it working on purpose for us."[5] This just might have been a steam engine, but the seeming ease with which it was set working strongly suggests a windmill.

The reclamation of Common Moor is interesting for another reason. It is one of the earliest examples in Somerset of the use of the procedure of a Private Act of Parliament (1721) to secure the enclosure of the land (with which the drainage was associated).[6] This method enabled any opponents of an enclosure to be overruled, provided that the proposers owned at least two-thirds to three-quarters of the land (by value). This draws attention to what was probably an even greater obstacle to reclamation than were any technical difficulties: namely, the opposition of the majority of the inhabitants of the Levels. At first sight this opposition (which was frequently formidable) seems irrational, since it was well known that drained and enclosed pasture was much more valuable than common grazing rights on floodable moors, but the matter is more complicated than appears at first sight. Drainage was expensive on two counts. Firstly, there was interest to be paid on the initial capital outlay (and the principal to be repaid), and secondly, there was the constant cost of maintaining the drainage rhynes, the river banks and their associated walls and ditches. All these sums were raised by special rates levied on the occupants by Courts of Sewers established for the purpose. For freeholders the enhanced value of their enclosed land ought to have been greater than the rates, but they also lost some valuable common rights in other parts of the moors. These included the rights of fishing, trapping or shooting wildfowl, cutting timber for fencing and firewood, and digging peat for fuel. When all this had been subtracted, the balance may not have been so favourable, especially as many of the earlier reclamation projects were not really successful technically. For instance, £60,000 were spent on the Brue valley drainage scheme of 1802–6, but the re-

[5] Cited by E. L. Kelting, "The rivers and seawalls of Somerset", *SANHS*, 112 (1968), p. 16.

[6] Tate, *Somerset Enclosure Acts*, p. 39.

Plate 13 A sea-wall at Wick St. Lawrence, south of Clevedon, it protects the rich reclaimed meadows on the left. This modern wall replaced much earlier ones. Sea-walls alongside the Axe Valley are mentioned in documents of 1129, and archaeological investigations have even hinted at Roman origins for some of them.

Plate 14 Highbridge clyse, near Burnham-on-Sea, at the mouth of the river Brue. Its gates will swing outwards to allow the river to flow into the sea at low tide, but the rising tide closes the gates and prevents the sea from entering the river.

Plate 15 Peat-digging in the Levels near Shapwick. The peat blocks are stacked in the traditional manner. The woodland behind shows the natural vegetation of the Levels when untouched by man.

Plate 16 Athelney "island" reclaimed. The low hill where the cows are grazing was surrounded by water when King Alfred took refuge from the Danes there in 878. He later founded an abbey on the site, but all that now remains is his Victorian monument, visible on the horizon (right).

Plate 17 The landscape of enclosure. Parkland and forest at West Bagborough on the western slope of the Quantocks. Prior to enclosure in the early nineteenth century, the Quantocks were a huge unfenced sheepwalk. The landscape seen here is a mid-Victorian creation.

Plate 18 The landscape of enclosure. New farmsteads on former common meadows. A substantial Victorian farmhouse on the Levels near Burrowbridge. Note the construction of redbrick and tiles in place of the traditional timber and thatch.

Plate 19 Quintessential Somerset. Cattle grazing on reclaimed pastures beneath Glastonbury Tor, the landmark visible from all round the county. Note the characteristic pollarded willows.

Plate 20 The King's Sedgemoor Drain, looking westwards from the central Levels. Dug in 1796, it provided a new channel for the river Cary, which had previously flowed into the Parrett. It now flows straight to the sea at Dunball, north of Bridgwater. This channel is the key to the drainage of all the Levels between the Polden Hills and the river Parrett.

claimed lands were still subject to frequent flooding.[7] For tenants the situation was of course much more unfavourable. A sharp rise in rent was certain, as was the loss of common grazing rights: the gains in productivity were much more speculative. It is noteworthy that, even during the high prices for food prevailing during the Napoleonic Wars (1793–1815), it was still necessary to use the enforced procedure of the Private Parliamentary Act to overcome popular resistance to many of the reclamation schemes.

The ferocity of the opposition was not to be taken lightly. Richard Locke, of Pillsmouth Farm, Burnham, who was an early enthusiast for reclamation, has recorded how, when he was out surveying some moors in 1769, he was "stoned, bruised and beat by the mob till the blood has issued from my nose, mouth and ears".[8] Perhaps the opposition involved more than mere calculations of profit and loss. It may have reflected a sense of restricted freedom where the extensive moors over which people could roam in search of game or fuel, or perhaps merely for enjoyment, would be cut up and confined by thousands of rhynes and fences. Perhaps people lamented that it would be not only their livestock who would be constricted by the new, orderly landscape of drainage and enclosure. The number of people affected by such schemes was also considerable. For instance, at Huntspill in 1776, Locke recorded that 161 people had ancient commons rights (known as austers) on the moor (with twelve more doubtful claimants).[9]

Early attempts at reclamation

We have already discussed some of the schemes prior to the major efforts which began in the 1770s. The earliest attempts were probably concerned with reclamation from the sea in the clay belt, either along the coastline or in tidal estuaries. This was done by sea-walls, behind which tidal mud flats could be quite rapidly turned into valuable pastures or meadows, known as warths.

[7] Williams, *Somerset Levels*, p. 138.
[8] Ibid., p. 125.
[9] SRO, Survey of old Austers in Huntspill, 1776 (D/P/b on S./23/7).

These sea-walls, which stretch all along the low parts of the coast from the west of the Parrett estuary to the mouth of the Avon at Portbury, are of great antiquity, although no one knows their precise date. The late Louis Kelting, formerly chief engineer to the Somerset River Authority, has speculated on the possibility of some of them having Roman origins. He noted that a stone with a Roman inscription on it was discovered in a collapsed sea-wall on the Welsh side of the Bristol Channel, and that the site of the Roman villa at Wemberham, about two miles down the river Yeo from Congresbury, would be flooded twice daily by tides were it not protected by sea-walls. This raises the possibility that some of these defences may have been Roman, but there is also doubt as to whether the tides rose as high in Roman times as they do today. The site of Wemberham may have been dry when the villa was built, but the Romans were good engineers, and there is nothing inherently improbable in the supposition that some at least of the sea-walls were started by them. [10]

When sea-walls first appear in medieval documents (they are mentioned alongside the river Axe as early as 1129), it is clear that they already comprised quite an extensive system (Plate 13). Special arrangements were made for their maintenance by tenants known as wickmen or moor-men, who held their land on condition of maintaining the sea-walls. A document of the early thirteenth century reveals that there were then four in South Brent, four in Lympsham, and three in Berrow. [11] Later, these feudal duties were converted into money rents, and a survey of the sea-wall at Highbridge in the eighteenth century shows the tenants being assessed for certain sections of the walls. Elizabeth Standley was responsible for three ropes (a rope was 20 feet) and thirteen feet; Henry Allan for two ropes and twelve feet; the late Richard Gould for nineteen feet and three inches—amongst many others. [12] This minute sub-division of responsibility meant that the work was fairly equitably distributed, but it also put the defence against flooding at the mercy of any defaulters

[10] Kelting, "Rivers and Seawalls", pp. 12–14.
[11] Williams, *Somerset Levels*, p. 44.
[12] SRO, Survey of Highbridge Rhine Sea Wall (D/P/b on S./23/5).

(especially in the days when the labour had to be carried out personally).

Many of these medieval reclamations may still be seen. In the great loop of the river Axe south of Weston-super-Mare, called Bleadon Level, many small fields are formed from twisting rhynes and are surrounded by a circular wall, called the "Old Wall" on the 2½″ O.S. map. These reclaimed pastures are referred to in a document of the thirteenth century. In old documents they are called the innynges or warths. They belonged to the Bishop of Winchester, who made arrangements for his tenants to maintain them.[13]

The gradations of such reclaimed lands may be seen in an eighteenth-century map of the northern part of Lympsham parish, lying along the south bank of the river Axe. The warths closest to the river are referred to as "salt warths" (Glebe and Smeath salt warths), while the warths a little farther from the river, and more fully protected by walls, are called "dry warths". Behind yet further walls, we find the fields called New Croft, New Lands and New Close, though they may already have been ancient when the map was made.[14]

As we have seen in chapter 5, medieval reclamation was by no means limited to the claylands behind the sea walls; an attack was launched on the Levels themselves, especially the alluvial Levels surrounding the many islands, like Zoy and Wedmore, and drainage was further facilitated by diverting the river Brue into a new channel. The main locations of reclamation work before 1400, and some idea of its extent, are provided by Fig. 17. It can be seen that the area where reclamation was most intense was in the marshes to the south of "Sowy" (Zoy) "island", which have already been discussed. These reclamations were carried out by Glastonbury Abbey, and it is hardly surprising that the other main area should have been the moors near to the abbey itself. These lay between Glastonbury and Meare, and were centred on Godney Moor (Plate 19). All was, however, not plain sailing in this area, for the abbey's ancient rivals, the bishops, deans and canons of Wells Cathedral, also claimed rights in these moors, and both parties were inclined to

[13] Williams, *Somerset Levels*, p. 44.
[14] SRO, D/P/b on S./23/15.

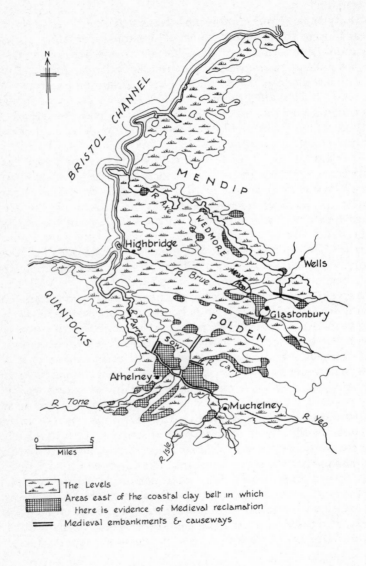

Fig. 17. Reclamation of the Levels before 1400

assert themselves forcibly. They destroyed one another's pig-
geries, set fire to woods and turves, and stole one another's
cattle, until a series of compromise agreements led to the
division of some of the moors, itself a precursor of their eventual
enclosure and reclamation. The ditch called Bounds Ditch,
which demarcates the parish boundary between Meare and
Wedmore, was dug as the result of one such agreement in 1327.
It was agreed that "a new dyke shall be cut and raised, upon
which shall be erected four stone crosses, two at the charge of
either party."[15] It was south from Mudgley on Wedmore
"island" to Westhay Bridge over the river Brue, about a mile to
the west of Meare. The abbey's lands lay to the east of it, and the
bishops' to the west.

On the whole, medieval reclamations were piecemeal and on
a small scale, concentrating on the moorland edges. The
resultant landscape which emerged was similar to that shown in
Fig. 18, where the south-eastern edge of Greinton parish is
illustrated in 1773, before the enclosure and drainage of King's
Sedgemoor (Plate 20). A large rhyne separated the village lands
from the moor, but the arable fields (still in commonable strip
cultivation) were set back some distance from the rhyne. Between the two lay numerous strips of meadow land (partly
enclosed by rhynes and hedges, but not every line on the map
was such a boundary—many simply denoted property divisions
which would not have existed physically on the ground). These
meadows were probably gradually reclaimed from the moor in
medieval times. There were also two "islands" in the moor,
where slightly higher ground had been reclaimed and enclosed.
The easternmost was inhabited by the family which farmed
Nythe Farm.

Another feature of medieval reclamation was the construction
of extensive embanked causeways. These served both to carry
roads from one "island" to another (such as Greylake Fosse—
built c. 1302—linking Sowy to Greinton), and to prevent
floods from moving from one part of the moors to another. Such
walls often ran alongside rivers, as well as dividing moors. The
massive Burrow Wall was built about 1255 to separate Southlake Moor from Earlake Moor. It runs along the southern side of

[15] Williams, *Somerset Levels*, p. 36.

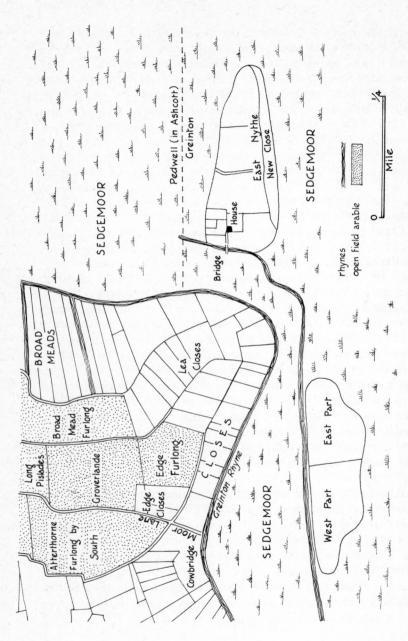

Fig. 18. The south-eastern edge of Greinton parish, c. 1773, before the reclamation of King's Sedgemoor, showing enclosed meadows (probably medieval reclamations from the moor's edge) and the two "islands" of reclaimed land in the moor

the modern A361 road from Burrowbridge to Othery, and still acts as an effective protection against floods. The Southlake Wall from Burrowbridge to Pathe was built before 1311. It follows the east bank of the Parrett from Burrowbridge nearly to Stathe, and then cuts northwards across the moor to the hamlet of Pathe, just south of Othery. About the same time (c.1300), Othery was also linked to the hills around Aller to the east by Beer Wall across King's Sedgemoor.[16]

The period of stagnation and disappointment, 1350–1770

After its promising medieval beginning, the reclamation of the Levels entered into a prolonged period when very little progress was made, and many frustrating disappointments were suffered. The long depression following the Black Death (1348–9) destroyed the financial incentives for reclamation, and when the more buoyant economic conditions of the sixteenth century promised a renewed attack, the dissolution of the monasteries (c.1536–9) destroyed the centralised ownership and control which had been responsible for organising the medieval activity. The monasteries were replaced by Courts of Sewers, which could levy rates for maintenance but could not commission new works.

Williams estimates that by the year 1600 about one-third of the Levels had theoretically been "reclaimed" from the swamps, but he points out that much of this work was not really effective; flooding had certainly been reduced, but it had by no means been ended.[17]

If this was not a period of great achievement, it was at least a time of considerably renewed interest in the problems of reclamation, and the early seventeenth century was alive with grandiose improvement projects. These no doubt were partly stimulated by the disastrous floods of 1607, when the sea-walls were breached and the flood-waters reached the foot of Glastonbury Tor, fourteen miles inland. The flood-levels were recorded in the local churches, and Kingston Seymour church was said to have had five feet of water in it for ten days. The chiselled

[16] Ibid., pp. 47–55.
[17] Ibid., p. 85.

high-water mark is 24.4 feet above the average sea level (Ordnance Datum Newlyn). Contemporary descriptions vividly describe the havoc such floods could cause:

> In a short tyme did whole villages stand like Islands (compassed round with Waters) and in a short tyme were those Islands undiscoverable, and no where to be found. The tops of trees and houses onely appeared (there where the country lay lowe) as if at the beginning of the world townes had been builte in the bottome of the Sea, and that people had plaide the husbandmen under the Waters.[18]

The prospect of making a profit from reclamation projects appealed to the impecunious Stuart kings, and in 1618 James I, who owned King's Sedgemoor (which had passed to the Crown at the dissolution of Glastonbury Abbey), began negotiations with the twenty-five manorial lords whose properties surrounded the moor. The lords were enthusiastic, but the commoners were opposed, and no progress was made. When Charles I succeeded to the throne in 1625, he took up the scheme again and hoped to obtain a rental of £20,000 from letting his share of the reclaimed moor. Once again shortage of money and the opposition of the small freeholders prevented any activity, and in 1632 Charles sold his 4,000 acres to a syndicate, which later came to include Sir Cornelius Vermuyden, the famous Dutch drainage engineer. Vermuyden hoped to begin work in 1638, but the outbreak of the Civil War shortly afterwards ended this scheme, just as it destroyed his more famous works in the Fenland. After the Civil War he brought his drainage schemes in the Fens to a successful conclusion, and in 1655 he petitioned Oliver Cromwell for permission to drain Sedgemoor. Eventually his petition was brought before Parliament as a Bill, and rejected because "the tenants and freeholders did not consent." Thus the people of Sedgemoor defeated the most famous drainage engineer of his day.[19]

The period from 1650 to 1770, which saw so much general economic progress throughout the country, might have been

[18] Ibid., p. 87–8.
[19] Ibid., pp. 95–101.

expected to be a period when reclamation would have been pushed more vigorously, but it was not so. The period was a particularly poor one, when Williams estimates that only some 2,250 acres were reclaimed. More than half of this was in Heath Moor in the Brue valley south of Meare, and most of the rest was in Alder and Common Moors, around Street and Glastonbury, which were reclaimed under the 1722 Private Act of Parliament already referred to.[20] There are several possible reasons why progress was so slow in this period. One was technical: most of the more easily drained alluvial moors had already been tackled—what remained were the much less fertile peat moors, which were also more difficult to reclaim. Another reason was probably economic. The marked improvements in agricultural productivity in other parts of the country in the late seventeenth century, coupled with the large expansion in overseas trade, had increased the food supply, with a consequent lowering of prices for corn and livestock—especially after about 1720.[21] Consequently the expected profits from further reclamation would have been considerably reduced. No doubt apathy, technical ignorance and popular opposition also played their part.

There was, however, one success story to record in this period—the reclamation of the Meare fish pool, which was carried out in stages between about 1620 and 1740 (Plate 36). This pool lay just to the north of Meare village, and was the result of the rivers Sheppey and Hartlake from the north-east adding their waters to the Brue. John Leland, the antiquary, described it in 1537. "The mere is as at high waters in winter a 4 miles in cumpace, and when it is lest a 2 miles and an half, and most communely 3 miles. This lak or mere is a good mile yn lenght"[22] (compared to its circumference of 3–4 miles). The details of its reclamation are not fully known, but in 1638 Mr William Freake owned 480 acres of new ground on the northern side of the pool which were described as "lately a Fish pool". However, Christopher Cockerell's attempts to grow flax on

[20] Ibid., pp. 110–11.

[21] For agricultural progress in other parts of England, see E. L. Jones, ed., *Agriculture and Economic Growth in England, 1650–1815* (1967), and for foreign trade, R. Davis, *The Rise of the Atlantic Economies* (1973).

[22] L. Toulmin Smith, ed., *Leland's Itinerary in England*, I (1907), p. 149.

reclaimed land in the same year were wrecked by severe flooding. It seems that the "New Cutts" (or Decoy Rhyne) were dug about 1660, but Strachey's map of 1736 still shows an extensive pool in the southern area between the rivers Sheppey and Brue. However, this had gone by the time of Bladeslade's map of 1741, and it would appear that the rivers Sheppey and Hartlake were canalised into the River James Wear and the Division Rhyne sometime in the late 1730s.[23] (See 2½" O.S. map of the area.) The existing rhynes show hardly any change from those in William White's map of 1803.

The drive for comprehensive reclamation, 1770–1840

Since the general picture of the causes and chronology of this movement have already been discussed in chapter 5, it is not necessary here to do more than give a brief summary before looking at some details of the kind of landscape which emerged. In general, enclosure under a Private Act of Parliament provided the framework for more comprehensive drainage and reclamation schemes, which were built up around the rhynes used to sub-divide the newly enclosed fields.

The activity started in the 1770s in the Brue valley, between the Poldens and Wedmore. Between 1780 and 1800 the work was completed in the Brue valley and was started up in the Axe valley (between Wedmore and Mendip) and in the Cary valley, including King's Sedgemoor (between Zoyland and the Polden Hills). The northern Levels (comprising the moors lying to the north of Mendip and to the south of the Failand ridge near Clevedon, as well as the Gordano valley farther north) were not tackled until the first decade of the nineteenth century. Finally, the more difficult southern Levels (the valleys of the Parrett, Tone, Isle and Yeo, and West Sedgemoor) were attempted in the period 1810 to 1840. Over 80 per cent of all the wetlands enclosed and drained (in so far as they were drained) were peat moors, presenting particularly difficult problems, not only of reclamation and conversion to useful pasture, but also of access, since building roads on these spongy and damp soils was not easy.

[23] Williams, *Somerset Levels*, pp. 106–7. However, Dr B. Harley of Exeter University informs me that Strachey's map may not be very reliable.

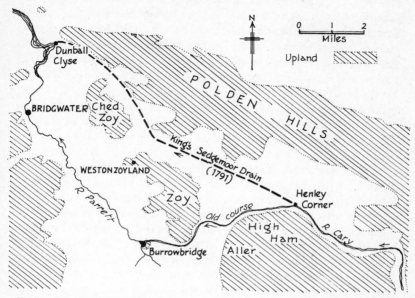

Fig. 19. The re-routing of the River Cary, showing the old course and the new one, the King's Sedgemoor Drain, from Henley Corner to Dunball, begun in 1791

The most dramatic single change in the landscape occurred when a new channel was dug for the river Cary (Fig. 19). This is the channel known today as the King's Sedgemoor Drain (Plate 20), and it took the waters of the Cary directly north-westwards through Sedgemoor to a new outlet (and clyse) at Dunball on the east bank of the Parrett estuary. Formerly the Cary had flowed westwards along the south edges of Sedgemoor and Zoyland to join the Parrett at Burrowbridge. This twisting and unsatisfactory course had led to flooding not only in Sedgemoor but also in the Parrett valley below Burrowbridge, because the Parrett could not cope with the waters of the Cary in that part of its valley. The new course ran for about twelve miles from Henley Corner to Dunball, and gradually got wider and deeper as it proceeded westwards. Its top width increased from twenty-six feet six inches at Henley Corner to fifty-five feet at Dunball, and its depth from five feet six inches to fourteen feet. However, the Dunball clyse was unsatisfactory, and its sill was four feet

163

too high, so that the flow down the river was slowed, and silting took place. In addition, several bridges over the lower part of the cut were too narrow and further impeded the drainage. As a result, the scheme, though it caused a great improvement on the previous situation, did not improve the drainage as much as had been planned, and reclamation was on occasion still affected by serious flooding.[24]

Because of the very large numbers of people who had rights to common grazing in the moors (the austers) the pattern of fields which emerged from an Act of Parliamentary enclosure was often extremely complex. This was especially so when numerous rights to cut turf existed and had to be compensated. Each holder would be given a small strip of land in what had previously been the common turbary (turf lands), and, of course, access roads had to be provided as well. An example of the pattern which emerged may be seen in Fig. 20, which shows the scores of tiny strips into which the turbary at Glastonbury Heath was divided in 1803. In theory each person was entitled to dig a rhyne around his allotment, but modern maps show that this was not done in every case. Very few rhynes were dug on the north side of Rock's Drove, although quite a few were dug on the south side. Further west, in the parish of Catcott, near Catcott Burtle, in another turbary area, the modern map shows extreme subdivision of strips, but the normal arrangement was to try to obtain a rectangular or square field of three to five acres. This size fits in well with modern ideas about rotational grazing, since cattle and sheep waste less grass if they are confined to several small paddocks for short periods and then moved on, rather than being allowed to spread out over a large field.

The ending of common rights also enabled building to take place on the moors, which had not been possible before. Naturally such low-lying and muddy sites did not commend themselves on a large scale, but farmsteads were no longer confined to the restricted village and "island" sites, and were enabled in suitable cases to move out into the centre of their new fields. Such farms were often built in brick instead of the traditional silver Liassic stone, and hence are usually fairly easy

[24] Williams, *Somerset Levels*, pp. 144–9.

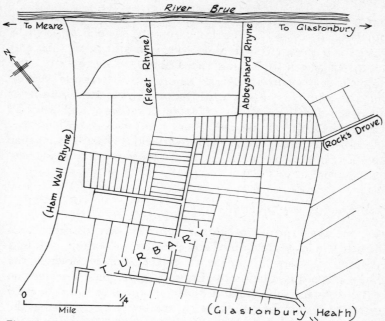

Fig. 20. The pattern of Parliamentary enclosure in allotted fields about two miles west of Glastonbury (Sharpham Civil Parish) in 1803

to identify. A comparison of old and modern maps will also reveal the new farms. For instance, none are shown on White's 1803 map of Glastonbury Heath, but the modern map shows a farmstead (with a small orchard attached) called Rice Farm, situated in the western corner formed by the Fleet Rhyne and the River Brue. This is typical of a number of other farms built out on the moors, like Laurel Farm and Brook Farm in Godney parish. But generally the moors did not provide very many suitable sites, and the opportunity for building a new, modern farmstead on the newly enclosed land did not occur in the same way as when dry land was enclosed.

The other great opportunity which reclamation might have provided was for new and straighter roads to be built, connecting the main centres around the Levels. A comparison of the roads shown on Day and Master's map of Somerset in 1782 with those of Greenwood's map of 1822 does indeed show that many miles of new road had been built, but surprisingly few were

165

through roads. Almost all either linked villages and hamlets or provided access to new enclosed pastures.[25] The great main trunk roads through the Levels—the Taunton, Bridgwater and Bristol (now the A38) and the Taunton—Glastonbury road (now the A361) already existed before the reclamation. A possible exception is the new road that was made westwards from Meare to Catcott Burtle, and then northwards through Mark to Tarnock on the A38 between Brent Knoll and Axbridge. This has, however, never been a main road, and the fact remains that the enclosure of the Levels did not provide any important new through roads.

Problems of the new landscape

By 1840 the central wetlands of Somerset had in theory been drained, enclosed, reclaimed and freed from flooding, enabling a completely new landscape to evolve, but in practice the achievement was much more limited. Inadequate work on the initial drainage schemes and insufficient money from the local rates to pay for regular and efficient maintenance meant that the area was still subject to dangerous winter floods, and that much of the potential value to be obtained from the reclaimed land had not been realised. Severe floods occurred in 1853, 1872-3, 1876-7, 1891, 1917, 1919 and 1929. The Land Drainage Act of 1930 set up the Somerset Catchment Board with unified control over all the river valleys in the Levels and adequate financial powers, but the severe depression of the 1930s upset plans involving any large-scale expenditure, and it was not until the outbreak of war in 1939, and the setting up of an ordnance factory at Puriton, near Bridgwater, with a very large daily water requirement, that action was taken. This situation coincided with the arrival of Louis Kelting as chief engineer of the Catchment Board, and his drive and acumen resulted in an ingenious solution which provided the factory with water and greatly improved the drainage in the Levels (especially the Brue valley) at the same time. His solution was to dig a new, wide channel for the river Brue for five miles westwards from Gold Corner to the Parrett estuary, known as the Huntspill river. In

[25] Ibid., p. 191.

winter (when water for the factory was no problem in any case), this new channel greatly assisted the drainage of the Brue valley. In summer, when water tended to be short, it acted as an immense elongated reservoir. It could be sealed by retention sluices at either end, and could be kept full, if necessary, by pumping extra water into it from the surrounding peat moors. It was built in 1940 and, with various associated new channels and pumping stations, has virtually ended flooding in the central Levels.

The problems of the Parrett valley and its tributaries, the Tone, Yeo, and Isle, are more difficult to solve. The absence of a clyse on the Parrett below Bridgwater enables the tides to flow up these rivers, but it is not clear whether a clyse would solve the problem, which stems mainly from the large quantities of *fresh* water flowing down the rivers after heavy rains. The provision of relief drainage-channels upstream together with constant pumping has greatly reduced the extent of flooding, however, without eliminating it.[26]

Thus the wetlands have been considerably relieved (though not freed) from the flooding problem in the last forty years, and have become much drier and more productive, but this change has come about by measures which have not had much visual impact on the landscape. Apart from the large new cut of the Huntspill river, most of the new relief drainage channels and pumping stations are fairly inconspicuous.

Communications and the growth of towns

By their nature the Somerset wetlands were not a good place for towns, and those which are important today can be divided into two distinct categories. First there are the ancient market centres, of which Bridgwater and Glastonbury are the chief, and second there are the new seaside resorts, which improved communication and the reclamation of their hinterlands allowed to develop from mere villages in the nineteenth century. Weston-super-Mare is much the most important of these, but Burnham-on-Sea to the south of it, and Clevedon to the north, although more modest in size, have also enjoyed

[26] Ibid., pp. 197–256.

quite rapid growth in the last century. The construction of the Great Western Railway in 1841 stimulated the process, and it has accelerated still further since the opening of the M5 in the mid-1970s.

In many ways Bridgwater was the ancient centre for the Levels, being at the mouth of the Parrett and thus the chief outlet for the trade of all the lands watered by the Parrett and its tributaries. Despite its long history it had only attained a population of some 3,000 by the first census in 1801, but it began to grow more rapidly as the improved communications of the nineteenth century assisted its transformation from a trading and market centre into an industrial city. In the early eighteenth century, Defoe had commented on Bridgwater's role as an importer and distributer of coal, and the opening of the Bridgwater–Taunton canal in 1827 enabled this trade to expand further, prior to the arrival of the main line of the Great Western Railway.[27] By 1901 the population had reached 14,900, and by 1971 it had grown to 26,700.

The town expanded mainly in a haphazard and piecemeal way, but an attempt to introduce a more planned appearance was made by the Duke of Chandos when he acquired the manorial lordship of the town in 1721 (Plate 43). He hoped to develop the port and to make Bridgwater a commercial rival to Bristol. To this end he laid out a square of red-brick Georgian houses on the site of the old castle keep (King's Square) and linked it to the quayside by a short, sloping street of similar houses (Castle Street). Now mainly occupied by solicitors' and doctors' offices, this street has suffered very little change, and still retains the spirit and feeling of the eighteenth century. Modern Bridgwater has become highly industrialised, especially on its northern side, where the ancient manor house of the Sydenhams has been engulfed by a huge cellophane factory (it has itself been converted into a staff club). Factories for making shoes, shirts, furniture, and a variety of light engineering components testify to Bridgwater's solid industrial prosperity, if not to its aesthetic charm. The old port has decayed and stands surrounded by the remains of the extensive brick and

[27] Hunt and Sellman, *Somerset History*, pp. 47–9; B. Little, *Portrait of Somerset*, pp. 141–2.

Plate 21 Blackmoor Farm, near Cannington. A traditional manor house in red sandstone, almost unchanged externally since it was built in the fifteenth century. The protruding wing was a private chapel.

Plate 22 Rexworthy, a moated farmstead on the plain between Bridgwater and the Quantocks. The term ''worthy'' is Saxon for an isolated farmstead. The farmhouse has been substantially modernised, but retains some early features.

Plate 23 The Priest's House, Muchelney. A rare survival of a medieval dwelling house, it was built by the monks of Muchelney Abbey for the vicar of the parish church in 1308. The fine windows were later medieval improvements. It is now owned by the National Trust.

Plate 24 Church and dovecot, Norton-sub-Hamdon near Montacute. Described by Pevsner as "an uncommonly perfect church", it is built in golden Ham stone from the nearby quarries and has a classical Somerset tower from the best period, c. 1500-10. The dovecot belonged to an adjacent manor house (now demolished). It is rare to find one so close to a church.

Plate 25 West Bower Farm, Durleigh near Bridgwater. A converted fifteenth century gatehouse, probably built by a local lawyer, Alexander Hody, who died 1461. The water in front is the recently created Durleigh reservoir – making for an attractive blend of old and new.

Plate 26 Spargrove, north of Bruton. This Victorian house occupies a moated site, whose earlier manor house is gone. The stables on the right date from the mid-eighteenth century. In 1791, Collinson, the Somerset historian, recorded six houses here, in addition to the manor. Extensive disturbance of the ground round about indicates where the former settlement stood.

tile works which were once the homes of a thriving Bridgwater industry. Bridgwater was also famous for Bath bricks—a scouring agent made from the fine silt deposited in the Parrett estuary by the ever-restless tide, which sends a minor version of the Severn bore through the town.[28]

In contrast to that of Bridgwater, Glastonbury's growth has been very modest, and would have been more modest still had it not become to some extent linked with its remarkable southern neighbour, Street. This place was a village with only 540 inhabitants in 1801, but it was here that a local Quaker family, the Clarks, established their shoe-making business in 1825. As mechanisation replaced hand work, the business grew and thrived, and the town with it. The population had reached nearly 4,000 by 1901 and is over 8,000 today—compared with Glastonbury's 6,580. Much of Street was laid out under the direction of the Clark family, who were responsible for designing and building many of their workers' houses. Local stone has been used in most cases, and the town has many attractive streets and residential quarters. Glastonbury has grown more as a tourist centre, based on the ruins of its famous abbey, than for other reasons. Local entrepreneurs placed great hopes in the Glastonbury to Highbridge canal (1834–53) and the Somerset and Dorset railway, which linked Glastonbury to the Bristol Channel port of Burnham in 1858 and the English Channel port of Poole in 1863. However, neither stimulated much industrial activity in the town, which remained instead a peaceful country market.[29]

The seaside resorts presented a quite different picture. Burnham was the largest in 1801, with 653 people; Clevedon came next with 334, and Weston was an insignificant little place with a mere 138 inhabitants. In 1851, ten years after the opening of the Great Western Railway, the picture had already changed significantly. Weston had expanded to a population of 4,034, helped also by the draining of the common marshes to the south of the old village; Clevedon had advanced to 1,905, and Burnham, although it had moved to 1,701, now lagged

[28] Aston and Leech, *Somerset Towns*, p. 13–19.
[29] See B. Lehane, *C. and J. Clark, 1825–1975* (1975), and Hunt and Sellman, *Somerset History*, pp. 43–9.

behind the other two. Perhaps it was less convenient as a residence for Bristol commuters. Since then growth has continued—at a respectable pace in Burnham and Clevedon, which in 1971 had 12,690 and 15,140 people respectively, and at a headlong pace at Weston, which now contains over 50,000 inhabitants. It extends all along the magnificent beach from Worlebury Hill in the north to the old village of Uphill in the south, while the lines of villas have climbed up the southern face of Worlebury Hill.

Despite an unattractively murky sea (the Bristol Channel no longer enjoys unpolluted waters) and extensive mud-flats beyond its beaches, Weston became popular as a seaside resort because it had bracing sea air, a vast extent of superb sands, and attractive views in all directions. The Welsh coast opposite closes the view to the west and is offset by the two islands in the Bristol Channel, the precipitous and craggy Steep Holm, and the less dramatic Flat Holm with its lighthouse. To the south is the sinuous mass of Brean Down with its ancient field system and its ruined Victorian fort, while to the north lies the similar but smaller mass of Middle Hope. Both these downs are extensions of the Mendips which jut into the Bristol Channel.

Weston's sea breezes were thought by doctors to be healthy, and its development received a fillip in the early nineteenth century when the Bristol physician, Dr Edward Long Fox, built the bathhouse at Knightstone, then a tiny island at the north end of the beach, but now linked to the mainland by a causeway. He and others began to build Regency-style villas, such as those in Park Parade with their views south-westwards towards the Quantocks and distant Exmoor on the far horizon. However, the gently curving Royal Crescent (Plate 45), though evocative of Regency Brighton, was not actually built until 1847, and hence is as Victorian as most of the rest of Weston. The town stands as a monument to Victorian prosperity and self-confidence, as well as to an eclecticism of architectural taste which is as distressing to classical purists as it is exciting to lovers of Victoriana.[30]

[30] B. Little, *Portrait of Somerset*, pp. 72–6, and N. Pevsner, *The Buildings of England, North Somerset and Bristol* (1958), pp. 336–8.

SELECT BIBLIOGRAPHY

Williams, M., *The Draining of the Somerset Levels* (1970).

Kelting, E. L., "The rivers and seawalls of Somerset", *SANHS*, 112 (1968).

Hawkins, D., *Avalon and Sedgemoor* (1973).

Collinson, J., *The History and Antiquities of the County of Somerset* (1761), 3 vols.

Billingsley, J., *A General View of the Agriculture of the County of Somerset* (1795).

7. Exmoor and the western hills

Enclosure on the Blackdowns. Enclosure on the Quantocks. Enclosure on Exmoor and the Brendon Hills. The western towns. Industrial and post-industrial landscape.

EXMOOR AND ITS eastern extension, the Brendon Hills, form the most distinctive landscape region in Somerset, and it is convenient to include the Quantock Hills and the Somerset section of the Blackdowns in the same region, since, despite some structural differences, all these western hills show landscape characteristics which are very different from those found in the lowlands. Hamlets and isolated farms are the predominant form of settlement on the hills, rather than compact villages, and the density of settlement is low, with woods, moors and heaths frequently more numerous than cultivated fields.

This, of course, does not mean that the appearance of these hills is similar. Exmoor and the Brendons are mainly treeless on their higher slopes, where wide expanses of open hillside are covered with heather, gorse, bracken and moorland grasses like purple moor-grass (also known as flying bent) and cotton-grass, except in the boggy patches where large clumps of rushes flourish. The heather moorland predominates around Dunkery Beacon, Winsford Hill, Withypool Common and parts of the eastern Brendons, while grass moorland is more common in the area of the old royal forest in the high country all around Simonsbath. It is thought that extensive sheep-grazing since very early times has destroyed much of the natural heather in this area and assisted the conversion to grass—though the reclaiming activities of the Knight family and their tenants after the enclosure of 1819 also played a part.

In recent years many of the lower slopes of the Brendons have been planted with conifer trees, like those at Holnicot and Croydon Hill. The Quantocks and Blackdowns are also fairly well wooded. The remains of the ancient Neroche Forest survive on the Blackdowns' northern edge around Corfe and Staple Fitzpaine, though parts of the plateau around Churchingford have been largely converted to pasture. The central and southern Quantocks are also extensively wooded, but these are not the remains of the ancient oak and beech forests, but are evergreen plantations of larches, firs, and pines, like those on the Brendons planted by the Forestry Commission since 1927 (Plate 17). Intense local resistance to these "foreign" trees has recently slowed down the re-afforestation programme.[1]

Since a brief summary of the grazing economy of these uplands, and the eventual enclosure of most of them in the nineteenth century was given in chapter 5, it need not be repeated here. However, before looking at the enclosure process in more detail, it is interesting to note the way in which attitudes to the wild and open uplands have changed. Today, conservation of the last remaining commons is a widely supported aim, but in the past these areas were considered useless and were regarded with distaste. John Leland, who travelled in Somerset between 1535 and 1543, commented, when riding across Exmoor from Exford to Simonsbath, that he passed "all by forest, baren and morisch ground, wher ys store and breading of yonge catelle, but little or no corne or habitation". Thomas Gerard in 1633 thought it "a solitarie place . . . the more commodious for stagges, who keep possession of it", while Daniel Defoe, with his passion for improvement and modernity, regarded Exmoor (c. 1725) as "a melancholy view, being a vast tract of baren and desolate lands"[2] Incidentally, wild deer still inhabit Exmoor, as do the Exmoor ponies, which are probably descended from the wild ponies of Bronze Age times. They are exceptionally hardy.

[1] See N. V. Allen, *The Exmoor Handbook and Gazetteer* (1974), and V. Waite, *Portrait of the Quantocks* (1969), pp. 158–62.

[2] Toulmin Smith, *Leland's Itinerary*, I, p. 168; E. H. Bates, ed., "The Particular Description of the County of Somerset, 1633" (by Thomas Gerard), *Som. Rec. Soc.*, XV (1900), p. 1; P. Rogers, ed., Daniel Defoe, *A Tour through the whole Island of Great Britain* (1971), p. 252.

In contrast to the dislike felt for the bleak high moors, the lower stretches, where the small fields of the hill farms had been carved out of them, were pleasurably regarded. Celia Fiennes, crossing the Blackdowns from Wellington to Cullompton in Devon in 1698, ascended "a high Ridge of hills which discover a vast prospect on each side full of inclosures, good grass and corn beset with quicksetts and hedg rows".[3]

Enclosure on the Blackdowns

We noted in chapter 5 that Charles I had ambitious schemes to raise money by enclosing his royal forests, and how his plan to enclose Exmoor collapsed. However, he had better luck in the early 1630s with Neroche Forest on the eastern edge of the Blackdowns. Despite the opposition of Lord Poulett of Hinton St George, who had been keeper of the Forest since 1619, and who resented the loss of his hunting there, dis-afforestation was carried out. In return for surrendering his exclusive hunting rights and agreeing to enclosure, the king was allotted one-third of the land in the Forest, about 1,634 acres, which he soon sold. The king's allotment was enclosed at this time, and shortly afterwards, the lord of the Manor enclosed another third. At the beginning of the Civil War (1642–3) "the Rabble broke up all hedges and fences and laid all in Common again", and in legal proceedings against objectors to the enclosure in 1658, some 2,000 people claiming common rights gave evidence. In the event, the enclosure of the king's former third was confirmed, but not the third which the lord had enclosed; so about two-thirds of the Forest remained open (some 3,268 acres).[4]

Sporadic piecemeal enclosure followed during the next two centuries, but as many as 2,357 acres (in thirteen parishes) were mentioned as commons in the Enclosure Act of 1830. These commons were enclosed in 1833. The reasons for the survival of so much common grazing were no doubt partly technical—the sheer difficulty of enclosing lands on the steep hill-sides and

[3] C. Morris, ed., *The Journeys of Celia Fiennes* (1947), p. 244.
[4] T. G. Barnes, *Somerset, 1625–40*, pp. 156–9; R. A. Sixsmith, *Staple Fitzpaine and the Forest of Neroche* (1958), passim.

bringing them into cultivation—but probably equally important was the fact that farmers in so many of the surrounding
parishes possessed rights of common grazing in Neroche Forest.
Ilton, Barrington and Whitelackington had rights, and with so
many interests to be considered it was naturally difficult to
obtain agreement. For instance, Barrington Hill, between
Bickenhall and Broadway, was a detached part of Barrington
parish, which had common grazing rights on about 1,200 acres
of the hill. About 1631 this land was divided between the lord
of the manor and the customary tenants, and some of it was
enclosed for growing wheat, but other parts remained as common grazings and woodlands until 1833.[5] Timber rights were
important to the lowland parishes, both for firewood and building. There are some fine timber-framed buildings in Barrington
village, some dating from as early as the fourteenth century. No
doubt villagers clung to their timber rights for as long as they
could.

When the Parliamentary enclosure came in 1833, the
parishes mainly concerned were Buckland St Mary, Curland,
Bickenhall, Broadway and Ashill where most of the surviving
forest was situated. After enclosure many new farms were built
on the former forest and the common pastures. Some of these
may be seen on Fig. 21, which contrasts Windmill Hill in
Ashill parish in 1809, before enclosure, with its layout in 1905,
seventy-two years after the enclosure of 1833. Cage Bush Farm,
Windmill Hill Farm and Forest Farm are amongst many in the
neighbourhood which were new creations.

The western Blackdowns were also partly involved in Parliamentary enclosure. For instance, 781 acres were enclosed in
West Buckland parish in 1815 and this was followed soon
afterwards (in 1820) by 355 acres in Wellington Without. This
land lay in a long line along the scarp of the hills, and included
the land on which the monument to the Duke of Wellington
now stands. Most of the land belonged to him, and he seems to
have been the chief sponsor of the Enclosure Act of 1816. These
must have been the last surviving areas of Wellington's commons, showing that earlier enclosures by agreement had pushed

[5] *VCH*, IV, pp. 116–17.

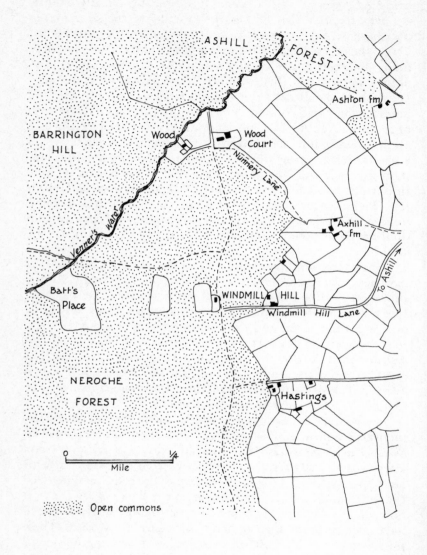

Fig. 21. Windmill Hill in Ashill parish before enclosure, 1809

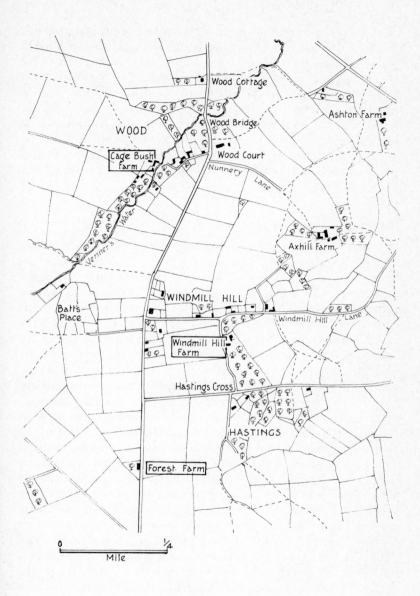

Windmill Hill in 1905, seventy-two years after its enclosure in 1833

the farmed land right up to the steepest part of the escarpment.[6] Much of this land is now wooded, and some of it belongs to the National Trust as land of outstanding beauty. A new farm called Monument Farm was created on the flat land to the south of the scarp. It is shown on the 1888 edition of the 6" O.S. map. A much larger area around Corfe, Pitminster and Otterford survived as commons until 1851, when it was included in an Enclosure Act relating to Taunton and many of its surrounding areas (not all of them on the Blackdowns). This Act authorised the enclosure of 2,430 acres, mainly on the hills between Corfe and Otterford.

Enclosure on the Quantocks

Here enclosure has never been completed, because the northern part of the range—much of which is over 1,000 feet high—has never been attractive for settlement, and is of little use except for rough grazing or forestry. Consequently extensive commons survive, and the Quantock ridgeway and its offshoots provide superb, unencumbered walks in the area between Wills Neck and Quantoxhead. The southern Quantocks lie at a somewhat lower altitude, and were gradually enclosed and partially brought under cultivation before the nineteenth century. However, much common pasture and scrubland survived, particularly on the steeper scarps. Some attempts to enclose this were made in the nineteenth century, such as the enclosure of West Bagborough Hill Common in 1810. The map attached to the enclosure award shows that about 1,200 acres were involved. The hill common was divided up into sixty-three allotments. Some were quite large, but about fifty were smaller (mainly about ten acres in size) and were laid out in strips running up the hill. It is, however, doubtful whether this land was ever actually enclosed and fenced, since none of these allotted closes appears on the 1888 O.S. map, when the whole hill was already a vast plantation attached to the grounds of Bagborough House. It is still thickly wooded. It looks as though the owners of the original allotments may have sold their lands rather than face

[6] SRO, Wellington Hill Enclosure Act (1816), and Award (1820), C.R. 48.

the costs of enclosing them. Thus the landscape planned by the enclosure commissioners of 1810 was replaced by a quite different pattern. The award does, however, reveal an aspect of enclosure which is not always noticed—namely the exchange of old enclosed fields in order to reduce the fragmentation of farms. Fragmentation was often quite serious, as a result of earlier piecemeal enclosure arrangements. In West Bagborough no fewer than forty-four closes (most of them very small) were exchanged. Some of these closes were near West Bagborough village, while others were in the hamlets of Shopnoller and Seven Ash.[7] One of the advantages of these exchanges was that little closes, once acquired, could be amalgamated with neighbouring small fields already in the new owners' possession to make new fields of a more convenient size. Thus Enclosure Acts were a method not only of bringing common pastures into individual ownership, but also of arranging quite substantial alterations in the shape, size and layout of farms already enclosed. This aspect of Parliamentary enclosure might merit further investigation.

Enclosure on Exmoor and the Brendon Hills

Parliamentary enclosure of common pastures was much more important on the Brendons and Exmoor than it was on the Quantocks. In the Brendons, eleven parishes were subject to Enclosure Acts between 1798 (Exton) and 1866 (Dunster). The areas involved could be tiny, like the 62 acres enclosed at Ashbrittle in 1858, or extensive, like the 2,700 acres enclosed at Exton near Cutcombe in 1798, and the 2,500 acres taken in at the joint award for Brompton Regis, Upton and Skilgate (all lying high up near the Devon border) in 1804. On the other hand, some of the Brendon parishes like Treborough and Luxborough were never affected. At Luxborough the farmland was gradually extended up the hillsides at the expense of the old commons until the commons themselves were small enough to be enclosed. The Tithe Map of 1841 shows this process completed, with former commons in the south of the parish adjacent to the ancient ridgeway along the Brendon hills divided up and

[7] SRO, West Bagborough Enclosure Award (1810), C.R. 50.

included in the farms of South Colly Hill, Kennisham, Beerland, Langham and Blindwell. However, cultivation has to some extent receded from this exposed area, and in 1978 only Langham still survived as a farmstead. South Colly Hill was in ruins, and the sites of Kennisham, Beerland and Blindwell had either vanished entirely or survived only as earthworks.[8]

Nearly all Exmoor parishes lying to the west of the main road from Dunster to Dulverton (A396) were affected by Parliamentary enclosure, and much of this was surprisingly late. Although the Royal Forest of Exmoor was enclosed in 1817, many of the commons in the other parishes were not enclosed until after 1850. One of the largest areas was the 2,912 acres enclosed in Oare parish in 1863. In 1867 Porlock took in 1,860 acres, but the commons at Wootton Courtenay (1,084 acres) survived until 1872. This was the last Parliamentary enclosure on Exmoor.[9] By this time Britain had become dependent on cheap imported food. Farm land had fallen in value and reclamation schemes were uneconomic. In fact, the amenity value of open commons for recreation was coming to be recognised as their greatest asset.

The largest single enclosure scheme on Exmoor was that involving the Royal Forest, where some 22,400 acres were involved under the Act passed in 1815. This was the most inaccessible and remote part of the moor, and one from which the Crown derived little profit (as we saw in chapter 5). The occasion of the enclosure was the government's need for increased timber supplies for the navy at a critical period of the Napoleonic wars. This coincided with the expiry of Sir Thomas Acland's lease as warden, and his request for a renewal in 1810. Plans were drawn up to enclose the moor and to reserve 10,000 acres to the Crown for timber production, and these were eventually embodied in the Enclosure Act of 1815. However, after the victory of Waterloo and the end of the war, the need for naval timber was much reduced, and in 1818 the Crown decided to sell its allotment by auction.[10]

[8] See map in E. F. Williams, *Parish Surveys in Somerset*, 2, *Luxborough* (1978), p. 27.
[9] See Tate, *Somerset Enclosure Acts and Awards*.
[10] MacDermot, *History of Exmoor*, pp. 407–36.

Intending buyers were asked to send in sealed bids, and Sir Thomas Acland, who as warden of the Forest had a shrewd idea of its value, is believed to have put in a bid of £5,000, representing twenty years' purchase on its annual net income of about £250, being the agistment rents received from the surrounding lowland farmers for grazing their sheep on the moor during the summer. In 1816 some 25,000 sheep from fifty parishes had fed on the moor. Their owners had paid 5d. a sheep unless they came from bordering parishes, when the charge had been 2½d. per sheep. Possibly Acland had underestimated the potential improvement of which the enclosed moor was capable, because another neighbouring magnate, Earl Fortescue of Castle Hill, in north Devon, who knew the moor well, was much later (in 1930) revealed to have offered £30,000. Although it was not known at the time what the local magnates had bid, it must have come of something of a surprise when the local press announced that a wealthy Worcestershire ironmaster and landowner, John Knight, from Wolverley parish near Kidderminster, had paid £50,000 for it. This was ten times what Sir Thomas Acland had offered, and was a relatively immense sum, nor was it influenced by any calculations of mineral wealth beneath the soil, for although John Knight had taken the precaution of buying the mineral rights, the Crown had sold these to him for a mere three shillings (15p.) an acre because they had no "reason to suppose that there are mines or minerals of any value under the property in question'. Although John Knight did try to develop a small copper mine (Wheal Eliza), he accepted that there were no significant quantities of minerals on the moor, and his son's unfortunate attempts to exploit iron ore in the 1850s show that this decision was correct.[11]

John Knight had thus paid £5 an acre for a vast expanse of moorland which was devoid of roads, hedges, trees and habitation except for a single farmhouse at Simonsbath, built about 1654, when a farm of 108 acres had been enclosed in a sheltered part of the Barle valley. The rest of the property would have fitted the description, penned by Edward Hutton in 1912, of a remote part of the moor which was never enclosed: "A bare

[11] Orwin and Sellick, *Reclamation of Exmoor*, pp. 37–56.

rolling waste very like the sea, with its long heaving monotony of grey water, without a voice, without life, and without human habitation; there is only the sound of wind and of running water. That is the moor, and its face is the face of eternity."[12]

But John Knight saw it differently. He was a lifelong enthusiast for agricultural improvement. Born in 1765, a contemporary of Arthur Young, Knight had studied Coke of Norfolk's reclamation works on the sandy marshes of the Norfolk coast, and had already had experience of reclaiming and farming heathlands in Worcestershire. To him there seemed no reason why the moors and peats of Exmoor should not be drained, ploughed, grazed and limed, and brought into cultivation. He believed that a regular sheep-corn cultivation, using the famous Norfolk four-course rotation of wheat, turnips, barley and clover, would be successful on Exmoor. He was not deterred by Exmoor's eighty inches of annual rainfall, nor by its extensive bogs, its bitter winds and its freezing late springs and early winter snows with their massive drifts. He had been a successful businessman used to operating on a large scale, and it would seem that he regarded the taming of Exmoor as yet one more great challenge which would exhibit his patriotism as well as his skill and determination. John Billingsley, when surveying Somerset for the Board of Agriculture in 1795, had declared that "a very large proportion of the whole needs but the spirit and fortune of some one or more of our wealthy gentlemen of England, whose attention . . . would render the Forest of Exmoor in a few years as fair a prospect as the surrounding country." It would appear that Knight agreed with him, though he neglected an important piece of advice also given by Billingsley—that success would depend upon the settlement of the moor by artificers and husbandmen who would build houses and farms surrounded by hedges and plantations of trees for shelter belts. Instead, John Knight tried for some twenty years to farm Exmoor as a huge demesne farm, worked by unmarried ploughmen and shepherds lodged in bothies in Simonsbath.

[12] Cited by N. V. Allen, *Exmoor Handbook and Gazetteer*, p. 17. In fact, Hutton was exercising poetic licence. Exmoor had been colonised by trees like birch and Scots pine after the Ice Age, and had been cleared by early man, beginning perhaps 10–12,000 years ago.

Despite the construction of numerous roads and an immense boundary fence around the whole property, it is hardly surprising that his farming operations were disastrous. His crops failed to ripen, and his livestock to thrive. His son, Frederic Winn Knight, who took over the management of the property in 1841, and ran it until his death in 1897, used to say that his father expected to farm on Exmoor as he had in the Midlands; nevertheless he recorded in 1845 that John Knight had been responsible for converting some 2,500 acres of rough moorland into enclosed pastures of improved grasses and white clover.[13] Much of this reclamation has proved permanent for, as C. S. Orwin recorded in 1929, the land remained free-draining even after heavy rainfall, where John Knight's sub-soiling operations had broken the hard, impervious clay-with-iron pan which underlay the boggy peat soils. Once moisture could drain away, the Exmoor soils needed only lime to neutralise their acidity for a permanent improvement to occur.

However, despite what must have been huge financial losses, John Knight's attempts to reclaim Exmoor only nibbled at the edges of the problem. It was left to his son Frederic Knight to carry out the changes which have led to the permanent alteration of much of the Exmoor landscape. In essence, he recognised the wisdom of Billingsley's early advice, and realised that only by the creation of tenant farms and cottages occupied by settled families could the moor be successfully tamed and brought under cultivation. His idea was that the tenants could be induced to undertake the reclamation work if they were granted leases at a low rent, and given compensation for their improvements on the expiry of their leases. From about 1844 he began letting farms of about 500 to 1,000 acres each (Fig. 22) on leases of twelve to twenty years. Rents began very low and rose every four years as the land was reclaimed and brought under cultivation. In theory this was a sensible scheme, but Knight over-estimated the extent to which the moor could be raised in value, and many of his tenants were attracted by the initial low rents, without realising the costs of reclamation that would fall on them (and in some cases without any intention of undertaking

---

[13] Orwin and Sellick, *Reclamation of Exmoor*, pp. 57–72.

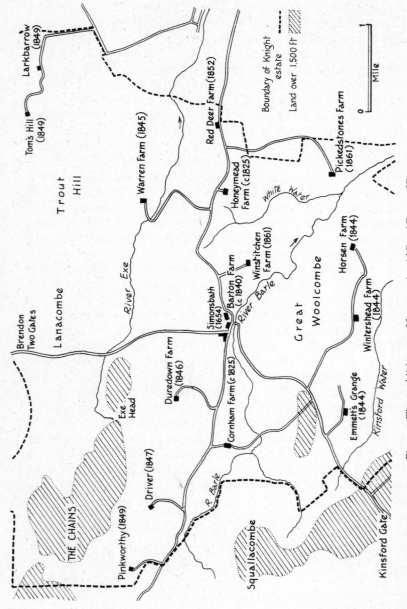

Fig. 22. The establishment of farms on the old Royal Forest of Exmoor

Plate 27 Mells Manor, near Frome. Originally owned by the Abbots of Glastonbury, it was bought by John Horner ("Little Jack" of nursery rhyme fame) in 1543, and later enlarged and embellished to become a classic Elizabethan mansion in Mendip limestone.

Plate 28 This picture of St. Catherine's Court and church in the Cotswolds, north of Bath, was taken about 1910. Once owned by Bath Abbey, it illustrates the close association of manor and church found in many (though not all) Somerset villages. It also highlights the importance of the garden in the country-house scene.

Plate 29 The church at East Lyng surrounded by a cider orchard – a picture typical of central Somerset, a landscape where orchards and elegantly decorated church towers form a recurring theme.

Plate 30 Dodington Manor on the eastern foothills of the Quantocks. A fifteenth-century dwelling with a later addition on the right. A largely unspoilt example of an old Somerset manor house, which escaped the extensive enlargements and alterations applied to so many others in Georgian and Victorian times.

Plate 31 Tilley Manor in West Harptree village beneath the northern edge of Mendip. A good example of a small manor house, it bears the date 1659, but the charming façade was added in the early eighteenth century.

Plate 32 A rare survival of an early sixteenth-century cottage at Stocklynch, near Ilminster. The original cob walls may be seen on the left. To the right the cob has been replaced by stone. The dormer window and upstairs storey were probably added later.

Plate 33 Somerset regional architecture at its prime. A cottage residence, once a small farmhouse, at Dowlish Wake, south of Ilminster. The treatment of the windows, especially, shows the quality of domestic building in stone in the seventeenth century.

the task). Not surprisingly there were unhappy experiences with tenants brought from far afield who used inappropriate systems, soon became discouraged, and quit their holdings. The amused locals said "they came in their po'chaises and left in their dung-carts." Before long Knight introduced local tenants, who used the traditional livestock husbandry in a modified form. His father's exotic cattle and Spanish merino sheep were replaced by the local red Devon cattle and Exmoor sheep. The attempts to grow cereals were abandoned (except for small acreages of oats for livestock feed) and eventually some sixteen extensive livestock farms were built on the more sheltered, south-facing slopes of the river valleys; most of these have survived as going concerns to the present day. Nor did Frederic Knight ultimately lose money over his Exmoor project. When he inherited the estate from his father in 1850, acquisitions subsequent to the purchase of the Crown allotment had increased its acreage to 21,893, and when he finally sold the reversion to the estate to Earl Fortescue in 1886 he made a respectable capital gain, despite an outstanding mortgage debt of £123,060. He secured £193,060, subject to his life interest (and he remained in possession, enjoying its rents and profits for another eleven years). His decision to sell occurred after the untimely death of his only son in 1879. Orwin calculates that the estate would have fetched £246,060 with possession. Discounting certain unimproved parts of the estate in Devon, he estimates that the Knight family spent about £78,000 on their lands in Exmoor Forest, and obtained effectively £200,000 for them as a result of their reclamation. He does not provide precise figures for the cost of the reclamation, but gives some estimates which indicate that it was about equal to the purchase price—making a total cost of £156,000. If this be deducted from the sale price of £193,000, it can be seen that Knight made a capital gain of £37,060 on the sale of the reversion—and this was not in an inflationary era. He would of course have made even more if he had given up his life interest. No doubt the Knights would have made more money if they had invested their capital in something less speculative than trying to reclaim Exmoor, but ultimately the project was not the financial fiasco it had once threatened to be. Yet it is still something of a puzzle

that Frederic Knight persisted for as long in his Exmoor scheme
when its annual returns were so low and so uncertain. The
answer seems to be that, when in 1850 he inherited the property
in a largely unimproved state, he could not have obtained a
reasonable price for it if he had sought to sell it, and also that at
this time his advisers told him that a fortune in iron ore lay
beneath the moor. By the time he realised that his mining
ventures would come to nothing (about 1860), his tenants were
beginning to improve their farms and were in a position to pay
increased rents. But although there was a gradual improvement
in the financial returns from the Exmoor farms during Frederic
Knight's lifetime, there can be little doubt that his primary
aims were not economic. He had been brought up on Exmoor
(he was six years old when his father bought it) and the life of a
hunting squire appealed to him, especially as land ownership on
such a large scale brought immense social prestige in Victorian
England. No doubt he also derived considerable satisfaction
from seeing his critics confounded, and from watching the
barren moorland gradually yield to the art of cultivation. He
was ultimately regarded as a substantial benefactor to his
country, and was rewarded with a knighthood in 1886.

In all, Frederic Knight seems to have converted some 7,000
to 8,000 acres of his estate (roughly one-third of it) from rough
moorland into improved permanent pasture, and to have left a
legacy of metalled roads substantial hedgerows (many crowned
with beech trees to provide additional shelter) and solid farmsteads. These latter were apparently designed by Knight himself, and were constructed from local stone—but roofed with
slates brought over from Wales. The style is a severe and plain
late Georgian, not without a certain stately elegance. Most of
the farmsteads are surrounded by plantations of beeches and
sycamores for shelter, and are well supplied with barns, cow-
sheds and outhouses.

The Pattern of Expansion of Knight's Exmoor Farms

Name of Farm	Date of creation	Initial acreage*
Honeymead	c. 1825	2,100
Cornham	c. 1825	545
Simonsbath Barton	c. 1840	1,030

Emmett's Grange	1844	1,300
Wintershead	1844	200
Crooked Post (Litton)	1844	350
Horsen	1844	400
Warren	1845	700
Duredown	1846	900
Driver	1847	400
Pinkworthy	1849	400
Tom's Hill	1849	207
Larkbarrow	1849	600
Red Deer	1852	124
Winstitchen	1861	407†
Pickedtones	1861	385†
	TOTALS:	9,256

*Some of the farms were later reduced in size.   †Formerly in Honeymead.

The settlement at Simonsbath also underwent a transformation—changing from an isolated farm housing a family of five in 1820 to a sizeable village with a population of 339 at its peak in 1871. In addition, a new farm (Simonsbath Barton), a hotel, a church, a school, a post office and some cottages were built, and the former extra-parochial settlement was made into a parish in 1856.[14] Although the population had fallen to 181 by 1971, Simonsbath is still an attraction to tourists and holiday-makers.

We can form some idea of what life on Exmoor was like during these years of transformation from the diary of William Hannam, who was the unfortunate tenant of Cornham Farm from 1845 until his losses forced him to give it up in 1858. Hannam came to Exmoor as a young married man of thirty-four from the neighbourhood of Wincanton, in south-eastern Somerset, where his father was a successful grazier and butcher. William Hannam was a younger son who had failed to prosper on a seventy-acre farm in North Cheriton. Dairying and cheese-making were his speciality, and, owing to his shortage of capital, his father agreed to be joint tenant with him. Hannam had had no experience of sheep (which were the essential back-

[14] Ibid., pp. 73–138.

bone of Exmoor farming) and he was no doubt ill-equipped to take on the rigours of hill farming on a desolate moor; yet the sad account of his disappointment and failure was not un-influenced by bad luck (he caught typhus fever in 1847) and by the encouragement he had received from Frederic Knight and others to commit himself to reclamation works and rising rents which were not realistic.

He was first attracted to Exmoor when visiting it to buy store cattle for his father in 1844, an abnormally fine summer. After hearing favourable reports from some of the other tenants and "many Darey Peeple" who were working for them, and "seeing the Beautifull crops of Corn they were just beginning to harvest and everything looking so prosperes", he asked Frederic Knight if he could rent a farm, and finally arranged to take Cornham with his father for twelve years, from Lady Day (25 March) 1845. The farm consisted of a house (not yet built), various farm buildings (also incomplete), three cottages, 545 acres of partly-reclaimed land (Cornham had been one of John Knight's original farmsteads) and 500 acres of rough grazing on the Chains (an extensive upland bog).

However, when he struggled up to Exmoor in March 1845 he was filled with depression:

> There was a certain part of the Buildings on each farm to be gott readey by Ladey Day but it turned out such a severe winter nothing scarceley could be done to Building—Things now had quite a different apperance from the September preveos—there had bin a Deal of Cattle lost During the winter and a great Deal that was living was looking misabrly Bad . . . the Forrest was looking very Barren not a Green Blade to be seen.

The trip to Exmoor indicates what the roads were like in those days. His family travelled in a "coverd Carr" accompanied by three wagons and two carts. He and his family intended to cover the sixty odd miles from Wincanton in one day "but could gett no farther than Exford as the Roads were in such a state after the severe frosts the Horses could scarce gett along." He and his family reached Simonsbath the next morning and he returned to the Brendon Hills to assist his wagons and carts, which had proceeded much more slowly. As they approached Cutcombe, a thick fog and the onset of dusk slowed them down further, especially as neither of his men "knew the least part of the Road and before we gott Half the distance it was so dark we could not see a yard—The roads were in such a state after the Frost and having very Heavey loads the wheels Cutt over the Fellows nearley every step they moved so that we could but just make a moove onwards." Nevertheless, they persevered, and Hannam survived twelve years on the moor—much longer than most of the early tenants.

He records different methods he used to reclaim land. One field was improved by manuring and mowing; another, which was too wet and infested with rushes, was improved by cutting irrigation ditches and "by paying attention to the water and woishing the Dung down over it Brought [the Redd Clover] up as thick as it could come and by alternateley Mowing it cleened it of the Rushes". But the costs of reclamation were much higher than he had realised, and he records that "I pared and Burnt and Broke 100 Acres or there about that had not bin Broken before which with Paring and Burning, Liming and Grass seeding cost me over £500." He drifted ever deeper into debt, and in 1857 his creditors forced him to sell all his livestock. The next year he left the moor, and, his mind unhinged by anxiety, took to the roads as a tramp, abandoning his family. Though Hannam was no doubt an extreme case, his experience suggests that the costs of reclaiming Exmoor may have been high in human as well as financial terms.[15]

The western towns

The towns in this part of Somerset are fewer and smaller than elsewhere in the county. For people living on the southern Quantocks and the Brendons, Taunton was the main market, while for people living around the northern and eastern Quantocks, Bridgwater was the centre of attraction. The true western towns are Dunster, Minehead, Watchet and Dulverton. It is

[15] Ibid., pp. 237–91.

noteworthy that proximity to the sea was important for three of them: Minehead and Watchet are ports, and Dunster was a port in medieval times, when the river Avill was still navigable up to the town. Thus Dulverton, the market centre for southern Exmoor, is the only real inland town. Ports were very important in this region where the roads were so bad. Travellers and goods frequently went by ship between Watchet, Minehead and Porlock rather than use the inadequate roads. The cross-Channel shipping trade with Wales was also popular, especially for importing coal and exporting food.

Dunster

This little town, which had a population of only 815 in 1971, is one of the most attractive in the region, and has changed very little in modern times, so that it still shows many of the characteristics of the old west Somerset towns. (see Plate 46) It seems to owe its origin to three causes which were important in town formation—seaborne trade, the presence of a castle, and the presence of a monastery. Situated on the coastal plain at the gateway to the western hills, it had a small port on the river Avill which used to be wider and deeper than it is now. This port area has now disappeared, but it was situated at the foot of the rugged hill on which the castle was built. The Mohun family probably converted a Saxon fortress into a Norman castle of the motte-and-bailey type, after the Norman conquest. The castle still stands and, although it contains many medieval features, none of the masonry of the stone-built castle known to have existed in 1138 has survived the frequent rebuildings since that date. The descendants of the Mohuns sold the castle to the Luttrell family in 1376, and they remained the owners until recently, when they gave the castle to the National Trust. Originally Dunster was simply an agricultural village lying to the north of the castle along Castle Hill and Church Street, but with the establishment of a Benedictine priory (before 1177) a little to the north of the castle, a further prospect for urban growth arose, as such places always attracted pilgrims and visitors. (The priory was dissolved in 1539, and only a tithe barn and dovecot now survive.)

The Mohuns set up a borough in the thirteenth century, and the cloth trade developed. A fulling mill was recorded c. 1259, and as early as 1266 "Dunsters" were recorded as a specific type of cloth. Owing to the constricted site between the castle and the priory, development proceeded in a linear fashion both northwards and southwards. Thus a broad market street (High Street) was laid out to the north of the castle, while further expansion occurred to the south-west along West Street. Later a new street, Water Street, connected West Street to the river Avill, and south of the river further medieval development occurred around Gallox Street. There is evidence that the town shrank in the sixteenth century, when ships became larger and could no longer ascend the river to Dunster, and began to use the port of Minehead instead. The old port area has now disappeared and has been included in the park of Dunster Castle. There was formerly a small suburb beyond Gallox Bridge, and another to the north-east of the High Street, where there was a chapel dedicated to St Thomas. Although most of the buildings in the town are of seventeenth- and eighteenth-century date, there are some ten of medieval origin (one of the best being a row of tile-hung medieval tenements, mistakenly called the Nunnery). Since there has been little modern development, the form and shape of the town is still medieval, even if its appearance is not, and for tourists it is one of the most popular towns in Somerset.[16]

Minehead

Topographically and scenically Minehead is one of the most interesting towns in Somerset, despite a good deal of modern development which has greatly altered its original character. Its name has nothing to do with mining, but is a corruption of the old British word *mynydd*, meaning hill, referring to the immense headland lying behind the town. The topographical interest of Minehead lies in its development from three originally separate settlements none of which had an urban character in 1086. All are probably extremely ancient. The

[16] Aston and Leech, *Somerset Towns*, pp. 45–50.

original settlements were known as Quay Town, High Town and Lower Town. Quay Town lay along the coast, and the original harbour was probably a little further south than the present one, which was built (or perhaps rebuilt) in the 1690s, when the Luttrells obtained a statute from William III to enlarge and repair the harbour.

High Town lay on the slopes of the hill around the church of St Michael, where many picturesque old cob and thatched cottages survive along the steep lanes (some of them stepped) leading up to the church. About half a mile to the south of High Town (and about the same distance inland from the sea) lay Lower Town, with its buildings straggling around a roughly rectangular market-place. There is no evidence of planned expansion, and the town seems to have grown up naturally along the ancient network of lanes and paths. After great prosperity in the early eighteenth century, when its ships traded as far afield as the West Indies and Virginia, the town declined somewhat (its population fell from 1,800 in 1705 to 1,128 in 1783). By 1791, when a serious fire occurred, many houses were already empty or ruined, and another fire in 1815 caused further damage, but in the nineteenth century a slow recovery began, as Minehead became popular as a tourist resort, especially after the arrival of the railway in 1874. Residential development filled up the gaps between the three original settlements, and wide new streets, like the Parade, were built to connect Lower Town with Quay Town. Expansion along the sea-front linked the railway station in the east with the harbour in the west. By 1901 the population had reached 2,782. However, it was only in the present century that the rate of growth became significant. By 1971 there were 8,055 residents, but the influx of summer tourists provides a much higher seasonal population.[17]

Watchet

Unlike Minehead, Watchet was an ancient port with a history going back to Saxon times. However, it is not situated on such

---

[17] F. Hancock, *Minehead in the County of Somerset: a history of the parish, the manor and the port* (1903).

an attractive part of the coast and consequently has not been so popular with tourists as Minehead. Its 1971 population was only 2,900. Watchet is still a working commercial port, which handles not only imported raw materials for its large local paper mill but also a wide variety of imports and exports to places as far afield as Portugal, the U.S.S.R., Zambia and Malaysia. The value of its harbour has nearly tripled from £2,285 in 1955/6 to £6,446 in 1971/2, (inflation, of course, affected the figures but this was not too serious before 1973).

Topographically, the old heart of the town lay in a rectangle behind the harbour, on slightly rising ground which it is thought may be the remains of a former promontory extending out into the area now occupied by the harbour, and bounded on the west by the Washford river and on the east by a marsh which has subsequently been filled in and built over. The present Market Street would thus have been more in the centre of the old town, and Swain Street, running north-south, would have been its main thoroughfare. If this theory is correct, the original Saxon *burh* would have needed walls only on the south side, across the neck of the promontory between the river and the marsh (roughly where Mill Street and Anchor Street now run). However, the remains of walls have not yet been found. Most of the buildings in the old part of the town appear to be of eighteenth-century or nineteenth-century date, but, as is the case of so many towns, these may be later façades fronting much older buildings.

Watchet enjoyed considerable prosperity in the period 1850 to 1880, when the harbour was rebuilt to take 500-ton sailing vessels carrying the iron ore from the mines on the Brendon Hills, which reached the port by the West Somerset Mineral Railway (the remains of the mines and the railway are discussed in the next section). After the end of iron-mining in the 1880s, the town's prosperity was threatened, but the growth of several modern industries enabled its expansion to continue, and the modern built-up area in the south-east of the town is now larger than the area of the old borough.[18]

[18] A. C. Wedlake, *A History of Watchet* (1973).

Dulverton

This attractive little town, nestling in the Barle valley at the foot of Exmoor, is quite a contrast to Watchet. It has a population of only 1,346, and is to a considerable extent dependent on its extensive summer tourist trade. The river Barle flows through a picturesque valley, flanked by wooded hills. Dulverton does not seem to have been more than a village in 1086, and the first reference to its urban status was in 1306, when King Edward I granted a market and a three-day fair to William de Hugteburgh at Dulverton. The topography of the town suggests some attempts at planning at about this time, because it seems that the town may originally have been built around a large market-place stretching from the church almost down to the river. This is the area now occupied by High Street, Queen Street and Broad Street, so that there has been considerable encroachment on the original market-place. The topography of the medieval town requires further investigation.

Dulverton had a cloth industry, but after the whole town was given to the Augustinian priory at Taunton in 1340, it seems to have stagnated. In 1555 it was said to be "in decay and the poor inhabitants in great want", and as late as 1791 it consisted merely of "two streets, paved, with channels of water down them". Most of the buildings appear to be of nineteenth-century date, but here again a detailed survey might reveal older buildings behind more recent façades. There has been very little modern development (and that mainly in a new suburb to the east), and so the town retains much of its medieval plan and shape, except for encroachments in the original market-place, most of which probably originally took place in Tudor and Stuart times. The medieval bridge over the river Barle is a scheduled ancient monument.[19]

Industrial and post-industrial landscapes

Except for the paper mill, shirt factory and other light industries around Watchet, there is at present little industrial activity in the western hills, but it was not always so. At various

[19] F. J. Shell, *Dulverton and District* (1924).

times, but specially during the nineteenth century, mining for mineral ores was carried on extensively. The most important area was on the Brendon Hills between Luxborough and Withiel Florey, where iron ore was mined in a large way in the mid-nineteenth century. A secondary area was around the Quantocks, where copper mining was more important than iron, though there were a few small iron mines. The main copper mine was at Dodington near Nether Stowey in the north-east Quantocks. As we have previously noted, a great effort was also made to exploit iron ore on the Knight estate on Exmoor, but, despite a considerable investment by the Dowlais Iron Company of South Wales, all the finds of ore proved to be very small and quite uncommercial. Frederic Knight was reluctant to accept this, and believed that, if he could construct a railway from central Exmoor down to the quay at Porlock Weir, other iron companies would be attracted to Exmoor. However, he was unable to finance the construction of the railway, though faint signs of the course which he laid out for it may be seen in places, most notably on Elsworthy Hill south of Larkbarrow. Visible remains of iron-mining activity are scanty.

The development on the Brendon Hills was, however, quite different. From the mid-1850s to 1879 the hills were a major supplier of ore to the Ebbw Vale iron and steel works, and a special railway (the West Somerset Mineral Line) was built to take the ore from the mines to the harbour at Watchet. The line was built between 1856 and 1861 (Fig. 23), and ran eastwards for about three and a half miles along the crest of the hills from the mines around Gupworthy and Langham Hill to the settlement at Brendon Hill. (Later it was joined by a short tramway which came from the mines further east around Burrow Farm and Raleigh's Cross.) At Brendon Hill the line plunged down the north scarp of the hills on a huge inclined plane three-quarters of a mile long. It descended 800 feet (at a gradient of 1 in 4) from the crest of the hills down to the valley of the Washford river at Comberow Farm, and thence to Watchet harbour. The wagons were raised and lowered on the incline by cables attached to massive drums eighteen feet in diameter, which were operated by steam power. They were situated in an

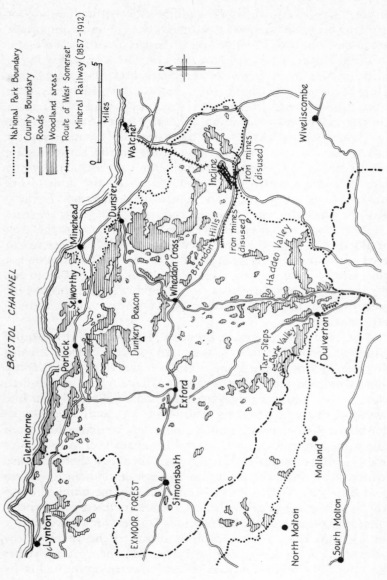

Fig. 23. Exmoor: woodlands and former iron ore mining areas

engine-house at the top of the incline. After a chequered career of closures and re-openings, the iron mines were finally abandoned in 1911, and the railway tracks were taken up in 1917–18 to provide wartime scrap metal.[20]

It is interesting (and encouraging) to see how quickly the natural landscape has re-asserted itself and practically obliterated all signs of this industrial activity. It has, of course, been assisted by deliberate re-planting of trees by private owners and the Forestry Commission. Evidence of the mines themselves is now quite hard to find, and the great incline has been so overgrown by trees that its course is unlikely to be spotted by anyone who does not know of its existence—except perhaps at the very top, where the engine-house was partly rebuilt in the late 1930s. Virtually all signs of the railway from Watchet southwards to Roadwater have also vanished, but from Roadwater to Comberow its track has been converted into a road, although few motorists would be likely to notice that they were on an old railway, because most of the stations and other railway buildings have been put to new uses. The old station at Roadwater, now converted into a bungalow, does, however, retain enough of its former character to be recognisable.

A similar return to earlier conditions has occurred at the site of the old copper mines south of Dodington on the eastern side of the Quantocks, near Nether Stowey. These were never very extensive or very deep, and during the two periods in which they were worked (1786–1802 and 1817–20) they failed to make a profit. However, two engine-houses, which still survive, were erected in the later period, and although the ruins of one of these are plainly visible from the main A39 road near Dodington, other signs of mining activity can only be discerned after careful searching. In comparison with other former mining areas, such as the Tamar valley, dividing Devon and Cornwall, where the remains are dramatic and extensive, the visible signs of West Somerset mining are surprisingly few.

Old factories and workshops can also blend back into a pre-industrial landscape with surprising ease, as does the former

[20] R. Sellick, J. R. Hamilton and M. H. Jones, *The West Somerset Mineral Railway and the Story of the Brendon Hills Iron Mines* (1970).

tannery in Holford Combe, also near Nether Stowey (Plate 49). This is now a modern hotel, but it retains the massive water-wheel which used to turn the machinery, and the outlying tannery buildings have all been tastefully converted to other uses. Here, the outward signs of former industrial activity have been rapidly re-absorbed into the rural scene. The result is a landscape which is surprisingly similar to its pre-industrial pattern, as we shall see also in many other parts of Somerset—most notably the northern coalfield. Only those with some prior knowledge and a sharp eye for detail can fully detect the very different history which lies behind so much of the bland appearance of Somerset's post-industrial landscape.

SELECT BIBLIOGRAPHY

Orwin, C. S. and Sellick, R. J., *The Reclamation of Exmoor Forest* (1970).

MacDermot, E. T., *A History of the Forest of Exmoor* (1973).

Waite, V., *Portrait of the Quantocks* (1969).

Webber, R., *The Devon and Somerset Blackdowns* (1976).

Sixsmith, R. A., *Staple Fitzpaine and the Forest of Neroche* (1958).

Sellick, R., Hamilton, J. R. and Jones, M. H., *The West Somerset Mineral Railway and the story of the Brendon Hills Iron Mines* (1970).

8. The Mendip–Avon country

Farming and enclosure. Country houses and parks. The towns.
Mining and industrial landscapes.

THE MENDIP HILLS and the undulating country which lies between them and the river Avon had always formed a distinctive
region of Somerset even before they were severed from the
county in 1974 and joined to south Gloucestershire to form the
new county of Avon. In terms of landscape this region has
several special features. Although much of the area between the
Mendips and the Avon was enclosed by private agreements
between about 1500 and 1780, the existence of extensive areas
of rough upland common pastures, not only in Mendip, but also
on Broadfield Down, the Failand Hills and the Dundry Hills,
meant that quite a large part of the region still remained to be
enclosed by Parliamentary Act. Most of this was carried out
between 1780 and 1820, giving rise to a much more planned
type of landscape on the hills than in the valleys.

Secondly, the region has long been subjected to the urban
influences of Bristol and Bath. Initially this gave rise to farming
systems geared to supplying dairy produce, meat and vegetables
to these towns and was a primary reason for the early enclosures.
Later, many small industries were established to serve the urban
markets, such as glass production at Nailsea, iron tool-making
at Mells, and printing at Paulton, and of course the expansion of
the old-established mining and quarrying industries, which
became so dominant between 1850 and 1950, when the coalfield was at its most flourishing. Finally, with the decline of
mining (though not of quarrying) the region became the
favoured residential area for the growing suburban and commuter population of the two cities, and especially of Bristol.
The opening of the M5 motorway in the mid-1970s has brought
Clevedon and Weston-super-Mare into close contact with
Bristol, but the motorway has also brought towns like Burn-

ham-on-Sea and Bridgwater into the commuter range, and this gives some relief from the pressure for housing-sites in the villages between Bristol and Mendip. Bristol itself has also extended rapidly since 1945, and its suburbs now stretch to the foot of the Dundry Hills. Keynsham, between Bristol and Bath, has also stretched out and has almost joined up with Bristol. Its population rose from 15,000 to nearly 20,000 between 1961 and 1971. Nor is there much open countryside left along the Avon between Keynsham and Bath. Although many of the people who have recently settled in this area are commuters to Bristol and Bath, that is not the only reason why the population has grown. Equally important has been the development of new light industries (especially those concerned with electrical components, engineering, and printing) in former industrial and mining towns such as Norton-Radstock, Frome and Shepton Mallet.

The region has long had a semi-urban character, not only because of the numerous mining villages, but also because of the widespread existence of the handloom-weaving woollen industry, which caused the expansion of older villages like Pensford and Chew Magna. The density of population in the rural areas of the region is now much above the county average. The census figures for 1971 show that for all the rural areas in the old county of Somerset the average was eight people per 10 hectares (roughly 250 acres), but in the northern rural districts of Clutton and Bathavon it rose to twelve, and in Long Ashton (just south of Bristol) to twenty-three. To highlight the contrast with western Somerset, the average for Williton rural district was four, and for Dulverton rural district (including most of Exmoor) only one. (Somerset is not, of course, as lightly populated as these figures for the rural areas above might imply. The average, including the urban population, was sixteen persons per ten hectares, so that on average each inhabitant had fifteen acres.)

Farming and enclosure

In chapter 5 we looked at some of the evidence for the early enclosure of the area between Mendip and the Avon, and saw that, for instance, in a village like Norton St Philip much of the land had already been enclosed by 1606. The chronology of enclosure is, however, difficult to work out in detail. Without any Parliamentary Awards to help, we cannot always be quite sure how many settlements had open fields in the Middle Ages, though from the evidence collected by Gray it seems likely that most villages had them. He noted evidence of open fields in eleven villages between 1201 and 1609. In the period 1210 to about 1325, his evidence related to Batheaston, Weston, Lyncombe and Englishcombe, in the immediate vicinity of Bath, and to Cameley, Coleford, Mells and Wookey Hole further afield. His early seventeenth-century examples were Norton St Philip, Corston and South Stoke. In South Stoke and Corston, although enclosed land was not negligible, the open fields were still dominant, as can be seen from the examples of farmers in the following Table.

Some examples of enclosure and open-fields in Corston and South Stoke,
1608–9 (after Gray)

CORSTON

Name of farmer	Acres in Holding	Acres Enclosed	Acres in Open-fields	% Enclosed
Thomas Coxe	65¾	8¼	57½	13
John Holbye	69	15	54	22
Flower Ford	62	10	52	16
Thomas Weekes	42	11	31	24
SOUTH STOKE				
William Hedges	36½	8½	28	23
William Mercer	68½	14½	54	21
Alice Willis	40¼	8¼	32	20
John Dagger	21¾	9¾	12	45

All these eight farmers had the larger part of their land lying in the open fields, and only one—John Dagger—had more than a quarter of it enclosed.[1] Yet if we look at the map of Somerset made by Day and Masters in 1782, we can see that by that time

---

[1] H. L. Gray, *English Field Systems* (1959 ed.), pp. 30, 97–101, 439, 494–6, 524–8.

nearly all the land between Mendip and Avon had been enclosed. Clearly the seventeenth century was an important period, but a map of the main roads, such as John Ogilby's, made in 1675, shows that the highway from Bristol to Wells was unfenced for its whole distance (except for the last mile down the Mendip scarp into Wells), and presumably passed through common fields—either arable strips or open pastures and meadows—for its whole distance. It ran through Bedminster (then a village a mile to the south of Bristol) to Bishopsworth, and over the Dundry Hills to Chew Magna; thence across the area now flooded by the Chew Valley Lake (where it probably followed the course of an old Roman road), then between Compton Martin and West Harptree, and up over Mendip to Wells. There was much fertile country along this route, apparently still unenclosed. It looks as though the century 1675–1775 may have been the critical one for enclosure in this area.

Enclosure in this period was associated with the desire not only to convert land into pasture in order to keep more livestock, but also to accommodate the new arable rotations, in which wheat and barley were grown in alternation with new fodder crops like turnips and clovers. This eliminated fallows, and increased the yields of the cereals by allowing the land to be grazed and manured by livestock in the years when the fodder crops were growing. An interesting (and fairly early) example of the arrival of the new crops is provided in 1683 by the protest of one of the old school of farm bailiffs at Kilmersdon near Radstock, who complained about "new improvements" like the cultivation of "parsley-seed, clover-seed, Tray-foyle, Turnips, Buckwheat and several other fantasyes, which I doubt will not pay half the charges".[2] It did indeed take a little while for the new systems to settle into a profitable pattern, but protests of that type were soon to be outdated.

If the enclosure of the relatively fertile and sheltered lands to the north of Mendip could proceed easily by private agreements, the attack on the high plateau of Mendip itself (much of it over 800 feet high) required an organised campaign and Parliamentary authority for its success. It may not be an accident that

[2] R. Atthill, *Old Mendip* (1971), p. 29.

most of it was carried out during the wars against the American colonists (1776–83) and France (1793–1801), when food imports were threatened or cut off. The campaign was led by John Billingsley, who in 1795 wrote the report on the state of Somerset farming for the newly-created Board of Agriculture. Billingsley lived and farmed on the Mendips at Ashwick Grove, near Shepton Mallet, and was not daunted by the unpromising Mendip environment so gloomily described by Collinson in 1791. For although Collinson conceded that parts of the plateau provided good grazing for sheep and young cattle, other parts were

> covered with heath, fern and furze. The air, especially in winter, is moist thick, and foggy, and so very cold that frost and snow inhabit these heights longer than they do almost any other parts of the county; and the few remaining trees, their leaves blasted and discoloured by the severe winds from the Channel, never attain to any considerable size.[3]

Billingsley and his like were convinced that with the growth of shelter-belts of timber and the construction of hedgerows and stone walls, these difficulties could be overcome, and productive mixed farms could be created where previously there had only been rough grazing. Between 1771 and 1813 about 24,000 acres were enclosed by Parliamentary Act, and another 3,500 acres were added in the central area of the plateau by private agreement. Williams has estimated that this involved the construction of about 1,650 miles of new fences and hedges and the creation of some fifty new farmsteads.[4] As always the cost proved to be much greater than had been anticipated, and the new farms tried to recoup their expenses by over-cropping with cereals at the expense of long-term fertility. By 1851 the situation had become so bad that Thomas Dyke Acland could write "assuredly, a large part of the Hill must be reclaimed again before it can be properly farmed."[5] Eventually a system

[3] Collinson, *History of Somerset*, III, p. 374.

[4] M. Williams, "The enclosure of the Mendip hills, 1770–1870", *Agric. Hist. Rev.*, 19 (1971), pp. 65–81.

[5] Sir Thomas Dyke Acland, "On the Farming of Somersetshire", *Journal of the Royal Agricultural Society of England*, 11 (1850), p. 666.

based primarily on livestock production was evolved, and although a few of the original farms, such as Fernhill Farm in Compton Martin parish, have been given up (it is shown on the 1887 6" O.S. map, but it is not a separate farm today), most of the new farmsteads have established themselves as successful enterprises.

Some idea of the changes which occurred in the Mendip landscape can be seen by comparing the two maps of Compton Martin (Fig. 24), which was enclosed in 1791. In 1790 the plateau consisted of open rough pasture intersected by a network of unfenced tracks meandering around the hilltop. By 1960 these had been replaced by two enclosed roads, but, more important, a substantial area of woodland had been planted to give shelter to the enclosed fields, creating a much more varied landscape than had existed in 1790. However, Billingsley's belief that the plateau would be extensively settled has not been borne out at Compton Martin. The only exception to this is the small settlement on the scarp marked "potato plots" on the 1960 map. This area, called the Wrangle, was where the commoners were given small plots in compensation for the loss of their grazing rights. These plots were mostly about half an acre in size, and a group of cottages was built to house the holders of them.[6]

Country houses and parks

Apart from enclosure, the farming countryside was subjected to two types of pressure, which increased in strength after 1700. One was the growth of rural industry, and especially coal mining, which we shall examine below, and the other was the growing fashion for extensive landscaped parks. As the work of men like William Kent and Lancelot "Capability" Brown became more fashionable, landlords vied with one another in the creation of deer parks, artificial lakes, vistas of trees, pleasure gardens, follies and the like. The spread of coal mining and of intensive agriculture to feed Bristol and Bath did not make this

[6] M. Williams, "Mendip Farming: the last three centuries", in Robin Atthill, ed., *Mendip, a New Study* (1976), pp. 111–18.

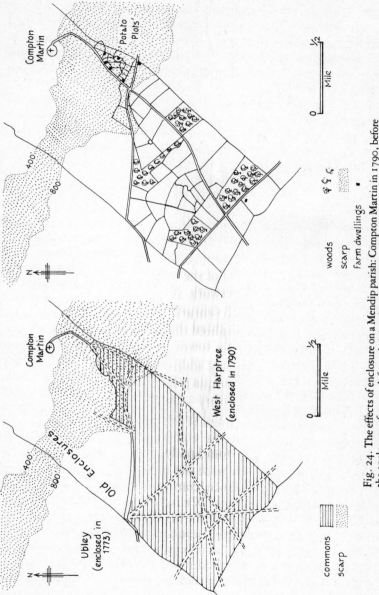

Fig. 24. The effects of enclosure on a Mendip parish: Compton Martin in 1790, before the enclosure of 1791, left; and right, fields and woods in 1960

woods

scarp

farm dwellings

commons

scarp

a particularly good area for such developments, but the fine views available in such an undulating country provided opportunities, and the region is not without some good examples of landscaped parks. Just south of Bristol is Ashton Park (now belonging to Bristol Corporation). Near Bath are Newton Park (now a teachers' training college) and just north of it, Kelston Park on a fine site overlooking the Avon. Between the Avon and Mendip are Sutton Court, Ammerdown Park (near Radstock), Mells (Plate 27), (now threatened with quarrying), and Orchardleigh, where an artificial lake covers the former village, but the ancient church survives on a small island.

The towns

The shape and functions of towns are subject to ever-changing pressures. The decline of population and trade in the late Middle Ages meant that there were more market towns than were necessary, so that some, like Axbridge or Chew Magna, declined (or at least stagnated). But these conditions also gave a renewed impetus to towns enjoying special advantages. Bristol, long the provincial capital of the west, was one such, and as its trading and financial network continued to grow with the expansion of the sixteenth century, it soon established a grip in north Somerset which blighted the chances of the other market towns in the region. Only towns with a specialised function, which could offer something additional, could hope to compete with Bristol. The best example is Bath, which was born anew in the late seventeenth century—shedding its old market and cloth-making functions, and re-emerging as a national spa. It expanded vigorously in the eighteenth century, drawing its fashionable population from London and its permanent service population from far and wide (its most famous architect, John Wood the elder, for instance, coming from Yorkshire, although he had been born in Bath). Wells, with its specialised ecclesiastical function as the seat of the bishop and his courts (as well as being a centre for quarter sessions), was another town in a favoured position which has enjoyed a modest growth.

Specialised industrial production was also a source of urban growth. Frome throve on its traditional woollen-cloth industry, and later on engineering and printing, while Norton-Radstock rose to prominence from village beginnings as the centre of the coal-mining industry. It too has survived the decline of its original source of growth, and continues to thrive on miscellaneous light industries. Finally, holiday and suburban residential facilities have caused the rapid growth of Clevedon and Portishead.

Bath (Plate 41)

It is not entirely clear why Bath was able to establish its dominance over all other fashionable spas in the eighteenth century. It was farther from London than Epsom or Tunbridge Wells, though a good turnpike road minimised this inconvenience. Its waters enjoyed a high medical reputation and its famous Master of Ceremonies, Richard (Beau) Nash (1674–1761) perhaps ensured that its frenzied gambling never became too scandalous. Perhaps not least of its attractions was the inspired architectural entrepreneurship of its great developer, John Wood the elder. The city grew at an astonishing rate. From a population of some 3,000 in 1700, it had reached 10,000 permanent residents by 1750, and was catering to another 12,000 who thronged it during the spring and autumn seasons. The first census (1801) showed that it had 32,200 permanent inhabitants and was the ninth largest city in England, bigger than such places as Sheffield (31,314), Hull (29,516) and Newcastle-on-Tyne (28,366), and far overshadowing such industrial giants of the future as Preston (11,886), Sunderland (12,412) and Bolton (12,549).

It was, of course, during this period of rapid growth that Bath became, what it still is today despite all the pressures of modern development, the finest Georgian city in England. The economic conditions for Bath's metamorphosis into an elegant classical city matured in the 1720s, and it was perhaps partly luck that brought the young John Wood back to Bath from Yorkshire at this critical moment. He had both the business acumen and the artistic talent necessary to preside over a series of imaginative developments which still dominate the city's architecture.

Although Wood hoped to be able to plan Bath according to the classical precepts of the Italian architect Palladio, he was in fact constrained by the availability of land. The land within the walls of the ancient city was owned or controlled by the corporation and was not made available, nor was land available in most of the surrounding countryside. The district was let on leases for three lives, which prevented the owners from selling land, even had they wished to do so. There was, however, one important estate, the eighty-five-acre Barton estate on the north-west side of the town, whose owner, Robert Gay, a successful London barber-surgeon, was anxious to increase his income by development. He and his family leased some forty acres on ninety-nine-year leases to John Wood the elder and his son (John Wood the younger) between 1728 and 1766. It was by sub-letting these leases to builders that the Woods were able to obtain the capital they needed for their part of the development, which consisted of laying out streets and squares, designing the houses and supplying essential services like water and drainage. Through covenants in these leases the Woods were able to control the style and standards of all the houses that were built on the land they had leased.

This accident of land-ownership ensured that Bath's Georgian expansion would be primarily in a north-western direction, but it did not, except in the most general terms, determine what shape that expansion would take. This depended primarily on John Wood the elder. He was a complex character who was driven by conflicting pressures and ideals. As a self-made entrepreneur he was concerned to make money (which he did) and to achieve recognition and success: yet he was also (in the words of R. S. Neale, the historian of Bath, "driven by a religious-aesthetic vision of a world different from the real one in which he was condemned to live and work", so that "his contribution to the Bath townscape is a statement about a system of religious belief and of a social order which was threatened" by the very people, including Wood himself, for whom he was building. He was called upon to provide elegant housing for "the rich, the powerful, the libertine, the gambler", and yet he believed that classical architecture was divinely inspired and that by building in this style he was carrying out a Christian duty to introduce God's conception of beauty and order into an earthly city. It is as if he had hoped to purify the worldlings who inhabited his buildings through the inspiration of their architectural style and planning. Both his masterpieces, Queen Square (1729–36) and the Circus (1754–8), were consciously planned with this aim in view. It was this strange conflict in his innermost being which, Neale believes, may account for the extraordinary originality and creativity of Wood's work at Bath.[7]

John Wood the elder died in 1754 and his work was continued by his son, John Wood the younger (1727–81), who brought it to a crowning glory with the Royal Crescent (1767–75). This has been called "the most dramatic building in Bath and one of the great set pieces of European architecture".[8]

By the end of the eighteenth century, classical Bath had not only spread up the north-western hills, with graceful terraces like Somerset Place and Lansdown Crescent, but had also expanded to the west and the south-west, with developments along Pulteney Street and the North and South Parades.

Bath's role as a fashionable spa began to decline with the re-opening of Europe after Waterloo (1815), and although it continued to grow modestly in the nineteenth century (reaching a population of 50,000 in 1901), its development henceforth depended much more on its little-known industrial activity than on the fashionable world. Crane-building, printing, corset-making and mixed engineering became prominent, and an important industrial suburb grew up along the river Avon to the west of the old city, and eventually engulfed the former villages of Twerton and Weston.

Yet the fabric of Georgian Bath survived, and it was not until the phase of post-war reconstruction in the 1950s and 1960s that it was seriously menaced. In that period some two thousand of Bath's stock of eight thousand Georgian houses were demolished to make way for flats, offices and shops, and it was even proposed to drive a motorway along the riverside and

[7] R. S. Neale, "Society, belief and the building of Bath", in C. W. Chalklin and M. A. Havinden, eds., *Rural Change and Urban Growth, Essays in English Regional History in Honour of W. G. Hoskins* (1974), pp. 253–80.
[8] C. Robertson, *Bath, an Architectural Guide* (1975), p. 109.

through the heart of the city (partly in a tunnel). Fortunately a massive protest campaign was organised locally and nationally, which led to a change of policy in 1973, and a recognition that the architectural heritage of Bath was of national—and international—importance. The most serious threats were stopped, but the struggle to maintain Bath as a living city without destroying its historic fabric continues—for mere preservation is not enough. Even Bath cannot survive simply as a museum, although it was originally built for tourists and pleasure-seekers. It is this continuing function which should ensure the survival of Bath as an organic city.[9]

Wells

The history of Wells is quite different from that of Bath, and its early history is shrouded in some obscurity. At the time of the Domesday Survey in 1086 Wells was not mentioned as a town, but it contained four manors with 132 recorded inhabitants—implying a population of 500–600. It occupies a well-watered and fertile site at the foot of Mendip, and it would seem that the original farming settlement probably grew up along the road from Glastonbury to Bristol, where it crossed the little stream which flows south-westwards from the springs, or wells, from which the town is named. As we saw in chapter 4, the town received two charters from its bishops (in 1166 and 1191), but what is not clear is why the bishopric had become established at Wells in the first place. It seems that the first church (dedicated to St Andrew) was built by Aldhelm around the year 700, and it may be that he selected the site because the wells were already regarded as holy, and were possibly a centre of pre-Christian religious worship. A charter of 774 mentions that Wells had become a minster, or centre from which a group of priests served surrounding villages, in an age before parish churches had been built and endowed.[10]

Wells must have been a thriving minster because in 909 it was decided to take Somerset out of the large diocese of

[9] A. Ferguson, "Bath", in *European Heritage, 3, Problems of Historic Towns* (1974), pp. 28–35.

[10] R. W. Dunning, ed., *Christianity in Somerset* (1975), p. 3.

Sherborne and to establish a new bishopric at Wells. The new bishop, Athelm, was appointed by King Edward the Elder. It is not clear why Wells, then still a small place, was chosen. Amongst its advantages were its roughly central position (almost halfway from Somerton and Ilchester to Bath) and its closeness to the royal palace at Cheddar, but the holy wells may have enjoyed a popular religious significance which has gone unrecorded.

The history of the town's topography is at present not fully understood, and the possible course of development (shown in Fig. 25) is suggested merely as a hypothesis based partly on the shape of property boundaries on old maps, and partly on documentary and archaeological evidence. The old road from Glastonbury to Bristol entered the town along the street called Southover, and then appears to have crossed the stream either by St John Street or Mill Street before turning eastwards to run up the High Street towards the cathedral. The present cathedral had not yet been built (work began c. 1184 and it was consecrated in 1239), and the road probably ran under where it now stands, before turning northwards again to ascend Mendip along the course of East Liberty. (This was the old road to Bristol which ran over Mendip via the Castle of Comfort Inn, Compton Martin and Chew Magna, and which was later replaced by the A39 via Chewton Mendip, Farrington Gurney and Pensford). Recent excavations by Dr Warwick Rodwell in the area to the south of the cathedral have revealed the remains of the old Saxon cathedral which was situated at the end of the High Street and on the same alignment, unlike the present cathedral, which is a little to the north of the High Street and on a slightly different alignment. [11]

For a short period between 1088 and 1136 the see was transferred to Bath, because Archbishop Lanfranc liked his bishops to reside in cities and not villages. However, with the election of Robert of Lewes as bishop (1136–66), Wells regained its cathedral status (although still sharing the title with Bath), and he was probably responsible for turning it into a town by laying out a planned extension between the old village

[11] See S. Minnitt and B. J. Murless, "Somerset Archaeology, 1978", in *SANHS*, 123 (1979), p. 94.

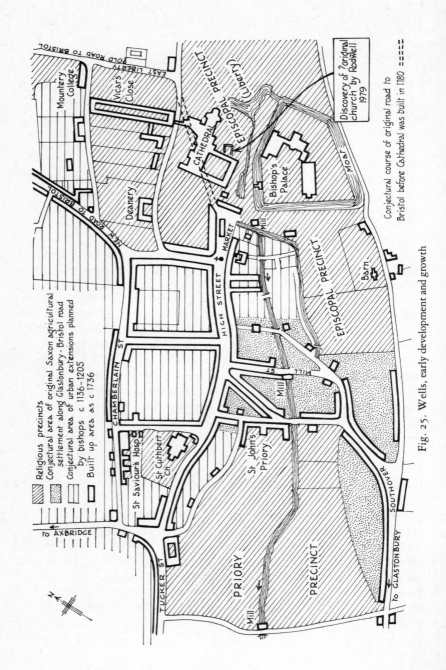

Fig. 25. Wells, early development and growth

Religious precincts

Conjectural area of original Saxon agricultural
settlement along Glastonbury - Bristol road

Conjectural area of urban extensions planned
by bishops c 1136-1205

Built up area as c 1736

to AXBRIDGE

TUCKER ST

CHAMBERLAIN ST

St Saviour's Hosp.

St Cuthbert
Ch.

St John's Priory

PRIORY

PRECINCT

to GLASTONBURY

SOUTHOVER

Mill

MILL ST

Mill

HIGH STREET

MARKET

Mill

Barn

EPISCOPAL PRECINCT

Bishop's Palace

Moat

EPISCOPAL
(Liberty)

CATHEDRAL
PRECINCT

Deanery

Vicars' Close

Mountery
College

EAST LIBERTY

OLD ROAD TO BRISTOL

NEW ROAD TO BRISTOL

Discovery of ?original
church by Rodwell
1979

Conjectural course of original road to
Bristol before Cathedral was built in 1180

and the cathedral (the rectangular area on the map to the north of the High Street where burgage plots were laid out). The bishop also probably extended the episcopal liberty northwards by diverting the Bristol road to a more northerly alignment.

As we have seen, the newly-planned town was given a second charter in 1191 by Bishop Reginald de Bohun (1174–99) and another by Bishop Savaric in 1201, and its market-place was established near the cathedral. Later, in 1210, St John's Priory was founded as a hospital with its own precinct on the western side of the town, and Tucker Street to the north of it shows that fulling (or tucking) had become a town craft (probably in the thirteenth century, when water-powered fulling mills were introduced to Somerset).

The west front of the cathedral was one of the earliest façades in England (c. 1230) to be elaborately decorated with sculpture (originally brightly painted and gilded), and it must have made Wells Cathedral one of the most dramatic sights in medieval England. Even today, much damaged by time, it remains superbly impressive, and has been enhanced by the wide green in front of it, which used to be a cemetery in the Middle Ages. The grandeur and wealth of the cathedral Liberty seems to have caused problems in the relationship with the town, for in about 1340 Bishop Ralph obtained a licence to build walls and a moat around his palace as well as "to erect towers, to divert streets and to place posterns and gates which could be closed at night". By this means the whole of the Liberty was enclosed by stone walls. He also built the Vicars' Close (1348), which was provided with a covered bridge (over the chain gate) to enable the vicars to enter the Cathedral without having to cross the street. Perhaps the bishop was mindful of the fate of Bury St Edmunds Abbey in Suffolk which had been utterly destroyed by its exploited and enraged townsmen in 1327. The city of Wells did not finally escape from episcopal control until the charter of Queen Elizabeth I in 1589.

Although the buildings in the cathedral precinct have been repeatedly enlarged and embellished since the early Middle Ages, the town of Wells has not grown much beyond its medieval core. Despite some development at its western end, it still retains much of the plan and character of a medieval cathedral town, with the countryside extending right up to the cathedral precinct on the southern side.[12]

Frome

Frome presents another contrast to Bath and Wells. It had long been a successful market town occupying an important cross-ing-point on the river Frome where main roads from Bath to the south intersected with east-west roads leading from Mendip and Wells into Wiltshire, but in the late seventeenth century it enjoyed a vigorous prosperity and expansion as a cloth-making town. When Defoe described it, c. 1725, he was deeply impres-sed—as he was with all the area involved in the broadcloth manufacture. The countryside in this region was

> . . . low and flat, being a rich, enclosed country, full of rivers and towns, and infinitely populous, insomuch, that some of the market towns are equal to cities in bigness and superior to them in number of people . . . these towns are interspersed with a very great number of villages . . . hamlets and scattered houses, in which, generally speaking, the spinning work of all this manufacture is performed by the poor people; the master clothiers who generally live in the greater towns, sending out the wool weekly to their houses, by their servants and horses, and, at the same time, bringing back the yarn that they have spun and finished, which then is fitted to the loom.
>
> The increasing and flourishing circumstances of this trade, are happily visible by the great concourse of people to, and increase of buildings and inhabitants in these principal clothing towns where this trade is carried on. The town of Froom, or as it is written in our maps, Frome Selwood, is a specimen of this, which is so prodigiously increased within these last twenty or thirty years, that they have built a new church, and so many new streets of houses, and those houses are so full of inhabitants, that Frome is now reckoned to have more people in it, than the city of Bath, and some say, than

[12] Aston and Leech, *Somerset Towns*, pp. 147–54.

even Salisbury itself, and it is very likely to be one of the greatest and wealthiest towns in England.

I call it an inland town, because it is particularly distinguished as such, being, not only no sea-port, but not near any sea-port, having no manner of communication by water, no navigable river at it, or near it. Its trade is wholly clothing, and the cloths they make, are, generally speaking, all conveyed to London; and, if we may believe common fame, there are above ten thousand people in Frome now, more than lived in it twenty years ago, and yet it was a considerable town then too. [13]

We may suspect Defoe of exaggeration, and his suggestion that Frome was larger than Bath and Salisbury was no doubt fanciful, but his references to rapid increases in population and the building of new streets of houses have been amply borne out by recent studies of the topography of the town. Roger Leech has shown how a whole new planned suburb of artisans' houses was developed by a family of clothiers, the Yerburys, between 1665 and 1725. This was the area of Frome known as Trinity, and may be clearly seen on Fig. 26 as the gridiron of streets to the west of Trinity Street. Many of the original houses still survive, and there was another suburb to the east of Trinity Street which has been recently demolished to make room for redevelopment. As can be seen, the area of new settlement in the seventeenth and eighteenth centuries was larger than the original medieval town. Seventeenth-century planned suburbs of this type are very rare, and that in Frome is of great interest as an example of planned layouts and house types. Trinity church is the one referred to by Defoe. The cloth industry has now left Frome, but it has been replaced by a range of new industries, like printing and electrical engineering, so that the town maintains its character as a small but vigorous industrial centre in a rural setting. [14]

[13] P. Rogers, ed., *Defoe's Tour*, pp. 260–1.
[14] R. Leech, *The Trinity Area of Frome, Somerset. A 17th and early 18th century housing development* (forthcoming). I am most grateful to Roger Leech for kindly allowing me to use some of his work prior to publication.

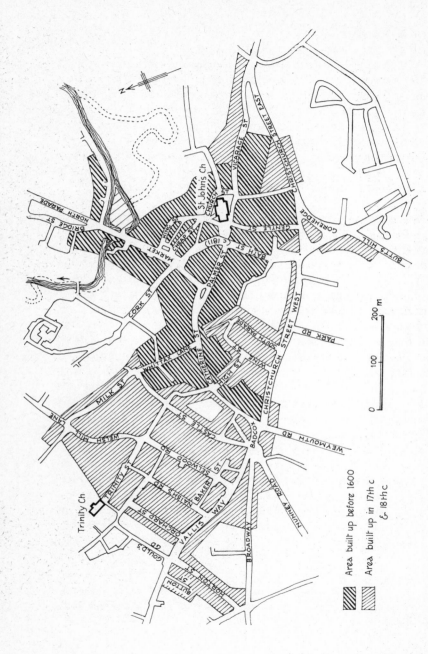

Fig. 26. Frome, development between 1600 and 1800

Area built up before 1600

Area built up in 17th c
& 18th c

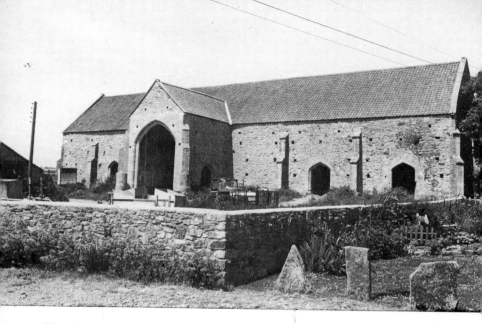

Plate 34 Tithe barn at Woodspring Priory near Weston-super-Mare. A magnificent example of medieval building for a practical purpose, yet revealing grace and style. The Priory's tenants brought their corn rents here.

Plate 35 A cattle shed and yard near Kilve on the north-west coast. The sturdy stone pillars and walls show that even mundane buildings could be given a touch of elegance.

Plate 36 Meare fishhouse, near Glastonbury. This medieval fishhouse belonged to Glastonbury Abbey. When it was built the low land behind it formed Meare pool, a large lake (drained c. 1630). The Abbey's fishermen lived on the second storey since the ground floor was liable to flooding.

Plate 37 A rare example of a small medieval tithe barn, at West Bradley, east of Glastonbury. Built for the Abbey in the fifteenth century, it incorporates the remains of a dovecot.

Plate 38 Mill and millhouse at Haselbury Plucknett, near Crewkerne. These handsome buildings in golden Ham stone illustrate the importance of watermills before the age of steam. The water-wheel was behind the mill.

Plate 39 Village lock-up at Pensford, south of Keynsham. Built in the eighteenth century, it was mainly used to house drunkards overnight.

Plate 40 Medieval houses in Axbridge. The house on the right-hand of the street at the end, fronting the market square, is misleadingly called "King John's hunting lodge". Actually a fifteenth-century merchant's house, it is now the town museum and is well worth a visit. Axbridge still retains the character of a Tudor market town.

Axbridge (Plate 40)

This little town has had a very different history from that of
Frome. It was a Saxon *burh*, called *Axanbrycg* in the Burghal
Hidage, a list of *burhs* compiled in c.AD 910. The name is
curious, since the river Axe is now about a mile to the south-
west of the town, but an old meander must have come close to
the town before the Levels were drained, and over this there
must have been a bridge. Axbridge was originally a fortress
protecting the western side of the royal manor of Cheddar,
where the Saxon kings had an important palace. It was probably
a minor port also, and the development of two new ports a little
downstream (Rackley, c. 1179–89, and Lower Weare, c. 1195–
1225) was probably connected with silting at the port of Axbridge. Neither of these ports throve, and they decayed long
before the drainage of the Levels brought navigation on the Axe
to an end. The site of Rackley (in Compton Bishop parish) has
disappeared almost totally, there being only a few farms and
cottages now on the river bank where the little port once stood.
Lower Weare still exists as a hamlet on the main road (A38)
from Bristol to Taunton, but it is hard to believe it was once a
borough with a market.[15]

Axbridge throve on the cloth trade in the Middle Ages and a
little later, but by the seventeenth century it had entered a
period of stability, since when it has altered little. As a result it
has a particularly fine collection of buildings of historic interest,
and maintains much of its original street plan. Apparently the
Saxon *burh* lay on the low lands to the south of the market-
place, but the medieval borough developed on an east-west axis
along the road at the foot of Mendip, connecting Wells to the
pass through the hills between Axbridge and Compton Bishop.
Almost every building in West Street, High Street and Market
Square is on the official list of historically interesting buildings.
There are three of medieval date, several which are Tudor and
Elizabethan, and many which appear to be Stuart or Georgian,
but more thorough investigation could well show these to be
later façades to older buildings behind them.[16]

[15] Aston and Leech, *Historic Towns*, pp. 7–11, 85–6, 117–18.
[16] Ibid., p. 8.

Clevedon and Portishead

These two towns were villages until the nineteenth century, when their attractive locations near the coast led to development as holiday resorts, places for retirement, and ultimately as commuter towns. In neither case was the original village on the sea coast. At Clevedon it was about half a mile inland, stretching along the road to Bristol beneath the shelter of Dial Hill, although its ancient church was (and is) on a low grassy hill by the sea, about a mile to the west of the village. Nineteenth-century development began along the sea coast to the north of the original village. The earliest villas were aligned to face south-west, with a view down the Bristol Channel. Gradually the villas spread southwards over the hill to join up with the original village. Coleridge was an early-nineteenth-century resident who lived at Myrtle Cottage at the end of the old village, and his lines from "Sibylline Leaves" were quoted in Murray's *Guide to Somersetshire* in 1869 to help popularise the place:

> Low was our pretty cot; our tallest rose
> Peeped at the chamber window. We could hear
> At silent noon, and eve, and early morn,
> The sea's faint murmur. In the open air
> Our myrtle blossom'd; and across the porch
> Thick jasmins twined: the little landscape round
> Was green and woody, and refresh'd the eye.
> It was a spot which you might aptly call
> The Valley of Seclusion.[17]

Yet Clevedon has never become popular in the same way as Weston-super-Mare, and it remains something of a treasure-house of Victorian domestic architecture.

The old village of Portishead was more than a mile inland, lying in the eastern lee of Portishead Down, but connected to the sea by Portishead Pill, a tidal estuary now converted into a modern dock entered by a lock. This enables ships to supply fuel

[17] Murray's *Handbook for Travellers in Wiltshire, Dorsetshire and Somersetshire* (1869), p. 343.

to the immense electric power station which has been built there, whose towers dominate the scenery for miles around. This industrial development has rather spoiled the Victorian resort which had grown up between the old village and the sea. Murray's *Guide to Somersetshire* in 1869 described it as

> a . . . pretty watering place and harbour in the Bristol Channel . . . [which] is growing in favour with visitors seeking health and pleasure; the site is eminently picturesque, the temperature equable, the air pure and envigorating. There is a good hotel near the pier; baths, lodging houses, etc. Delightful excursions may be made in the neighbourhood. The harbour is sheltered by a densely-wooded hill, rising abruptly out of the sea, commanding views of the Channel from the North Devon Foreland, the mountain-coast of Wales, King Road, and the River Severn. In the deep-water entrance to the estuary on the South-East a pier, of timber and artificial granite, has been constructed, used by Irish, Welsh, and other steamers, to avoid the tidal delays of the River Avon.[18]

To the west of the dock, and facing the sea, lies the attractively wooded East Wood Hill, culminating at its western end in Portishead Point where there is a lighthouse. Victorian villas abound on the lower slopes of the hill, and more modern development has taken place around the artificial marine lake next to Woodhill Bay on the westward-facing coast. Suburban development has sprawled rather extensively along the hilly coast to the west of the town.[19]

Mining and industrial landscapes

The term "industrial landscape" is something of a misnomer here, as in West Somerset, for although the landscape between Mendip and Bath shows signs of its industrial past (and contains substantial pockets of modern industry), it is visually rather a post-industrial scene. One can hardly believe that the visible

[18] Ibid., p. 339.
[19] See R. Whitlock, *Somerset*, p. 189.

signs of mining, relatively recently ended, should be so few (Plate 50). The last remnants of lead mining ceased on Mendip in 1908, and even though the last coal-mines closed only in 1973, it is already becoming difficult to see the explicit signs of mining activity, except perhaps for the long rows of miners' cottages in places like Radstock and Paulton, which have an unmistakable "coalfield" appearance. But even the spoil-tips of the mines are rapidly disappearing beneath a green mantle of grass, bushes and trees, as are the numerous little canals, railways and tramways which once connected the mines to the main railway lines and rivers. The density of settlement—the way in which villages and hamlets spread out and nearly touched one another, and the elaborate network of roads and trackways—indicates that this is not a landscape which has evolved simply from farming. The availability of a labour supply, and probably the ease of planning permission, makes the area attractive to modern industry. There is a constant immigration of new firms, or subsidiaries of firms, such as Clark's large shoe factory at Westfield on the southern outskirts of Radstock.

Mendip lead has been so famous since Roman times that we might expect to see considerable signs of mining activity in the landscape, especially as the lead was mainly obtained by open-cast mining. In fact, the remains (the "gruffy" ground, named after the trenches or grooves that were dug to obtain the lead), though extensive on Mendip, are not easy to identify, except in one or two places. This is because the growth of timber and bushes tends to obscure the sites. The best known of these are at Charterhouse, to the east of the former Roman mining town, and at Priddy to the east of the village. These places are the sites of "mineries" where the lead was smelted into pigs (often using coal from nearby mines such as those at Bishop's Sutton). The mining area was anciently divided into four sectors, each one controlled by one of the Lords Royal of Mendip who took 10 per cent of the lead, and administered claims, licences, etc. by an ancient mining law at special courts. The lord of Charterhouse had his minery there, while two other lords—the bishop of Wells and the lord of Chewton—had their mineries almost adjacent, at Priddy. The fourth minery, pertaining to the lord of Harptree, was on Smithan Hill, above East Harptree.[20] Lead mining was carried out on a small scale by men who were often farmers as well. Production seems to have reached its peak between 1600 and 1670 and then to have declined steadily until about 1800, when mining finally ceased.

There was, however, an important revival in the mid-nineteenth century, based not on renewed mining activity but on re-smelting the extensive spoil-heaps left by the old miners. Because the pre-1800 methods of smelting were very inefficient, much ore still remained in these heaps, and for fifty years or so Cornish mining engineers were able to thrive by re-smelting. Little of their buildings and equipment is visible now, but some long flue tunnels survive at Charterhouse. These were horizontal flues built along the ground between the furnace and its chimney. The smoke from the furnaces which smelted the lead contained much lead vapour, and this could be precipitated on the sides of the flue as it passed along towards the chimney. This lead deposit was then collected and sold. One of these tall furnace chimneys (built in 1867) survives at Smithan Hill, East Harptree, and may still be seen rising above the recently planted forest which surrounds it. The minery areas at Charterhouse and Priddy, though, are wild and extensive, and the mounds of shining black slag can give the landscape a moon-like appearance.

Zinc mining was important between about 1566 and 1850. It began on Worle Hill, behind Weston-super-Mare, where calamine ore (from which zinc was extracted) was first found. The hill today is pock-marked with pits (and also with limestone quarries). The industry later moved to the western Mendips where it became centred in the villages of Shipham and Rowberrow, which became prosperous in the early nineteenth century, supplying zinc to the many brass-works in Bristol. Around 1850 the industry died out, leaving another pock-marked landscape around Shipham, and rows of miners' cottages at Rowberrow.[21] Recently its ghost paid the area an unpleasant visit when modern quarrying operations disturbed

[20] This section is largely based on R. Atthill, ed., *Mendip, A New Study*, pp. 146–9.

[21] Ibid., pp. 149–50.

old zinc workings and scattered zinc dust over houses and gardens. Controversy has since raged about the seriousness of this type of pollution as a hazard to health, and the incident shows that the past history of the landscape is not always a subject which can be safely forgotten.

For a coalfield which boasted at least seventy-nine deep mines and hundreds of small open-cast pits, the visual remains in Somerset are surprisingly scanty. The density of village and hamlet settlement and the frequent occurrence of little rows of cottages in unexpected rural settlements are today the most noticeable legacies, the most important of these, of course, being the town of Norton-Radstock, with a population of 15,232 in the 1971 census. It grew from the amalgamation of the two small villages of Radstock and Midsomer Norton. At its mining heyday, around 1910, this town had twenty-one coal-mines, of which several, such as Norton Hill, Kilmersdon and Lower Writhlington, were the largest in Somerset. Topographically the town differs from all others in the county, and we shall look at it in more detail below.

Surprisingly, the remains of the mines themselves are not prominent. There are some dramatic spoil-heaps at Pensford, Camerton and Tyning (on the north-east of Radstock) but most Somerset mines had small buildings made of local stone and tiles, which could easily be converted to other uses. Several have become garages, workshops and depots, and some have been converted into farms, as at Charmborough on the road south of Radstock towards Holcombe. The signs of mining activity are soon obliterated, especially where no open-cast work was involved. Where coal outcropped on the surface, as in the medieval pit-mines on Stratton Common and around Vobster, the disturbance of the earth is much more noticeable. Of Stratton Common, the historians of the Somerset coalfield, Down and Warrington, have written that

the area concerned is a little over half a mile square. It is largely bare of covering rock deposits except at the northern limits, where the coal measures are overlain by dolomitic conglomerates, and the whole area is peppered with the lumps of early workings. Even today it is possible to trace the coal outcrop—black lines against the brown earth of ploughed fields.

Coal was being worked here as early as 1300, and in 1443 the Manor pits sold their coals for £2. 1s. 1d. A little further east around Vobster

dozens of pits were strung out along the outcrops like beads on a thread. To the immediate south and east of Vobster village there were at least fifty pits and probably as many again whose sites will never be known. Today the valley here is quiet and agricultural, but scattered in secluded places are the traces left by the men who persistently sought coal over the centuries.[22]

The Somerset coalfield was roughly triangular in shape. It extended from a northern point at Pensford southwards for about eleven miles to a base along the Nettlebridge valley in eastern Mendip, extending from Gurney Slade eastwards for about six miles almost to Mells. Its eastern boundary followed a billowing curve north of Mells, to take in an area to the east of Radstock and Dunkerton before returning to Pensford through Priston and Marksbury. Within this field, which is very hilly and dissected with deep valleys, there were three main mining concentrations, apart from the more northern outliers around Pensford, Bishop's Sutton and Compton Dando. The northernmost of the concentrations lay in the valley of the Cam brook, between Temple Cloud and Dunkerton. The next was the most important—the valley of the Somer river between Farrington Gurney and Shoscombe, which included Norton-Radstock. Finally came the southern region, which lay on the Mendip Hills around Stratton and eastwards down the Nettlebridge valley through Holcombe, Coleford and Vobster to the edge of Mells. This southern area was probably the earliest to be worked, and it throve throughout the nineteenth century, but very few of its mines survived beyond 1920. The Cam valley was

[22] C. G. Down and A. J. Warrington, *The History of the Somerset Coalfield* (n.d. but c. 1970), pp. 226–8.

the next to be developed, and it too enjoyed a period of vigorous activity prior to 1920, but only the mines at Camerton and Dunkerton survived for longer. The middle area around Radstock was the last to be worked, because the coal lay deep beneath the overlying rocks, and required steam pumping and a large capital before it could be worked. The successful sinking of Old Pit, Radstock in 1763 marked the beginning of this section of the field which was destined to be the most successful. The last two mines to close—Kilmersdon and Lower Writhlington in 1973—were both in this area.

Production statistics for the period before 1860 are not reliable, but it has been estimated that production first became significant in the mid-sixteenth century, when a shortage of timber, combined with new coal-using industries, like glass and brass-making, to boost demand. Production in this period has been estimated by J. U. Nef at about 10,000 tons a year for the Somerset and Bristol coalfields combined, which implies that Somerset pits may have been raising some 5,000 tons, but modern scholars consider Nef's estimates to be optimistic.[23] Production increased rapidly in the seventeenth century, despite the poor transport facilities which condemned the mines to rely on wagons and pack-horses on inadequate roads. Bulley has estimated that by the 1680s production may have been as much as 50,000 tons in a good year, but only 10,000 in a poor one.[24]

Steam pumping was slow to enter Somerset. Newcomen's atmospheric engine was working at Dudley in Staffordshire as early as 1712, but Somerset relied for long on water- and horse-powered pumping. However, by the 1780s steam pumps were being used. It was estimated by John Billingsley that production had reached 120,000 to 150,000 tons a year in the 1740s. Billingsley (the Mendip encloser whose work we have already discussed) knew the coalfield well.

To facilitate the marketing of this increasing production, the Somerset Coal Canal was built up the Cam valley from the Avon

[23] J. U. Nef, *The Rise of the British Coal Industry*, I (1932), pp. 19–20, for the estimates; but for a modern criticism see D. C. Coleman, *Industry in Tudor and Stuart England* (1975), pp. 45–9.

[24] J. A. Bulley, "To Mendip for Coal, a study of the Somerset Coalfield before 1830", part I, in *SANHS*, 97 (1952), p. 48.

at Midford to Paulton in the 1790s. Not long after this a branch was extended to Radstock. This widened the market considerably, and two Victorian mining engineers later estimated that the twenty-nine mines they knew of had been producing about 140,000 tons annually by 1800. The first railway (a G.W.R. branch from Frome to Radstock) did not arrive until 1854, and a proper network not until the 1870s, when Radstock was linked to Bristol (1873) by the G.W.R., and the Somerset and Dorset main line was extended from Shepton Mallet through Radstock to Bath (1874). The coming of the railways assisted production considerably. From 413,678 tons in 1867 it rose to its maximum of 1,250,000 tons in the years before the First World War (c. 1910–14). From then on a steady decline set in. There had been sixty-four mines working in 1868. By 1894 they were reduced to twenty-seven, and by the 1930s to thirteen. At the time of nationalisation in 1947, twelve still survived, and large new investments raised production from 589,214 tons in 1947 to a post-war peak of 690,827 in 1958. By then it was clear that Somerset coal could not compete with cheap imported oil, and a rapid run-down began.[25]

With the mines went the canals and railways. The Somerset Coal Canal survived until 1898 and was replaced by a railway between 1907 and 1910 (closed in sections between 1925 and 1951). The Bristol-Radstock-Frome branch of the former G.W.R. was closed in 1959, and the old Somerset and Dorset main line, which had connected Radstock northwards with Bath and the Midlands, and southwards with Shepton Mallet and Bournemouth, was closed in 1966. Now the dense network of major and minor roads is the sole surviving transport legacy of the coalfield.[26]

The town of Norton-Radstock is the most enduring memorial to coal. Coal mines were scattered all through it, and it seemed to have more railway lines than streets, with two intersecting main lines and some dozen branches, and narrow-gauge tramways connecting mines in all directions. The most

[25] Down and Warrington, *Somerset Coalfield*, pp. 1–55.
[26] Hunt and Sellman, *Somerset History*, pp. 43–50.

prominent feature of Radstock seemed to be its level crossing! Yet its houses and public buildings were well built of the local limestone, and although there are probably few people who would regard the town as beautiful, it has never exhibited the squalor of some northern mining towns. It sprawls at a low density and, now that modern electrically-powered industries have replaced coal-mining, it is clean and comfortable. The Waldegrave family of Chewton Mendip owned much of the area and in the late nineteenth century the Countess Waldegrave was concerned to see that the people who worked in her mines were well housed. This has given Radstock something of the aura of a magnified estate village.

Another landscape which was once industrial may be seen north of the coalfield in the peaceful rural setting of the Chew valley, where the remains of numerous mills (woollen, paper, brass and logwood amongst others) survive in various stages of preservation and decay, although it is very difficult to believe that this was once a noisy and hectic industrial area. The mills began near the head of the Chew valley at Sherborn (in Litton parish) where a former papermill survives. It has now been converted to other uses, like the old fulling- and grist-mills at Chew Magna. Further downstream, the remains of a fine old mill still stand at Stanton Drew, and the disused Bye Mills to the west of Pensford (Plate 53) were once used for paper-making, fulling and metal working. Pensford itself has the remains of several metal-working mills. Their buildings have gone, but the sites of two water-wheels still make a pleasant feature in a leat by the river, almost under the immense viaduct which used to carry the Bristol-to-Frome railway over the town. The railway has been removed, but the viaduct is to be pre-served. A mile to its south stands the huge spoil-heap of Pensford coal mine which was closed in 1958.

It is difficult to believe that Church Farm in Publow, stand-ing peacefully in a meadow by the river near the church, was once a busy metal mill, where iron, copper and brass were worked by water-power. The remains of a dam are barely visible next to Publow Bridge, but a shallow ditch, circling round the churchyard and across a meadow, indicates where the old leat flowed. A mile downstream, the attractive terrace of cottages at

Woollard, dated 1783, suggests that this little rural hamlet had an industrial origin, but a search is needed to uncover the traces of its three mills (one for copper-working, one for brass and one for tanning). Further mill-sites occur at Woodborough, Compton Dando and Chewton Keynsham, but the most impressive is the disused log-wood mill at the southern edge of Keynsham. Called Albert Mill, it is a sturdy building of the 1820s, now used as a storehouse, but with its large water-wheel still intact and visible outside the building. The machinery crushed red-wood logs imported from Brazil, to produce red dye for the woollen industry. Keynsham is still a busy industrial town, and near the confluence of the Avon and the Chew stands Somerdale, the huge chocolate factory built by Fry's in the 1920s (now part of Cadbury-Schweppes). Keynsham has been extensively modernised, and a huge dual carriage road passes right through the ruined nave of its former abbey.[27]

SELECT BIBLIOGRAPHY

Atthill, R., *Mendip, A New Study* (1976).
Atthill, R., *Old Mendip* (1971).
Down, C. G. and Warrington, A. J., *The History of the Somerset Coalfield* (n.d., but c. 1970).
Gough, J. W., *The Mines of Mendip* (1930).
Walker, F., *The Bristol Region* (1972).
Bettey, J. H., *Rural Life in Wessex, 1500–1900* (1977).
Robertson, C., *Bath, an Architectural Guide* (1975).
Buchanan, C. A. & R. A., *The Batsford Guide to the Industrial Archaeology of Central Southern England* (1980).

[27] I am indebted to the kindness of Dr J. H. Bettey of Bristol University Extra-Mural Department for showing me the sites in the Chew Valley, and for providing information about their history.

9. The Southern arc

The farming landscape. Mansions and parks. Rural settlements. The towns.

AS WE SAW in chapter 1, the southern arc is a far from homogeneous region, but comprises a group of geographically different areas united by devotion to mixed farming, but with a stronger element of arable cultivation than anywhere else in Somerset. Stretching from the foot of the Wiltshire Downs in the east almost to the Devon border west of Wellington, it is about forty-five miles long, but seldom more than five or six miles wide from north to south. On its northern side it blends imperceptibly into the wetlands, especially where the upper reaches of rivers like the Parrett, Yeo and Brue cut deeply into the region. Its southern edge is formed by the county's boundaries with Wiltshire, Dorset, and Devon. Yet for all its local variation in landscape detail, its common characteristics help to unify it. The absence of uplands and marshes and the relative importance of arable farming give it a very different appearance from that of the pastoral levels or the highland regions. It is also more densely settled than any other part of the historic county except the suburban belt between Bristol and Bath. Especially in its central section between Yeovil and Taunton, villages and hamlets cluster thickly on the ground, and the traveller has no sooner left a village like South Petherton than he finds himself entering one of its numerous neighbours (such as Martock or Shepton Beauchamp).

Within the region, landscape variation is affected by the lie of the land and the underlying geology as well as by historical processes. In the east, between the Wiltshire Downs and the low limestone ridge which runs north-south from Bruton down to Sherborne in Dorset, lies the northern part of the Vale of

Blackmoor—a flat valley lying on the heavy Oxford Clay. This area was formerly occupied by Selwood Forest, and is an exception to the statement about the predominance of arable farming. As the forest was gradually cleared between the late Middle Ages and the eighteenth century, small settlements devoted to dairying and livestock-raising expanded to fill the valley.

Farther west between Milborne Port and the eastern scarp of the Blackdowns lies a rolling countryside cut up by limestone hills and ridges, such as those on which Cadbury Castle and Montacute stand, but consisting in the main of fertile sands and loams. This was the area where the open-field system of arable farming was most widespread and most firmly entrenched. Indeed, in some villages like Barrington and Lopen open-field strips were still in use in 1918, while at Seavington St Michael they survived till 1932 in the Nether Field, and lands separated only by balks may still be seen (1980) in some of Seavington's fields.[1] Enclosure in this area was a long and complex process as we shall see.

To the west of Ilminster the plain meets the foothills of the Blackdowns, and the area of another former forest—Neroche—which, as we saw in chapter 2, was partly enclosed when disafforested in 1627, but not finally enclosed until 1833. In former forest parishes like Ashill and Broadway, the regular rectangular fields and straight roads characteristic of Parliamentary enclosure may be seen (though in this case it was common forest and pasture, not open-field arable, which was involved).

To the north of the former Neroche Forest begins the fertile Vale of Taunton Deane with its rich red soil and its alternating scene of corn, meadows and orchards. It stretches westwards along the route of the M5 to the Blackdowns and the Devon border, and spreads in a semi-circle north-west of Taunton to take in the rolling hill country between the Brendons and the Quantocks. At Lydeard St Lawrence (Lydeard means "gateway" in Old English) a low ridge of hills separates the Vale from the

[1] *VCH*, IV, pp. 117, 167, and 207.

Doniford valley leading northwards to Watchet and the coast in the western upland region.

The farming landscape

Generalisation about the emergence of the farming landscape is made difficult by the fact that this is an area which was affected both by early enclosure and by the long survival of open fields, so that the landscape was characterised by considerable variation from at least the sixteenth century onwards (and probably much earlier). Nor was this merely a question of a contrast between enclosed and open-field parishes (or "champaign", as the early writers called it), because one of the most noticeable features of enclosure in Somerset was its long-drawn-out piecemeal nature *within* villages. Totally enclosed places were rare, but so were totally "champaign" ones. Everywhere in this region there was an immensely complex inter-relationship between numerous fragmented common arable fields and equally numerous hedged closes.

This helps to account for the paradox that an early traveller like John Leland could ride from South Cadbury to Ilchester in the 1540s and note that "Al this way the pastures and feeldes be much enclosed with heggerowes of elmes", while passing through villages like Queen Camel and Northover on the edge of Ilchester, which were later subject to enclosure of open-field arable by Parliamentary Act; though by the time these enclosures took place (in 1798 and 1839) the surviving open fields had no doubt been reduced. At Queen Camel, in 1798, 650 acres still survived, though at Northover in 1839 there were only 178 acres still remaining.[2] But in 1605 most of Northover seems to have been under open-field cultivation.[3]

To someone like Leland, coming into Somerset from eastern England where "champaign" was the rule, enclosures naturally struck the eye, and, proceeding westwards from Ilchester to Montacute, he was impressed by the "good pasture and corne ground enclosed and meately will wooded", and again farther

[2] Tate, *Somerset Enclosure Acts*, pp. 31 and 55.
[3] *VCH*, III, p. 227.

west between Crewkerne and Hinton St George "by hilly ground but plentiful of corne, grasse and elme wood, wherewith most part of al Somersetshire ys yn hegge rowys enclosid". Yet east of Yeovil the situation was rather different. For instance, from Bruton to Castle Cary, "I rode from the bridg up a stony hill to a very fair and fruteful champain and so passid forth a 5 miles by little woode" to North and South Cadbury. From there he proceeded south to Sherborne (at that time only just in Dorset, the border was extended northwards in the late nineteenth century) "al champagne but fruteful ground".[4]

He shows that Selwood Forest was still quite extensive, but by no means so huge as it had been in the early Middle Ages, when it covered nearly two hundred square miles. Its northern edge came to within three miles of Mells, and it was "a 30 miles yn cumpace, and streachith one way almoste unto Werminstre [Warminster in Wiltshire] and a nother way onto the quarters of Shaftesbyri [in Dorset] by estimation a 10 miles".[5]

Leland has not left a description of the Vale of Taunton Deane, but this had long been enclosed, if indeed it had ever known open-field farming of the type prevalent between Ilminster and Yeovil. It is more likely that, being mainly a pastoral area, its small quantities of arable land (sometimes called "infields") had been early enclosed, leaving the more extensive common pastures to be gradually taken in. (These pastures had been occasionally cultivated for corn, and called "outfields".)[6] A few of these survived into the era of Parliamentary enclosure, such as the two hundred acres in five moors and heaths around Milverton which were enclosed in 1833, and the fifty-seven acres of wet Moor and Common Down at Halse, enclosed in 1857.[7] A few managed to escape enclosure altogether, like the extensive upland common to the west of Langford Budville. This partially wooded common is called Langford Heathfield, and has an interesting pattern of irregularly shaped fields on its south-western edge. In places these cut

---

[4] Tate, *Somerset Enclosure Acts*, p. 16.
[5] Toulmin Smith, *Leland's Tour*, pt. X, p. 105.
[6] See H. L. Gray, *English Field Systems*, for a discussion of what he calls the "Celtic" field systems; more accurately described as infield-outfield systems.
[7] Tate, *Somerset Enclosure Acts*, pp. 54 and 58.

deeply into the common, and bear all the marks of piecemeal medieval reclamation. At Ash Priors, about five miles north-west of Taunton, a much smaller common survives just to the south of the village, looking almost like a village green (although in fact it is not one). The parish boundary between Ash Priors and Bishops Lydeard runs north-south down the middle of this common, and it may owe its survival to the difficulty of arranging enclosures where more than one parish enjoyed common grazing rights.

These little patches of common would already have been anomalous by the seventeenth century, as is made clear by the descriptions of the Vale of Taunton Deane given by Thomas Gerard, a local antiquary, in 1633. The Vale had long been famous for its fertility, and in a walk from Bishop's Hull, a village to the west of Taunton, down the river Tone to Taunton, Gerard noted that

> . . . besides the River which is heare fayre and very clear, you have the prospect of many fair orchards, gardens, and cherry gardens, of which there are a great number here about, and there cherries ripe welneere as soon as at London, for [there] is rich redd earth which produceth all fruits not only in great plentye, but very early, insomuch that they have peas and other such fruites as soon as London; from this walke also you may see many and those most flourishing meadowes lying by ye Riverside.[8]

Of Orchard Portman, some two miles south of Taunton, he commented that it "well brookes the name, for it is sceated in a very fertile soyle for fruit; and the whole Countrey thereabouts seems to be orchards, insomuch that all the hedgerows and pasture groundes are full frought with fruite trees of all sorts fittinge to eat and make cider of".[9] Sadly there are no longer any orchards in the immediate vicinity, though they are still to be seen scattered about the Vale (Plate 29). The old type of orchards which grew trees known as "standards" are now giving

[8] Gerard's survey, *Som. Rec. Soc.*, XV (1900), p. 54.
[9] Ibid., p. 61.

Plate 41 Aerial view of Bath, showing the remarkable homogeneity of the eighteenth-century town planning and building, organised by John Wood and his son (see chapter 8). Queen Square (1729-36) is in the left-hand corner, the Circus (1754-8) in the right centre, and the Royal Crescent (1767-75) at the top centre.

Plate 42 Market Square Somerton, laid out in c. 1290 (see chapter 9). It is now surrounded by Tudor and Stuart buildings in bright silver limestone, garnished with quoins, window frames and drip mouldings in golden Ham stone, making it perhaps the most attractive small town in the county.

Plate 43 Castle Street, Bridgwater. The town was famous for its bricks, and the Duke of Chandos took advantage of this when having this delightful street built in 1723. It was part of a projected development to be based on expanding the port as a rival to Bristol. Only this street and part of King Square were built.

Plate 44 The rooftops of Taunton. The county capital lacks the elegance of Bath or Wells, but the church towers of St. Mary Magdalene (right) and St. James (left) are fine examples of the Somerset Perpendicular style (though both had to be rebuilt in the nineteenth century, to the original designs).

Plate 45 Royal Crescent, Weston-super-Mare (now a hotel). Built in 1847 in the heyday of Weston's hectic expansion as a seaside resort (see chapter 6), it is a late survival of the Georgian classic style into Victorian times.

Plate 46 Dunster. The castle (National Trust) dominates the little town, which thrived on the woollen trade in Tudor and Stuart times (see chapter 7). It has changed little since then and is a beautiful example of an old west Somerset town, with its broad market place and many attractive Stuart and Georgian houses.

place to the more intensive type where low-growing bush varieties are planted. The old apple-trees grew to a height of fifteen or twenty feet, and were planted well spaced-out from one another, so that livestock could graze beneath them. The bush varieties are planted close together, and produce a quite different landscape, almost akin to that of a vineyard in appearance.

There were a few villages where complete, or almost complete, enclosure was carried out by agreement before the seventeenth century. At Merriott, about two miles north of Crewkerne, the open fields were gradually enclosed during the fifteenth and sixteenth centuries, except for two pieces called Hychyns and Landshare. In 1559 and again in 1561 all the tenants were ordered to maintain the hedges around the corn-field called Hychyns, and a few strips survived there until about 1840, when all the rest of the village land had long been enclosed.[10] However, the details of the enclosure process have not survived at Merriott, unlike Cricket St Thomas, which lies on the southern slopes of Windwhistle Hill between Crewkerne and Chard. Cricket was the nineteenth-century country seat of Admiral Alexander Hood, 1st Viscount Bridport, and his descendants, who removed the remains of the small village in the early nineteenth century to extend their park, but the whole parish had been enclosed long before this. As early as 1459, a description of the farms shows that there were fourteen tenants, with most of their land enclosed, although there were references to six common fields. By 1534 only one of these, known as the Great Field, still survived, and in 1546 there was an agreement to enclose this and divide the land amongst the owners. Five arbitrators were appointed for this purpose, one for the lord of the manor (John Preston, whose grandfather had purchased the manor from the widow of Sir Robert Hungerford in 1466), one for the rector, and three for the tenants. This consideration for the tenants might seem unusual, since they were not land-owners, but some of them held their farms on leases for three lives, which gave them a kind of semi-freehold. Leases of this type were purchased for lump sums of cash.

[10] *VCH*, IV, p. 57.

The common pastures and woodlands at Cricket had also been partly enclosed in medieval times. References to enclosures at Marshwood (formerly a detached part of Cricket, now in Winsham) occur as early as 1300, and in 1539 there were several substantial closes of pasture. One tenant had a sixty-acre close, another had thirty acres, and another twelve acres. In 1541 it was agreed to enclose the common "moor" and to allot the land proportionately to each tenement and cottage.[11]

Although Cricket St Thomas survived as a village into the nineteenth century, there were many settlements, usually of the hamlet or small village type, which disappeared as part of the enclosure process. We have already in chapter 4 discussed the case of Nether Adber in Mudford. There were numerous others, especially in this region. Usually the places concerned did not disappear altogether, but were turned into a single farmstead. A good example is provided by Whitcomb Farm just south of Cadbury Castle hill-fort. The farmstead stands at the head of a broad combe surrounded by a ridge of limestone hills on all sides except the north, with a stream running down the middle of it. The land is all enclosed in fields of substantial size, but the remains of the former strips can still be seen on the hillsides to the south of the farmstead, while aerial photographs have revealed the site of the former settlement along the stream to the north of the present farm.

Cudworth, two and a half miles south of Ilminster, beneath the northern slopes of Windwhistle Hill, presents another variation on the desertion theme. Next to its little church lie the remains of an abandoned moated site, and round about are ample evidences of former medieval occupation, but on either side of this site lie two small hamlets called West Farm and East Farm, which are about half a mile apart. Field-names from early documents suggest that enclosure had already occurred by the late fourteenth century. The manor had been divided and held by absentee owners since the early fourteenth century, while the church had been given to Wells Cathedral c. 1186–8. The place had been reduced to fourteen households in 1563, but the two

[11] *VCH*, IV, pp. 133–7.

little hamlets and a few isolated farms had prevented it from becoming completely depopulated.[12]

At Redlynch, south of Bruton, the story is more similar to that of Cricket St Thomas, with the village disappearing to make way for the extension of the park surrounding the mansion. In the muster of 1569, ten able men over the age of sixteen were recorded, which implies a settlement of thirty-five to fifty people. Today the old village has gone, but a few estate cottages survive along the main road, probably built by Sir Stephen Fox when he rebuilt the former mansion of the Fitz-James family in 1672. Redlynch Park is beautifully landscaped and extends southwards down a limestone ridge to a large pond surrounded by trees. The house was enlarged in the eighteenth century by Fox's descendents, the Earls of Ilchester, but most of it was later destroyed by fire.

Another interesting site is Spargrove (Plate 26) in Batcombe parish, where a moated sixteenth-century farmhouse (almost entirely rebuilt in 1870) and some eighteenth-century stables are all that remains of the manor house. There is a farm which was once a mill, but all other signs of the settlement have gone, though its site is visible in aerial photographs, and to some extent on the ground. About half a mile to the west of Spargrove lies Milton Clevedon, where a moated farmhouse and a church are all that remain of the former village. Eleven men were mustered here in 1569, a few of whom probably came from outlying farms in the parish, but there are clear signs of denser settlement around the church. These are but a few of many examples which have recently been identified by Michael Aston. Future research will almost certainly bring more deserted sites to light.

The great forest of Selwood was gradually enclosed during the course of the seventeenth and eighteenth centuries, except for a few commons and marshes which survived into the era of Parliamentary enclosure, and were allotted under two awards in 1771 and 1821. The award of 1771 resulted from an Act of 1769 relating to the parishes of Wincanton, Maperton and Horsington, under which eight commons comprising nearly

[12] *VCH*, IV, pp. 141–4.

580 acres were enclosed.[13] This did not, however, include all the marshes along the banks of the river Cale south of Wincanton. On the first edition of the Ordnance map (Sherborne area), dated 1811, a line of marshes stretching southwards down into Dorset is shown as still unenclosed, and these were the areas to which an Act of 1814 referred. It related to 150 acres in the parish of Wincanton; to Charlton, South Marsh and Barrow Commons (comprising 100 acres) in the parish of Charlton Musgrove, and to Leigh Common (comprising 60 acres) in PenSelwood. Kilmington Common (covering 200 acres and now in Wiltshire) was also included. The act of 1814 was not implemented until the award of 1821, so that presumably there must have been some difficulty in sorting out conflicting claims.

The first edition of the Ordnance Survey (1809–17) also shows that only scattered patches of Selwood Forest still remained. Its enclosure history stretches back a long way. Some pieces had been enclosed in the early Middle Ages. A perambulation of the bounds in 1298 refers to "the gate of the hall of the lord king which stood there when the park of Witham was enclosed". This may refer to the foundation of Witham Priory by King Henry II about 1178–9 as part of his penance for the murder of Archbishop Thomas Becket, or possibly to an even earlier enclosure of part of Witham as a royal deer park.

No doubt piecemeal enclosure continued after that, but much of the woodland was protected by its inclusion in a royal forest in the technical sense (i.e. an area—not necessarily wooded—which was reserved for royal hunting). Special laws, designed to protect the deer, applied in such places, and these naturally made enclosure very difficult. However, in 1627, when King Charles I was desperately short of money to finance his mismanaged war against France and Spain, it was decided to disforest Selwood as well as Neroche (see chapter 7) and to sell the king's share (one-third). By these means he hoped to raise £20,000. The local "lords and owners of the soil" were also to have a third, and the final third was to go to the "commoners having the right of common for the depasturing of their cattle".

[13] Tate, *Somerset Enclosure Acts*, p. 40.

Power to convert the former forest lands to enclosed meadow and pasture was granted, and all the king's special rights and privileges were ended. The inconvenience of such rights can be gauged from the conditions attached to the charter of Bruton Abbey in 1252, when King Henry III granted the monks twenty-five acres in "his forest of Selewode, to be cleared and tilled, but subject to the run of the doe and fawn, and of other wild animals".[14] Clearly "enclosures" of this type were not all that agricultural improvers might desire.

Disafforestation was carried out during the 1630s, and no doubt was accompanied by a good deal of enclosure at the time and subsequently.[15] By 1791 Collinson could write that

> the woodlands in Frome parish, round the New Church of that name built in 1712 (i.e. in the hamlet of East Wood-lands) are now the only part of the ancient forest of Selwood which bear any resemblance to its former state, and have been within the memory of man, the notorious asylum of a desperate clan of banditti, whose depredations were a terror to the surrounding parishes . . . but the cutting down of large tracts of wood, establishing small farms and building the church have been the means of destroying their haunts and obliging the possessors to seek subsistence in honest and useful labour.[16]

In 1794 Billingsley put a figure to the extent of clearance by declaring that, out of an original forest of 20,000 acres, "18,000 had been cleared and converted into pasture and arable land, the remainder being chiefly in a state of coppice wood." Much of the coppice was oak and ash, and after about 1870 substantial replantings of timber took place, especially on the scarp of the Downs and along the ridge. The extensive Wiltshire estates of the Marquess of Bath at Longleat, the Duke of Somerset at Maiden Bradley, and the Hoares at Stourhead all

[14] Two Cartularies of the Augustinian Priory of Bruton and the Cluniac Priory of Montacute; *Som. Rec. Soc.*, VIII (1894), p. 19.
[15] T. G. Barnes, *Somerset, 1625–40*, pp. 156–9.
[16] Collinson, *History of Somerset*, II (1791), p. 194.

extended over the border into Somerset. All were prominent in converting their marginal lands back to forestry.[17]

Despite the enthusiasm for enclosure in the eighteenth century, some arable parishes in the Ilminster-Crewkerne area maintained their open fields for a surprisingly long time into the nineteenth century—and, as we noted earlier, vestiges still survive even today in places like Seavington St Michael. The dates at which Parliamentary enclosure occurred are shown on Fig. 22 (see chapter 5), but it has to be stressed that many of the parishes along the southern rim between Chard and Yeovil, which had no Acts, retained parts of their open fields for much longer than some of the places which were enclosed by Acts. As a general rule, it is safe to assume that if a village in England had no Parliamentary Act, its common lands (if it had any) were enclosed before the eighteenth century. But in Somerset such an assumption is most unsafe. For instance, the large parish of Crewkerne was not affected by Parliamentary Acts, except for about 130 acres of common pasture and march at Roundham in the west of the parish, which were enclosed in 1823 under an Act of 1814. The open arable fields of Crewkerne itself were gradually enclosed by private agreements, but the process was very lengthy, and quite a lot of land was still unenclosed as late as 1842. In the map in the *Victoria County History*, vol. IV, the town of Crewkerne is shown as surrounded on all sides by a scatter of open-field arable land. It is true that most of the parish had been enclosed and that the surviving common arable consisted of some fifty scattered blocks of land, representing un-enclosed furlongs in the main, but occasionally even individual strips. These were the survivors of Crewkerne's original three open fields—known as North, South and East—in the sixteenth century. The process of enclosure continued gradually after 1842 and was complete by 1931, but as late as 1886 a few isolated strips still survived in the North and South Fields, and several in the East Field, with characteristic names like Broad-shord, Long Strings, and Butts.[18]

[17] G. N. Wright, "A forest under the plough", *Country Life* (3rd February, 1972), pp. 254–5.
[18] *VCH*, IV, pp. 6–20.

In the area around Crewkerne there were quite a few similar examples. Much of Dowlish Wake was enclosed by agreement in the eighteenth century, but the process does not seem to have been complete until around 1838. At Seavington St Mary, some arable strips survived into the 1880s, and at Shepton Beauchamp, where an estate map of 1755 shows myriads of strips, open-field farming was still active in the early nineteenth century. It began to disappear after 1807, but Muchelditch Field was still unenclosed in 1853, and enclosure does not seem to have been completed until the 1880s. At Barrington there was still much open land as late as 1879, and Barrington, like nearby Lopen, still had a few strips in 1918. The longest survivor, though, seems to have been Seavington St Michael, where enclosure had made little progress by 1876, and where it was being actively pursued on the Winchester College lands in 1914–15. Yet by 1932 much of the former Nether Field remained open, and it was still unfenced in 1973, with grassy balks separating strips.[19]

Mansions and parks

Although Somerset was characterised by a surprising absence of resident peers, and even, in some areas, of resident gentry, this region nevertheless possesses a good selection of the country's more famous mansions and parks, ranging from well-known Elizabethan houses like Montacute, Barrington Court and Dillington House, to lesser-known fifteenth-century houses like Gaulden Manor in the Vale of Taunton Deane, and handsome Georgian edifices like Hadspen, a mile south-east of Castle Cary. The area between Yeovil and Chard is especially notable for country estates, for there are numerous others in addition to Montacute, Dillington and Barrington. There is a fine Elizabethan house at Newton Surmaville, to the east of Yeovil. Coker Court, south of Yeovil, is a fifteenth-century hall with later additions. Brympton d'Evercy, for many years one of the chief seats of the Sydenham family, has a Tudor west front and a magnificent Palladian south wing, once attributed to Inigo

[19] *VCH*, IV, pp. 117, 153, 167, 203, 207, and 215.

Jones, but now thought to be of later date. At Hinton St George the Earls Poulett had an extensive park and an imposing mansion, in which a medieval hall was encased in later additions dating from every century between Elizabeth I and Victoria. Part of it is now demolished and the remainder has been turned into flats. Other examples are Cricket St Thomas, where the large attractive park sloping down to the lake has been turned into a wild-life park, and North Cadbury, where Henry Hastings, 3rd Earl of Huntingdon, built a gabled Tudor house in grey stone on a hill overlooking South Cadbury hill-fort.

Somerset is fortunate in that a fair number of small, late medieval manor houses have survived. There are various reasons for this. The county had numerous gentry with small estates who were prosperous enough to build a good medium-sized manor house, but who never "rose" like the Pouletts and hence did not feel the need to make extensive additions to their houses. Cothay Manor, near the Devon border, is a good example of this type. Others, like Gaulden in Tolland, Blackford in Cannington, and Dodington (Plate 30) near Nether Stowey, belonged to families which, through inter-marriage, were absorbed by relations who already possessed more imposing seats, so that the fifteenth-century houses survived as dower houses or residences of junior branches of the main family. Blackford, in Cannington, now a farmhouse, is a superbly preserved example of a small medieval manor house, which was unaltered because let to tenant farmers at an early date.[20] Another particularly good example is Lyte's Cary, near Ilchester, now owned by the National Trust.

Montacute House, built in the 1590s by Sir Edward Phelips, a successful and wealthy Elizabethan lawyer, is perhaps the most famous of the county's great houses. The Phelips family had acquired the lands of Montacute Priory, and Sir Edward, who was soon to become Speaker of the House of Commons (1604) and Master of the Rolls (1611), was clearly anxious to announce his arrival in county society by building a suitably imposing

---

[20] I am indebted to Mr Lloyd Jones of West Lyng for his kindness in showing me many of these houses, and for introducing me to farmers in the Cannington area.

house in the new symmetrical and lavishly fenestrated Elizabethan style. A survey taken in 1667 shows what the house and grounds were like before various more recent alterations in the gardens and surroundings were carried out. The mansion was described as "a very faire Yellow Freestone house 3 storeys high with a faire hall" and numerous other rooms, which had cost at least £20,000 to build (a colossal sum, considering how much the pound sterling was worth at that time). To the east of the house there was a stone terrace and a walled courtyard entered through a "faire Gatehouse with lodging Chambers of Free-stone" (which has since been demolished). Beyond this there was another

large Court walled about and coped with Freestone sett with several walkes and Rowes of Trees, on the north side of Which Court is a faire Bowling Greene sett about with goodly rowes of Trees, and variety of pleasant walkes Arbours and coppices full of delight and pleasure.

On the North side of the house is a very faire Spacious Garden walled about and furnished with all sorts of Flowers and fruits and divers mounted walkes without which Garden there is a descent of about 10 stepps into Private walkes walled about and furnished with store of fruite, and at the end of the East walke there is a faire Banqueting house built and Arched with Freestone wainscoted within and leaded on the Toppe therof, and without the Walke of the Garden there is a faire Orchard furnished with good fruit and divers pleasant Walkes.

On the south side of the house there is a large Woodyard and necessary buildings for Daryes Washing Brewing and Bakeing, a Pigeon house, and on the South side thereof, and of the Courts before the house, are several Orchards of Cherryes, Pares, Plumbs, others of Apples, and also good kitchen gardens with 2 fishponds all incompassed with a wall.

On the West side of the house there is a large Voyd Court Sett with Rowes of Trees in order, of Elmes and Walnutts leading to the Stables Barnes Stawles and other large build-ings for servants Granaryes and other necessary uses where are also several Fish ponds and also a hopp garden of an Acre and a halfe.

All this containes 24 Acres or thereabouts and is Valued at £4,000.[21]

In contrast to the ostentatious splendour of Montacute, the elegant Georgian mansion of Hadspen, seat of the Hobhouse family, blends harmoniously into the rolling parkland in which it is set at the foot of a wooded hill in Pitcombe parish about a mile south-east of Castle Cary. Dated by Pevsner between 1750 and 1770, it is built of honey-coloured stone, and is one of the best examples of a Georgian house and park in Somerset.

The effect of the great house and its park on the landscape is a theme which could be illustrated at great length if space allowed. Here we have room for only one more, and a slightly different, example. At Hestercombe House, north of Taunton, a rather ungainly Victorian pile, now occupied by the Somerset Fire Service, is one of the county's most interesting gardens. It was designed by the famous architect, Sir Edwin Lutyens, between about 1906 and 1914, in collaboration with Gertrude Jekyll, one of the most skilful creators of gardens in that epoch. It is a variation on the theme of the so-called "Surrey garden", in which a series of stone-paved terraces and walled enclosures at differing heights are linked by steps and pathways. Ponds, streamlets, covered walkways, and arbours are all used with great charm and taste. The garden became derelict for a time, but Gertrude Jekyll's original planting plan was recently re-discovered and the garden is now being restored to its original form. With the wooded foothills of the Quantocks rising gently behind it, and an extensive view in front over the Vale of Taunton Deane to the Blackdowns on the horizon, the garden utilises a classical Somerset landscape scene to maximum effect. Another example of Gertrude Jekyll's work may be seen at Barrington Court, now owned by the National Trust.

Rural settlements

It is difficult to generalise about the layout and appearance of the rural settlements in this region, since they do not conform to

[21] *National Trust Guide to Montacute House* (1975), pp. 33–4.

any common pattern. Very broadly, hamlets and isolated farms predominate to the west of the Parrett, and villages to the east, but even in the classical territory of open-field villages around Ilminster and Yeovil there are large numbers of hamlets, whilst amongst the more scattered settlement pattern of the Vale of Taunton Deane there are some prominent large villages like Bishops Lydeard, Bradford-on-Tone and Norton Fitzwarren (now more or less absorbed into Taunton). In so far as there can be said to be a typical form of village, it tended to be one which stretched along a single street (as at Martock, for instance) rather than adopting a square or circular plan around a village green. Village greens are very rare in Somerset, though it is possible that some may have disappeared under subsequent development. Long villages like Martock usually have one or two streets intersecting them at right angles. Martock, in fact, is unusual because its long main street, which runs from north to south, continues southwards (after a couple of right-angled turns) to become the main street of the contiguous settlements of Hurst and Newton, before ending at yet another village within the parish, Bower Hinton. From the north of Martock to the south of Bower Hinton the road is continuously built up for nearly two miles, until Bower Hinton, where the houses spread out round a rectangle and a semi-circular enclosure. Such a pronounced example of linear development is unusual, even in this region where villages tend to merge.[22]

In villages which were planned as *burhs*, like East Lyng (Plate 29), there was one long main street intersected at right angles by "streets" which it was hoped to develop. These still exist as overgrown lanes, providing access for cattle to the surrounding marshland pastures, but no building has occurred along them. In fact, the area of East Lyng not liable to flooding is so small that it is difficult to see how it could have developed into a town except by linear growth westwards along the ridge leading to West Lyng. In any case East Lyng was too isolated on the edge of the wetlands to have much hope of becoming a market centre.

Villages like South Petherton and Montacute, which were once small market towns, naturally have a much more complex plan than agricultural places like Shepton Beauchamp or Hasel-

[22] *VCH*, IV, p. 80.

bury Plucknett. The nucleus of South Petherton developed round the church and market-place (now much reduced by subsequent building within it) on the west bank of a small brook, about a mile to the west of the river Parrett. Later development in the seventeenth century saw the little town spreading eastwards across the brook and southwards towards the Fosse Way along South Street, first mentioned in deeds in the seventeenth century. South Street and another street running parallel to it comprised a separate part of the town known as Hayes End. South Petherton declined from a market town with a population of 2,606 in 1851 to a large village with a population of 1,997 in 1901, but an influx of people working elsewhere had raised its population to 2,549 by 1971.[23]

Montacute has an interesting history because it developed from two planned medieval boroughs (established c. 1100 and c. 1240) built alongside one another, each with its own market and main street. In Saxon times Montacute was a village (called at first *Logworesbeorh* and later Bishopston) lying at the eastern base of a steep hill—the *mons acutus* on which Robert Count of Mortain had built his castle by 1086. Later (c. 1100), his son William established a borough which in 1102 was given to the Abbey of Cluny in France (along with other lands and possessions) for them to establish a priory at Montacute. The long, narrow, regularly laid-out plots, aligned on the street now called Bishopston, suggest that this was the original borough of c. 1100. The site of the priory lay to the south of it, and there seems to have been a small market place outside the priory gates. Apparently this borough did not yield the priory enough income, and by about 1240 Prior Mark had established a "new town" on the east side of the original one, with a larger market place. This was aligned along the street now called The Borough and probably ran farther north than it does now, up towards Montacute House; it included buildings which were demolished when the park and gardens surrounding the mansion were being extended in the seventeenth century.

Montacute thrived as a market and as a clothing town in the Middle Ages, and even returned two M.P.s in 1302, but by the

[23] *VCH*, IV, pp. 170–5.

sixteenth century its market was in decline, probably as a result of competition from Ilminster and Yeovil, which were more advantageously sited with respect to roads. The market finally ceased to be held in 1732, and by 1801 Montacute was only a village with a population of 827. Yet its handsome Ham stone houses reflect its former importance as a borough, as well as the influence of the wealthy Phelips family who, as we saw above, dominated the place from Tudor times until quite recently. They acquired it in 1539 at the dissolution of the priory.[24]

Building styles show considerable variety throughout the region. Prior to the seventeenth century, most houses were timber-framed, infilled with cob, and thatched with straw. After about 1600 timber became more expensive and was replaced (at least in the larger houses) by local stone. The villages in the east of the region used the grey, oolitic limestones (as at North Cadbury); those in the centre used the imposing Ham stone, and farther to the west around Crewkerne and Chard the complicated geological formation around the Windwhistle ridge provided a variety of building-stones—sandstone, limestone and greensand.

In the nineteenth century, brick-making developed in the region; bricks replaced stone in some proportion of new houses, and they were sometimes used as an infilling for timber-framed houses. Thatch also gradually gave way to locally-made red tiles, and later to grey slates imported from Wales.

The towns

Although there are no very large towns in the region there are at least fourteen settlements which may be regarded as urban, ranging from important places like Taunton and Yeovil to marginal cases like Bruton and Milverton. Consequently it is not possible to discuss the topographical development of each one individually, but we may consider them as groups in differing categories, of which there are four.

First comes Taunton, which as the county's capital and administrative centre is in a category of its own. Secondly, under the heading of industrial towns, comes Yeovil, which is

[24] Aston and Leech, *Somerset Towns*, pp. 104–9.

the only town in the region which really qualifies. Thirdly comes a group of towns which, while primarily regional market centres, also have quite important industrial components. These are Wincanton (dairy industries), Crewkerne (webbing and textiles), Chard (miscellaneous light engineering and electronics) and Wellington (woollens). Finally come the small agricultural marketing and rural distribution centres, of which there are eight in the region: Bruton, Castle Cary, Ilchester, Ilminster, Langport, Milverton, Somerton and Wiveliscombe.

Taunton (see Plate 44)

The county capital had a population of 37,444 in 1971, making it fairly small for a county town. Taunton lies in flat country, and until recently its bridge was the only one over the river Tone for several miles in either direction, thus making Taunton an important traffic centre. The medieval core of the town lies just to the south of the bridge. It was originally a triangular-shaped walled borough, with the base of the triangle running along the west side, and with the castle precinct in the north-west corner abutting on to the river. The main streets were T-shaped and joined at the old market-place (now no longer used as a market, having been replaced by a modern market to the north of the river). Although a certain number of old buildings in this area survive, such as the Tudor House, a timber-framed house, now a hotel, on the south side of the old market-place, most of the older buildings lie behind more recent façades, often red-brick Georgian or later in date. The town centre thus looks newer than it really is. With its narrow central streets, Taunton must always have presented a traffic problem, even before the motor-car added to the congestion. In the eighteenth century, a short but fine street of Georgian brick houses was cut from the market place to St Mary's Church (Hammet Street), and an elegant crescent was built to the west of the town, but these did little to relieve traffic congestion. This was helped c.1840 when a new street (Corporation Street) was cut between the market place and the western exit to the town, which relieved the pressure in the High Street. Eventually, with the development of ring roads in the twentieth century, the High Street was made into a pedestrian precinct, restoring some safety and amenity to the old town centre.

Suburban development prior to the railway age was mainly eastwards, but with the construction of the Bridgwater and Taunton canal in 1827 (and its continuation to Tiverton in Devon as the Grand Western in 1838) development began to the north of the river. When the Bristol and Exeter Railway opened its station in this northern area in 1841, rapid development as an industrial suburb began. Later, the cattle market moved up to be near to the station, and a second bridge was built over the Tone to help to relieve the traffic congestion on the old town bridge.[25]

Until recently Taunton never utilised its riverside, except industrially, but now some attractive riverside walks have been made in the centre of town, and the opening of new bridges (the M5 downstream at Bathpool, and a new bridge upstream at Bishop's Hull in 1979) have helped to ease the traffic flow somewhat. Modern Taunton is rather a sprawling, mainly brick-built town, but it has one rare amenity. A large, pleasant park, called Vivary Park, stretches southwards from the end of the High Street and abuts on to green fields stretching clear to the Blackdowns. There is thus a green-field triangular segment reaching right into the heart of the town.

Yeovil

Although Yeovil may conveniently be categorised as an industrial town, it also provides important agricultural marketing and general servicing functions. It is not a very large town, but its rise in population has been rapid in the last two centuries. With only 2,700 inhabitants in 1801, it increased over four-fold to 11,704 by 1901, and has more than doubled its population since then, reaching 25,503 in 1971. However, by then another 5,536 people lived in the suburbs of Yeovil Without, so the true total was 31,039. The medieval core of the town consisted of several small, narrow streets to the east of the

[25] R. Bush, *The Book of Taunton* (1977).

church, clustered round the old market-place, called the Borough. The ravages of fire and modern traffic have destroyed most of the ancient buildings. Despite its name, derived from the river Yeo, the centre of the town is in fact about half a mile to the west of the river, and shortage of water for fire-fighting was for long a serious problem, especially before 1700, when many houses were built of timber and thatch. In 1449, 117 houses were destroyed by fire; in 1623 there was another serious outbreak; and in 1640, 83 dwelling-houses and many other buildings, housing "six hundred persons at least" were swept away by "a sudden grevious misfortune of fire".[26]

Modern roads have been almost as destructive. In the nineteenth century, several new roads were cut in the heart of the town, especially to improve communications between Middle Street and South Street, which ran right through the town parallel to each other but with very limited connecting access ways. Mounting motor traffic in the twentieth century soon produced impossible congestion, and a series of ring roads was cut round the old town, involving much destruction of property in the inner suburbs, but restoring some amenity to the old town centre, where Middle Street has become a pedestrian precinct.

Yeovil's first staple industry was glove-making and its associated tanning, which still thrives. Modern tanning works have been built to the east of the town at Pen Mills on the river Yeo, and there has been considerable suburban expansion in that area. Later development spread westwards, with the expansion of the Petter Oil Engine Company into aircraft production at Westland during the First World War. In the 1920s, new works were built in this area. Later the company became part of the Westland Aircraft Group, which concentrates on helicopters, and has a subsidiary, Normalair-Garrett, which is one of Europe's largest specialists in pressure control, air-conditioning and hydraulic systems for aircraft. The Westland Group is the largest employer of labour in Yeovil, and gives the town an industrial core based on advanced engineering. Yeovil is free from the overcrowding and dirt often associated with

[26] L. Brooke, *The Book of Yeovil* (1978), pp. 122–3.

Plate 47 A vanishing part of the landscape. A withy-drying kiln at Stathe in the Levels. Withies were much used in basket-making and associated crafts, and these coal-fired kilns were once numerous.

Plate 48 Stembridge windmill at High Ham, near Somerton (National Trust). One of only a handful of survivors from over 100 which are known to have existed, located mainly on Mendip and in the Levels. Stembridge mill was built in 1822 and last worked by wind in 1898 (it continued under steam power till the 1920s). Its thatched cap is the last survivor in England.

Plate 49 A small rural tannery (now a hotel) at Holford in the Quantocks. The leat can be seen in the foreground leading the water over an iron bridge on to the huge overshot water-wheel which is set within the building below the bridge. The building opposite, with the perforated wall, was used for drying tanned skins.

Plate 50 A disused coalmine at Dunkerton, near Radstock. The viaduct of the former railway can be seen running through the centre of the village. The spoil-heap is just to the left, under trees. Opened in 1898, it became the largest mine in Somerset and was closed in 1927. Seen from a distance it has left remarkably little trace.

Plate 51 The Tonedale woollen mills (Fox Bros) on the edge of Wellington, west Somerset. The potato field leading right up to the factory is a good example of the way industry has blended into the rural scene in Somerset. The original works (buildings on the left) were built in 1803 and used water power. Later extensions were steam-powered as the chimney shows.

Plate 52 Canal versus railway. The bridge in the foreground carried the Grand Western Canal over the old driveway to Nynehead Manor, near Wellington, on its way from Taunton to Tiverton (in Devon). Opened in 1838, it was closed in 1867 owing to competition from the Great Western Railway, whose rival bridge can be seen in the distance. This section of the GWR main line to Exeter was opened in 1844.

Plate 53 Post-industrial grandeur. The magnificent disused railway viaduct at Pensford, south of Keynsham, seen behind Pensford parish church, flanked by a stream and leat once used to turn water mills.

industry and, although its topography lacks historical interest, its prosperous inhabitants live in extensive and pleasant suburbs, well spaced out and mostly fairly modern.[27]

The mixed market and industrial towns

This group comprises Wincanton in the east of the region, Crewkerne and Chard in the south, and Wellington in the west. Each is fairly small, but has important, though sometimes little noticed, industries. In 1971 Wincanton had a population of 2,576, Crewkerne had 4,821, Chard had 7,908, and Wellington had 9,359.

Wincanton was never a borough, and originated as a small agricultural settlement on the east bank of the river Cale where there was a good site for a mill. It later developed as a clothing town and a survey of 1558 shows that it had developed up the hill behind it to a market place where several roads met, and then extensively eastwards along the present High Street, where there are several attractive stone buildings of the Stuart and Georgian periods. Defoe described Wincanton (c.1725) as a centre for fine "Spanish" medley clothes and it also benefited from the coaching trade between London and the west country. It would, however, have declined without the large Unigate creamery, which is in the Cale valley to the south of the old town nucleus.[28]

Crewkerne also benefited from the coaching trade, being on the main road from London to Exeter and Plymouth (A30). In fact, it was an enterprising Crewkerne man, Thomas Hutchins, who in 1629 organised the first private letter postal service in England, persuading King James I to allow the royal postal service to be used for this purpose. Hutchins and his fellow western post riders secured authority to "undertake the speedy dispatch of all private letters weekly from London to Plymouth and from Plymouth to London" (and places within twenty miles of the main road) for a charge of 2½d. a mile.[29] In the eighteenth century Crewkerne specialised in the production of

[27] Ibid., pp. 119–41.
[28] Aston and Leech, *Somerset Towns*, pp. 155–8.
[29] J. Crofts, *Packhorse, Wagon and Post* (1967), pp. 99–100.

sailcloth and serges for the East India Company, but its modern expansion has been based on making shirts, webbing and gloves, and on light engineering.[30] The old heart of the town, with its pleasant stone buildings, suffers because the heavy traffic on the A30 passes right through it, but the industrial sections of the town lie to the south. At the webbing mill at Viney's Bridge there is an eighteenth-century building with a pedimented Tuscan doorway and a fanlight in the Adam style, which is, according to Bryan Little, "Somerset's most stylish surviving piece of industrial architecture".[31]

A few miles to the west of Crewkerne is Chard, with its elegant long High Street, which was laid out as part of a medieval planned borough (c. 1206–34) to the north of the Saxon village area around the parish church. Chard was originally developed by the bishops of Bath and Wells, and consisted of fifty-two long, narrow burgage plots, each of one acre, laid out on both sides of the new High Street, which was 2,600 feet (800 metres) long. Chard developed a thriving cloth trade which, in 1578, employed "many a thousand poor people within ten miles compass". Cloth-making continued until about 1830, when it was replaced by lace-making. In the later nineteenth century, engineering began, and today Chard, which looks so like a Georgian market town, has numerous and varied engineering firms. They include brass and bronze foundries, tool-making firms, specialists in aircraft systems and breathing apparatus, and several firms engaged in general mechanical and electrical engineering. The industrial area has developed mainly to the east of the old town in a valley where the disused canal and railway once ran. The canal linked Chard to Taunton (1842–67) and the branch railway linked the town to the G. W. R. system near Taunton and the southern system at Chard junction, about three miles south of the town. These lines were closed in 1962–4. The main street of Chard, with its charming Georgian houses in brick and stone, has a market-town appearance, and is one of the most attractive towns in the region. Yet John Stringfellow's lace works, where he flew the world's first steam-

[30]Aston and Leech, *Somerset Towns*, pp. 35–8; F. Walker, *The Bristol Region* (1972), p. 312.
[31] B. Little, *Portrait of Somerset*, p. 163.

driven model aeroplane in the 1840s, back on to his house in the main street, and in side streets are two large early nineteenth-century factory buildings.[32]

Wellington, six miles west of Taunton at the end of the Vale, has a similar early history to that of Chard, having also been planned and developed by the bishops of Bath and Wells around a single long street. Its name, derived from *weo-leah* (a temple clearing) suggests a pre-Saxon origin, but although it had a large recorded rural population in the Domesday Survey of 1086 (145 people, consisting of 53 villeins, 61 bordars and 31 slaves) there is no sign of it having been a borough. Mention in a charter of 1215 suggests that the planned urban development probably took place c.1190–1215. Development extended along a single street to the west of the church, and this street is now over a mile long. Wellington throve on the leather and cloth trades in the pre-industrial period, and the latter industry survived at Wellington, unlike so many other towns. The firm of Fox Brothers rose to prominence in the eighteenth century, and between 1801 and 1803 Thomas Fox built a handsome red-brick factory at Tonedale (see Plate 51) out of a disused flour mill. Situated about a mile to the north of the town, the Tonedale works originally relied on water-powered spinning and weaving machinery.[33]

Modern Wellington has a population of 9,359 (1971), and the life of the town still revolves around Tonedale works, though agricultural marketing continues to be important. Suburban development to the north and the south of the High street has occurred since 1945, and to some extent caters for people who commute from Wellington to jobs in other towns, especially Taunton.

The smaller market towns

No fewer than eight towns come into this category, and all are of historic interest. Although none are very large, they have a

[32] Aston and Leech, *Somerset Towns*, pp. 31–4; F. Walker, *The Bristol Region*, p. 311. I owe the reference to John Stringfellow's steam-driven model aeroplane to Professor E. L. Jones.

[33] H. Fox, *Quaker Homespun, the life of Thomas Fox of Wellington, Serge Maker and Banker, 1747–1821* (1958).

much more urban appearance than their population figures might suggest. Ilminster, Somerton and Wiveliscombe had between 2,000 and 4,500 inhabitants in 1971, while Bruton, Castle Cary, Ilchester, Milverton and Langport (including its suburb Huish Episcopi) had only between 1,000 and 2,000 each.

This network of market towns was suitable for an age when produce was carried by horse and cart, but with the advent of the railway and the motor-lorry, they lost many of their marketing functions to larger centres. Consequently, in their essential plan, and often in their appearance as well, they have changed little since the eighteenth century. Mostly they are constructed of stone and are of simple plan. Often one main street, as at Bruton and Longport, makes up the bulk of the town, but sometimes the plan is more complex, as at Castle Cary and Somerton. Since space forbids consideration of them all, we shall end with Somerton (Plate 42), the ancient centre of the county, as an illustration. With most of its houses built in the soft blue-grey limestone of the lower Liassic formation, and garnished with quoins, window frames and drip mouldings in the golden Ham stone, Somerton remains one of the most charming small towns in the county.

As can be seen in Fig. 27, the original Saxon settlement seems to have been to the north of the church in an area most of which was not included in the medieval town, but which has now been built over by modern houses. Possibly the former East Street, which was mentioned in seventeenth-century deeds, but which has now disappeared, was formerly the main street. It led directly westwards to Langport. The town prospered in the thirteenth century, and around 1290 a major expansion took place. A new rectangular market was established to the south of the church, and the present Broad and West Streets were developed to serve it. Expansion continued in later centuries with New Street, first mentioned about 1349, North Street about 1624, and Kirkham Street about 1664. Today most of the houses along these streets have façades dating from the seventeenth to the nineteenth centuries, but these often conceal older structures behind them, as at the White Hart Inn on the south side of the market-place. Here a mid-nineteenth-century re-

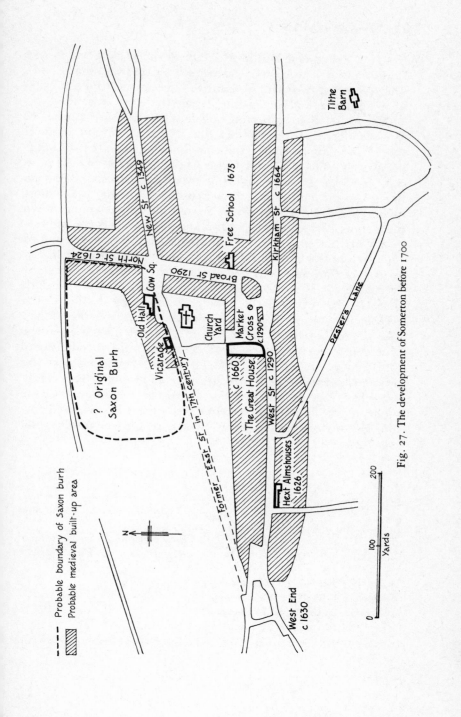

Fig. 27. The development of Somerton before 1700

- - - Probable boundary of Saxon burh

▨▨ Probable medieval built-up area

? Original
Saxon Burh

Old Hall
New St c.1349
North St c.1624
Cow Sq
Broad St 1290
Free School 1675
Kirkham St c.1664
Tithe Barn

Vicarage
Former East St in 17th century
Church Yard
Market Cross c.1290
c.1660
The Great House
West St c.1290
Pesler's Lane

Hext Almshouses 1626

West End c.1630

N

0   100   200
Yards

fronting conceals a building of late medieval date whose roof still survives. There is no evidence for the tradition that a castle once stood on this site; it seems to have arisen from confusion with Somerton in Lincolnshire, where there *was* a castle.

The belief that Somerton was once the ancient "capital" of Wessex derives from the fact that it was an important royal manor in Saxon times and was consequently visited by the kings of Wessex. The *witan* (or Great Council) met at Somerton in 949, but the West Saxon kings were peripatetic and had no fixed capital city—Winchester probably being their most favoured residence. However, Somerton was the county town for a short period between 1278 and 1366, reflecting its prosperity at that time. The clothing and leather trades sustained the town in the later Middle Ages, but by 1540 it was listed in an Act of Parliament as one of the towns which needed to be "re-edified". There seems to have been a revival of the cloth trade in the seventeenth century, followed by decline in the eighteenth. No serge-weavers are mentioned later than 1710. The population was only 1,145 in 1801; it fluctuated in the nineteenth century, rising to 2,302 in 1871 and then falling to 1,797 in 1901. By 1921 it was down to 1,776, but post-war residential development (much of it for commuters) has recently brought an upsurge which has carried the population over the 3,000 mark. Fortunately recent development has occurred outside the historic town centre, which retains its architectural unity and charm.[34]

SELECT BIBLIOGRAPHY

Dunning, R. W., ed., *The Victoria History of the County of Somerset*, Vols. III (1974) and IV (1978). These are devoted to parishes in the south of the county.

Bates, E. H., ed., "The Particular Description of the County of Somerset, 1633" (by Thomas Gerard), *Somerset Record Society*, XV (1900).

Bush, R., *The Book of Taunton* (1977).

Brooke, L., *The Book of Yeovil* (1978).

Couzens, P., *Bruton in Selwood* (1972).

[34] *VCH*, III, pp. 129–42; Aston and Leech, *Somerset Towns*, pp. 123–6.

10. Epilogue

AN IMMENSE PERIOD of time has passed since the earliest settlers began to influence the Somerset landscape by fire and axe in prehistoric times. We have seen how each successive age added its distinctive contribution. The task of future generations is not to stop all change, but to try to channel it in directions which will enhance the beauty as well as the utility of the landscape. We cannot prevent change, but we can look very suspiciously at proposals which might involve permanent damage to the landscape. We need to be very sure that the alleged advantages which they will offer are really worth the price. Once a piece of landscape has been destroyed by unwise "development" there is usually no way in which it can be re-created, as witness the huge stone quarries on the south face of Mendip.

Before looking at some of the possible directions which future change may take, we may perhaps take stock of how fortunate Somerset has been in the evolution of its landscape. The population of the historic county is distributed at an uncrowded density of sixteen people for ten hectares, or twenty-five acres (1971 figures, when the total population was a little over 680,000). This means that, on average, each inhabitant enjoys nearly two acres. But although Somerset gives the impression of being predominantly rural in character, it has a more industrialised economy than is at first apparent. Recent censuses have shown that only one occupied person in five works in agriculture and that industrial occupations are quite important. The reason why they impinge so little on the landscape is that industries in Somerset are not concentrated, but are spread out in small pockets all over the county. Nearly every town has some important factory, like woollen manufacturing in Wellington, or electronics in Chard, but they are seldom obtrusive and it is possible to pass through many small towns in Somerset without realising that they have any industrial component at all. The county is very fortunate in this balanced economy. It retains its rural appearance and yet manages to provide industrial jobs for many of its inhabitants (though not of course for all; its relatively slow population growth indicates that some proportion of the people who were born in Somerset have always had to seek work elsewhere).

The question for the future is: can the county adapt to the mounting pressures of a modern society without losing its admirable balance and charm? There are some hopeful signs. One of the most insidious of recent pressures has been the ever-widening use of motorcars and lorries, and the consequent demand for ever more (and larger) roads. For Somerset this culminated in the construction in the 1970s of the great M5 motorway which cuts a swathe through the county from Bristol to the Devon border west of Wellington. However, the effect of the M5 on Somerset has been much less than might have been expected, because the motorway carries so many people *through* the county rather than *into* it. It has relieved the appalling traffic jams which used to clog up towns like Bath, Wells, Bridgwater, Glastonbury, Taunton and Wellington (and villages for miles around) without doing too much damage to the landscape through which it passes. This of course is a subjective judgment with which others may not agree, but at least Somerset has avoided the environmental damage which can occur when a county is criss-crossed with motorways and "spaghetti junctions" as has occurred to some extent in Warwickshire. Fortunately there are no plans for new motorways in Somerset in the foreseeable future.

The second problem associated with motorcars (and linked to population increase) is urban sprawl and the rise of the commuter village. This has been most noticeable to the south of Bristol, where the ancient villages of Bedminster and Brislington have been absorbed into a sea of houses and roads. It has also occurred to some extent around Bath and Taunton, but on the whole the absence of really large cities in Somerset has prevented this problem from becoming too serious. But the marked tendency for farms to increase in size and to shed labour has resulted in a change in many villages. Increasingly, farmsteads and cottages are being taken up by urban commuters, and in-filling by new housing has become very noticeable in villages near to towns like Yeovil, Bridgwater and Taunton. As yet the change has been gradual, but the increasing popularity of Somerset as a retirement county adds to the pressure.

The new structure of agricultural prices, associated with the European Common Agricultural Policy, puts the emphasis on cereal production, and increasingly Somerset farms are being turned from their old specialisation in dairy products to corn production. This means larger fields, fewer hedges and less permanent pasture as the landscape assumes a more Midland or East Anglian appearance. There are some signs, though, that this movement may not continue indefinitely. The present structure of prices is highly artificial, and if it were to show signs of crumbling, Somerset farming might return to the predominance of pasture for which its wet climate makes it so suitable. Also, with industrial employment threatened by technological changes (robots, etc.) as well as cyclical economic recessions, and with the recent enthusiasm for self-sufficiency, the future may see a return to rural life. Some of the large farms may be subdivided again, and the drift to a prairie landscape may be halted—this could have great economic as well as aesthetic advantages.

The more extreme proponents of increased cereal production have proposed a scheme for a more comprehensive drainage of the Levels, which would end for ever the threat of flooding, and allow mechanised corn growing to take place on the central marshland pastures. For technical and economic reasons this is likely to be a very expensive and complex scheme. It would have far-reaching effects on the flora and fauna of the region. Rare and valuable species of plants and animals would disappear, and the character of this distinctive region would be permanently altered. Because of the technical difficulties of draining such a large area, which is beneath the tidal level of the Bristol Channel (and is supplied with a massive quantity of river water from its surrounding hills) the viability of this scheme must always be in doubt. The cost is bound to be immense and the chances of it being successfully carried out cannot be regarded as bright.

Exmoor has been subjected to a different threat. The farmers around the edges of the national park are paid grants by the Ministry of Agriculture if they reclaim adjacent moorland, and they are naturally keen to do so. However, people who are concerned with environmental issues, and the many thousands of tourists who like to visit Exmoor, equally naturally deplore this tendency. A compromise solution lies ironically in paying farmers *not* to reclaim land. They can also be paid to continue exercising their common rights to keep sheep and cattle on Exmoor in order to obtain control over bracken which spreads unwantedly, when the traditional (and somewhat uneconomic) practices of livestock husbandry are abandoned.

Reservoirs are another source of conflict. As the population rises, new ones are needed. There is general agreement that they should not, if possible, be sited on good agricultural land. This makes remote areas, like Exmoor, seem desirable sites, but defenders of the few remaining tracts of natural landscape point out that these are in very short supply, and that reservoirs inevitably attract sight-seers, hikers and fishermen, who demand roads, café's, pubs and all the other attributes of modern life which are inimical to solitude. In this, as in other matters, it is necessary to strike a balance. Reservoirs can undoubtedly be attractive, and Somerset has some good examples, like the Blagdon and Chew Valley lakes north of Mendip, Sutton Bingham, near Yeovil, and Clatworthy in the Brendons. The big new reservoir at Wimbleball, in wooded country south of Exmoor, near Dulverton, will also no doubt become a beauty spot when the initial disruption to the landscape has had a chance to settle down. Yet the destruction can be considerable, and proposals for new reservoir sites need to be considered with great care. It was encouraging at Wimbleball that the environmental effects on the landscape were appreciated from the beginning, and that steps were taken to ensure that the reservoir would be blended into the surrounding landscape with the minimum of disruption, by special landscape planning arrangements.

Another proposal which could have a profound long-term effect on the landscape is the scheme to erect a barrage across the Severn estuary to generate tidal electricity. Various sites have been suggested, some as far west as the area between Minehead and Aberthaw in South Wales, but the most likely would be somewhere between Weston-super-Mare and Penarth, probably linked with the islands of Steep Holm and Flat Holm. This is a very ambitious and costly scheme, with so many implications for the economy and environment of the region that the government has set up a feasibility study to be carried out over the next few years at a cost of three to four million pounds to assess its practicability. Its proponents argue that it could ultimately supply as much as 12 per cent of the nation's electricity from turbines turned by the tides, and hence it would be cheap in the long run, though expensive to build initially, since two barrages would be needed to ensure continuous generation. It is also argued that it would assist shipping in the upper estuary by reducing the tidal outflow at high tides, and that it would improve communications to south Wales if a bridge were built on top of the barrage.

The basic reasons are thus economic (and are especially connected with long-term fuel conservation), but some environmental advantages have also been put forward. It is claimed that lower tides above the barrage would reduce the risk of sea-water flooding, and would enable tidal mud flats, which are not now utilised, to be reclaimed for agriculture or recreation. Against this both environmentalists and economists have raised numerous objections. The economic objection (apart from inevitable disputes about what the costs of generating electricity would really be) are centred on the fact that this is a high-risk enterprise, where unknown factors like the degree of sedimentation and pollution behind the barrage cannot be accurately forecast. In addition, there is the inconvenience and high cost of the disruption which would occur during the construction period—which could take twenty years! Construction would be noisy and dusty and would generate huge traffic flows in areas where roads are sparse, narrow and winding. In addition a vast amount of stone and concrete would be required—throwing a heavy burden on areas of supply such as the Mendip quarries. Thus environmental damage could be generated over a wide area.

Environmentalists and biologists, concerned with the balance of plant and animal life in the estuary region, also have particular concerns. A higher average water level *above* the barrage would reduce the salt marshes on which wading and migrant birds now breed, while higher tidal variation *below* the

259

barrage could endanger the waders' breeding-grounds on the south side of Bridgwater Bay, which is recognised by an international convention as a "Wetland Site of International Importance". In addition, increased tidal flows up the Parrett valley (at present unprotected by a clyse) could substantially increase the risk of flooding over a wide area of the southern Levels. Finally sewage emptied into the estuary above the barrage could congeal into liquid mud emitting noxious odours.[1]

It is clear that the implications of the proposed Severn barrage for the landscape are very considerable, and might lead to widespread environmental damage. However the possible long-term energy savings could be considerable, but it would not seem that there is any great urgency about the matter, and it is to be hoped that very thorough studies of the environmental effects will be carried out before any decisions are taken.

The pressures on the landscape are bound to mount from all sides in future, and there can be no ideal blueprint for how to proceed. It is useful to remember that the landscape has taken thousands of years to evolve and grow, and that it is part of the heritage which has been handed down to us. We should treasure it accordingly.

[1] I am grateful to Dr Alan Carr of the Institute of Oceanographic Sciences at Taunton for information and advice about the Severn barrage proposals. See also T. Shaw, ed., *An environmental appraisal of tidal power stations with particular reference to the Severn Barrage* (Pitman, 1980); R. T. Severn, D. L. Dineley and L. E. Hawker, eds, *Tidal power and estuary management* (Colston Papers, No. 30, University of Bristol, 1979); T. Shaw (ed.) *An environmental appraisal of the Severn Barrage: a collection of 17 essays by different authors* (Dept. of Civil Engineering, University of Bristol, 2nd ed., 1977); and *Fourth report from the select committee on Science and Technology, the exploitation of tidal power in the Severn estuary* (HMSO, 1977).

Index

Aberthaw, 258
Abonae, 66, 71
Acland, Sir Thomas, 180, 181, 203
aerial photography, 50, 117, 118
Aethelburg, Queen, 82
Age of Arthur, The (Morris), 80
Agricola, 63
agriculture – and Domesday Survey, 97–104; early, 42–3, 45–6, 48–9, 50; and enclosures, 123, 124–7, 202–3; harvest failures, 115; medieval, 110, 116; modern, 257; on Exmoor, 182–9; orchards, 232–3; Roman, 61–4; Saxon, 75, 86, 89–90, 91–3; *see also* enclosures; estates; farms
Alcock, L., 58, 61, 76
Alder Moor, 161
Aldhelm, Bishop, 210
Alfoxden, 36
Alfred, King, 34, 93, 94
Allan, Henry, 154
Aller, 93, 125, 130, 159
Almisworthy Common, 51
Ammerdown Park, 206
Anglo-Saxon Chronicle, 67, 75, 76, 79, 82
Applebaum, Professor Shimon, 61, 63
Aprise, Alicia, 128
Aquae Sulis see Bath
architecture – domestic, 138–40, 164, 186; Elizabethan, 241; industrial, 227; religious, 120–1; 129; Wells Cathedral, 213; timber-framed, 175; town, 244–5; Bath, 208–10; Frome, 215, Norton-Radstock, 226; Somerton, 252; Weston, 244–5; village, 243; *see also* manor houses
Arthur, "King", 75–6
Ash, 107, 108
Ashbrittle, 179
Ashill, 175, 229
Ash Priors, 232
Ashton Park, 206
Ashwick Grove, 203; Park, 133

Asser, Bishop, 93
Aston, Michael, 235
Athelm, Bishop, 211
Athelney, 34, 110, 111, 136, 137; monastery, 93, 94, 130; manor of, 109
Avebury, 51
Avill river, 190, 191
Avon, county of, 30, 60, 199; river, 29, 30, 31, 37, 66, 71, 76, 154, 199, 200, 206, 209, 218, 227; canals linking, 141, 224; valley, 29, 30, 58, 78; enclosures in, 200–4
Avonmouth, 66, 145
Axbridge, 32, 104, 111, 206; history of, 217; road link to, 166
Axe river, 33, 71, 217; and flooding, 151; and river Brue, 110, 111; clyses on, 136; sea-walls on, 154, 155; valley, 162
Axmouth, 80, 114

Badbury Rings, 76
Badon *see Mons Badonicus*
Bagborough House, 178
Bagendon, 52
Bagley, 117
Ballynagilly, 47
Banwell church, 129
Barbury Castle, 76, 78
Barle river, 37, 127, 181, 194
Barrington, 175, 229, 239; Court, 239, 242; Hill, 175
Barrow Commons, 236
Barrow Gurney reservoir, 145
barrows, long, 49; round, 50
Barwick, 113
Batcombe, 117, 235
Bath, 29, 30, 32, 40, 69, 70, 89, 140, 206, 211, 214, 219, 256; abbey, 102, 112; manor of, 109; ancient settlements in, 58; and *Mons Badonicus* battle, 76; architecture of, 208–9; expansion of, 145, 199, 200, 207–10; in Domesday Survey, 104; in Middle

Pilrow Cut, 111
Pilton, 89, 117
Pinhoe, 80
Pitcombe, 242
Pitminster, 89, 178
Pitney, 60, 61, 63, 80
place-names, 43, 46; field-names, 234, 238; Saxon, 72, 79, 84–6, 88, 251
Plymouth, 249
Polden Hills, 33, 34, 70, 93, 94, 136, 149, 162; ancient tracks on, 48–9, 54; peat-digging on, 144; Roman roads on, 59, 63
Poole, 66, 115, 143, 169
Porlock, 180; Common, 51; Weir, 195
Portbury, 154
Portishead, 136, 140, 207; development of, 218–19
Poulett, Earls, 35, 174, 240; family, 124, 126
Preston, John, 233
Priddy lead-mining settlement, 31, 84, 220–1; Circles, 45, 50; excavations at, 47
Priston, 223
Publow, 226
Puriton, 59, 113, 166

Quantock Hills, 34, 36, 45, 86, 90, 97, 99, 113, 189, 229, 242; copper mining on, 195, 197; early settlements on, 50, 80; enclosures on, 178–9; hill-forts on, 53; landscape of, 172–3; round barrows on, 51
Quantoxhead, 34, 178
quarrying, 90, 140, 144, 199, 206
Queen Camel village, 230

Rackham, Oliver, 73
Rackley, 217
Radstock, 144, 202, 206, 225; coal mining at, 31, 40, 131, 140, 220; *see also* Norton Radstock
Rahtz, P. A., 81
railways, 131, 141–4, 168, 192, 195–7, 225, 247, 250
Redlake river, 91
Redlynch, 235
religious sites, early, 49–50, 51, 54; in Bath, 66; in Glastonbury, 210
Rennie, John, 136

reservoirs, 145, 167, 258
Richard I, 112
Richmont castle, 114
Rimpton, 85
rivers – anti-flooding measures, 135–7, 149–59, 160; alteration of courses, 110–12, 162–4
roads, 202; A30, 35, 249, 250; A38, 88, 166, 217; A39, 211; A303, 107; A361, 159, 166; M5, 55, 59, 132, 145, 168, 199, 229, 247, 256; ancient tracks, 48–9, 54, 55, 86, 89; building of, 40, 137, 140, 165–6, 204; Fosse Way, 59, 66, 69, 73; importance of, 114, 124, 131–2; Roman, 59–60, 63, 66, 69, 70, 71, 78, 81; Saxon, 75, 94–5; state of, 188, 189
Roadwater, 197
Rock's Drove, 164
Rodwell, Dr Warwick, 211
Roger family, 130
Roman settlements, 33, 38, 52, 55, 57, 58–71, 73, 74; in Bath, 30, 59, 60, 66–7; in Ilchester, 59, 60, 63, 67–9; mines, 220; sea-walls, 154
Rowberrow, 221
Ruishton, 89
Runnington, 85

Salisbury, 71, 76, 143, 215; Plain, 42
Savaric, Bishop, 213
Saxon settlements, 33, 57, 58, 60, 190, 193, 217, 244; advance into Somerset, 76–81; agriculture of, 89, 92–3; churches, 91, 211; consolidation of, 84–92, 93–6; in Bath, 67; in Ilchester, 69; in Somerton, 252, 253, 254; nature of, 72–5
Sea Mills, 66
Seavington St Michael, 229, 238, 239
Sedgemoor *see* King's Sedgemoor
Selwood forest, 42, 78, 91, 109, 229, 231; enclosures in 235–7
Seven Ash, 179
Severn river, 76; Sea, 32; tidal electricity scheme, 258–60; valley, 52
Shapwick, 47, 144
Sheppey river, 161, 162
Shepton Beauchamp, 34, 133, 228, 239, 243
Shepton Mallet, 32, 69, 133, 140, 200,